Soldier On

Soldier On

by
James A. Sesnak

Written and Produced by James A. Sesnak
Entropic Publishing
Sedona, Arizona

ISBN 978-1-7338722-0-1

Book design and layout by Marion Johnson
The Memory Works, LLC
Sedona, Arizona
www.memoryworkspublishing.com

*To my lovely wife Alice,
who proved to me
there is life after death.*

Contents

Prologue

"The pain I feel now is the happiness I had before.
That's the deal."

—C.S. Lewis

C.S. Lewis's memorable quote summarizes my life as I write these words. My thirty-year marriage ended when my wife succumbed to ovarian cancer. The initial surgery proved a success and the routine check-ups offered no cause for alarm. For many years the cancer simply remained a background noise, and we lived as if nothing had happened.

That abruptly changed when the last seven years of our lives became a slow-motion disaster. Cancer screamed in the background of every discussion but screeched even louder in our quieter moments. As the disease advanced, our conversations progressed from cancer to cures to spirituality. I don't know which proved harder, the sleepless nights providing care with the hope of recovery or the sleepless nights providing comfort care with no hope of recovery. Throughout our cancer journey the goal posts for remission were constantly moving, and that specific moment when we both finally accepted that Kath's days were numbered became very blurred.

Once, I woke up in the middle of the night to find her staring at me, and through my sleepiness I heard her say, "I love you." My half-opened eyes saw the unbearable sadness in her face and my ears heard the reluctant resignation in her voice that conveyed a deep despair. That unnerving moment had quietly arrived when she finally realized exactly how her life journey would end, and she started her goodbyes in the only way she knew how

Our conversations never focused on the morose. There were no dramatic emotional outbursts or breakdowns. It was a remarkable moment when we finally realized that her life's dreams and aspirations were gone—poof. There would be no more planning, no more scouring the Internet for the next cancer breakthrough, no more doctor appointments or distracting movies to watch. All of that had been replaced with an eerie calm that filled the air.

A deep sadness filled my soul as I kept vigil over my sleeping spouse. I couldn't believe the wedding vows I had taken so long ago were coming to an end. Months later I felt privileged to witness her last breath and she would die holding my hand. This is her story of how she faced the last full measure with more class and grace than any character in a Hollywood movie.

In The **1**Beginning

"**I**never asked to be born" is a refrain often heard by disciplining parents from their frustrated children, but Kath considered that statement to be fundamentally flawed. She believed all sentient beings are reincarnated with an ethereal spirit that willingly chooses its future life and readily agrees to play its part for the greater cosmic good, being fully aware of the inevitable tragic events the earthly incarnation will endure. But Kath's soul seemed to have last minute second thoughts about the human journey she had volunteered for.

Kath remained in utero for several days past her due date before her forty-one-year-old father, Robert C Wilson, drove his pregnant wife, Carol, to the hospital through the frozen, snow-covered streets of Detroit for the birth of their fourth daughter. Barbara Kathleen Wilson embarked upon her new life on December 28, 1951, at 3:40 AM at Providence Hospital in Detroit, Michigan.

Kathy Wilson grew up to be her own woman, but many of her personal traits and odd quirks could be traced directly to the genealogical linage of a family tree that produced a true cast of characters that shaped her life.

Grandpa Frank Rosebaum came from a long line of Freemasons. He became a *Lewis* by the age of sixteen and rose to the thirty-third degree, the highest level possible in that mystical organization, just as his father had done before him. He received an engineering degree from the University of Detroit, but how the son of a working-class Belgian immigrant managed to fund his education remained a family mystery. His wife, Lucy, had little formal education but remained active in the local Lutheran church. They met at a dance in the social hall and soon married.

Lucy and Frank shared a deep spiritual connection and remained life-long Lutherans, but Frank continued to partake in the Masonic rituals and their secret handshakes. The Freemasons played a large part in Frank's life, and he used his connections to land a lucrative engineering job at the newly built Ford plant in suburban Detroit. Kath's mother, Carol, was born to Lucy and Frank on Christmas Day 1912, the year the Titanic sank.

Viola De LaPlace, Kath's paternal grand-mother, laid claim to the Daughters of the American Revolution. Viola's father, John, afforded her a comfortable middle-class life, but his strong-willed Christian Science wife, Anna, clearly wore the pants in the family. John had a penchant for the occasional poker game, and Anna was not pleased when he lost his paycheck at a late-night game. That unfortunate loss ultimately led Kath's paternal Grandpa, Ernie Wilson, to meet and marry Viola De LaPlace.

Ernie was one of five children born on a farm in Bay City Michigan. He grew up to be a larger than life figure and an overbearing man.

As a youth, Ernie piloted the milk wagon pulled by a horse to Detroit where he negotiated the milk prices and quickly learned the art of the financial transaction. He always managed to get premium prices for the family goods and always flashed his father's money around when he returned.

The affluent amenities of the big city and the ability to make money in the bustling metropolis greatly intrigued Grandpa Ernie. When Ernie turned seventeen he ran away from the farm to make a name for himself in the burgeoning city of Detroit, which sat on the verge of an unprecedented economic boom.

He went from job to job, smoking cigars and living large, with no visible means of support, but always managed to procure those finer things in life. Grandpa Ernie claimed he spent his evenings playing bridge, which may have been true in his later years as a member of the Detroit Yacht Club. But the local poker tables provided the necessary cash flow for his extravagant lifestyle, which he supplemented with his bookmaking business. He had a hound dog's sense for sniffing out card games and a magical ability to win at the high dollar tables. The well-bred high-stakes poker players often said that no one could be that lucky, and his questionable reputation often kept Ernie out of some really big games.

Grandpa Ernie always made it his business to know something about the people seated at the card table before he ever sat down to play. On Valentine's Day, he watched in restrained delight as John De LaPlace, an inexperienced card player, took a seat at the table.

That night John lost his entire paycheck to Grandpa Ernie, and as he pushed himself away from the table lamented that he could no longer buy his daughter a present for her upcoming twenty-first birthday.

Ever the opportunist, Ernie showed up unannounced at John's house one week later with an Edwardian hat from Paris, neatly packed inside a gift-wrapped box with an oversized red bow and a card that read "Happy Birthday, Viola." Family legend says he handed the box to John when he answered the door and grinned a wiry smile before he simply walked away. Anna gave her husband a chastising look when she gaped at the expensive hat from Paris and wondered how he even knew where to buy such a hat, let alone pay for it!

Before long before Grandpa Ernie returned to the De LaPlace's front door dressed in a well-cut sack suit over a tall-collared white shirt with a wide red tie, a bowler hat, leather shoes with spats, and the ever-present cigar. John did not invite him inside. Instead, he squeezed out the front door, pushing Ernie slightly backwards on the small porch where the two men stood face-to-face.

Grandpa Ernie's intentions were no mystery to Viola's father, but Ernie held all the cards and John saw no way out of his dilemma. They both knew Anna's Christian Science beliefs frowned upon gambling, and the birthday hat had already put John in hot water. The two men briefly discussed Ernie's intentions, but John knew his poker nemesis had once again outplayed him. With a reluctant handshake John finalized his daughter's courtship agreement.

Ernie held his cigar securely in his mouth as he floated down the stairs and triumphantly walked away, completely unaware that one hundred years later, the cosmic plan he had unwittingly set into motion would result in such tragic consequences.

Ernie Wilson properly courted Viola De LaPlace with new gifts of perfume, fancy gloves, and wardrobe accessories but successfully concealed the hard-nosed temperament he learned at the card table and the bookmaking business. Viola's parents questioned the legitimacy of his funds and demanded that Ernie demonstrate a viable income before he could marry their daughter. Ernie used his illicit winnings to establish a haberdashery and clandestinely solidified his bookmaking business under the same roof. Now that he had a legitimate business, he could finally get married.

Either by incredible foresight or dumb luck, Grandpa Ernie set up shop, not in Detroit where the police had already partnered with much bigger boys than Grandpa Ernie, but in the growing suburb of Grosse Pointe Park. Grandpa Ernie made friends with the local police who visited his hat shop regularly and did his best to mitigate any unexpected gambling losses that his illustrious clientele might have encountered. Since he had no real competition within the small city limits, his customer list grew and his business boomed. Yes, Grandpa Ernie did quite well financially, and he even sold some hats.

Ernie and Viola became parents on June 16, 1910, when Kathy's father, Robert C. Wilson, was born. The demands of Viola's first-born child quickly overwhelmed her and forced her mother, Anna, to step in. As the reality of Viola's new life slowly emerged, she withdrew emotionally, refused to get out of bed, and complained of a variety of ailments that the doctors could not cure. Today her symptoms would be called postpartum depression. Viola's emotional antics and the demands of his new-born son never affected Ernie. He continued to have the time of his life, and for two weeks anyone who came into the hat shop got a free cigar.

Viola eventually recovered from her maladies and soon focused all of her energy on her first born. The Wilson household continued on for two more years before Ernie fell in love with Betty, his second born. As much as Viola doted over Robert, Ernie spoiled Betty, and a sibling rivalry was established that lasted a lifetime.

Ernie always looked for ways to make money. The passage of the 18th Amendment afforded him a business opportunity on the Canadian side of the Detroit River at the Hiram Walker plant in Windsor, Ontario. He had never been a seafarer, but his disposable income dramatically increased after he purchased a small boat. Ernie did quite well on a haberdasher's income, and his small family enjoyed all the amenities of an upper-class lifestyle.

Detroit's vibrant economy soon transformed the city into the Paris of the Midwest. The American culture had changed, but Ernie refused to adapt to the new social order and held steadfast to his old chauvinistic ways. Traditionally, the woman ran the house but in-reality Ernie ruled the roost. No one ever suggested physical abuse within the family dynamics but Ernie psychologically bullied his wife. He always had the last word in any discussion and regularly reminded her that he paid the bills. His financial generosity insured that Viola never wanted for material things, but she paid a price.

Bob Wilson grew up trying to earn his father's respect. He worked hard, went to school, and did everything his father expected of him, but he received little recognition for his efforts. Ernie's flashy lifestyle made Bob uncomfortable. He preferred a less ostentatious approach to life. Bob embraced conservative monetary management and developed old school social habits. He always stood up whenever a woman entered the room and remained firm in his belief that proper table manners mattered. His very traditional mother greatly influenced him, which guaranteed that he would always be a proper gentleman.

Carol's family life proved far less flamboyant. Lucy became the family anchor that instilled a sense of love for self and others, which her daughter fully embraced. Carol displayed a great tolerance for divergent views and agreed with the Christian Science tenet that man is a spirit, but she strongly disagreed with their "heal-yourself" philosophy. She refuted fatalism and never blamed others for troubles that came her way. She always tried to find the good in people and make the best of every situation. Her great love of music and singing kept her involved at the Trinity Lutheran Church and out of the clubs. Although prohibition and speakeasies still dominated the landscape in the early 30s, she never considered herself a flapper. She enjoyed the cultural beauty of art and had a penchant for museums. A short streetcar ride took her to her favorite place, the Detroit Institute of Art.

She took this trek many times but always remembered the 1933 unveiling of the controversial Diego Rivera fresco. She witnessed firsthand the condemnation of the famous mural by the

Catholic and Episcopalian clergy, who labeled it a blasphemous abomination. But the twenty-one-year-old Bible-reading Lutheran could never see the blasphemy in that beautiful work.

In 1937, during one of her visits to the Art Museum, Bob and Carol coincidentally met for the first time under Rivera's fresco. She expressed her views to him on the clerics' edicts that dominated its inaugural unveiling. Some may have perceived her diatribe as a bit forward or even offensive, but Bob found it intriguing, particularly when viewed through his Christian Science upbringing. As their conversation carried on to the John James Audubon exhibit, he found himself deeply infatuated with her, but when she spoke about her love of horses, he fell head over heels for her. That chance encounter developed into a relationship that spanned over fifty years. They married later that year, on June 17, 1937.

Ernie helped the young couple purchase a house on Audubon near his own home in Grosse Pointe Park and set the stage for the newlyweds to start their family. Bob continued to drive a gas truck for his first job as a married man, but Ernie eventually took the profits from his various business adventures and invested his new-found wealth into a start-up called the OverHead Door company. The small manufacturing firm specialized in large and small garage doors that folded upward much like every garage door that operates today, and Bob became the main company guy.

Grandpa Ernie lived only two streets away, which proved convenient for family gatherings. Ernie continued to make sure everyone knew he remained the alpha male of the family. He would bang his walking stick on the floor if he wanted something. Carol would usually come running, while a frightened Kath scurried away in the opposite direction.

In 1951, Viola's health suddenly deteriorated when she developed significant cardiovascular disease, but she adamantly avoided medical doctors and relied instead on her Christian Science faith to heal her. Unfortunately, she became catastrophically infirm, and Bob, not Ernie or Betty, delivered all of her nursing care. Bob attended to the private bodily functions of his incapacitated mother, which left him uneasy and angry.

Six months after Kath's birth her grandmother died from apoplexy, an outdated term for a stroke. A few months later Bob experienced increasingly debilitating emotional issues that appeared for no apparent physical reason. He remained in bed for days at a time while Carol brought him food and drink, which sustained him until he snapped out of it. At other times, he worked nonstop at both the office and around the house. Those activities curiously seemed to coincide with bouts of insomnia and eventually earned the nickname "Rapid Robert." As a young girl, Kath had no idea that her father exhibited well-defined bipolar behavior that continued throughout his life.

The lifestyle of Bob's only sister stood in sharp contrast to his chosen path. Betty's lack of participation in Viola's nursing care and her extravagant tastes that she had learned from Ernie, set the stage for endless family feuds. Betty never held a job, but her husband, Saul, participated in the family business. Bob frequently complained of Saul's excessive drinking and wanted him out, but Ernie insisted otherwise.

Bob taught his girls the value of money, but much to his chagrin, Betty exerted some influence on his family. The girls witnessed her free spirit and flashy ways with the finances to pursue it. Smoking, drinking, laughing, and exhibiting a debutante lifestyle seemed far more appealing than the conservative work ethic espoused by their father. Betty also taught the girls the value of antiques, Persian rugs, and various well-priced collectibles, but Bette's unspoken embrace of financial privilege greatly upset Bob.

Bob never spanked or physically abused his youngest daughter, but his booming voice frightened Kath, especially during heated family discussions. Her fear of loud and powerful men carried over into her adult life. His aberrant behavioral episodes took a toll on his wife, but Carol found solace in her youngest daughter, which created an exceptionally deep bond that grew more profound over time.

Bob sold the OverHead company in 1957 and successfully invested those profits in land development, which allowed him to retire financially secure at fifty-seven years old. In 1967, he purchased a large farm in the rolling, green country hills, sixty miles north of Detroit, and fulfilled his lifelong dream of raising thoroughbred race horses. He moved the family from the affluent suburb of Grosse Pointe Park to the small farm town of Leonard, Michigan, just outside the equally small town of Romeo.

Unfortunately, he failed to discuss that life-changing move with his sixteen-year-old daughter and totally underestimated the tumult it would cause in her academic and social life.

The 2 Sisters

For nine months Bob had convinced himself that his firstborn would bear his name, and in 1939 the newlywed couple named their daughter Roberta. The eldest child quickly became the built-in babysitter for the three other children that followed. Roberta approached that task with a motherly affection that forever left a loving imprint on Kath.

Roberta followed in the footsteps of her father and received an engineering degree with honors from Purdue. The sights and sounds of academia that Kath experienced on the many family trips to Lafayette, Indiana, left a lasting impression on the young girl, and her father's admiration of her older sister did not go unnoticed.

Joan, the second daughter, left a lifelong impact on Kath. Joan took her impressionable younger sister under her wing and taught her the things that parents tended to avoid. Kath enthusiastically joined the family on their regular trips to Ann Arbor to visit her older sister at the University of Michigan. Once again Kath became so enthralled with the academic landscape that the young girl vowed that she too would walk the storied halls of that famed university.

Joan exposed Kath to modern-day romance when she met her fiancé and followed him to Thailand. Her tales about that faraway, exotic world introduced Kath to the world of Buddhism and sparked her interest in Eastern spirituality, as well the occult. Joan also introduced her sister to modern-day divorce when she left her husband.

In 1969, Kath's big sister took her to Paris for Bastille Day where the lessons of Bohemian love flourished in the air with the sights and sounds of French celebrations, including men that followed their every move. As an active participant in the 1960s sexual revolution, Joan went home with a *"homme"* and left Kath to find her own way back to the hotel. At seventeen, she had no trouble finding an escort, but her shyness left him standing on the hotel steps.

Joan introduced her youngest sibling to the concept of contraception. She emphasized how an unplanned pregnancy would adversely impact her life. She actively promoted the newly introduced birth control pill, which ultimately played a role in Kath's eventual demise.

Marianne, the third child in the family, arrived three years before Kath and eventually proved to be a study in contrast. One of Kath's earliest memories was of Marianne trying to suffocate her with a pillow while she laid in her crib. Their tumultuous relationship unceremoniously erupted at unpredictable times throughout their lives. But at other times, they shared a genuine fondness and sisterly-love that shined brilliantly. Throughout their lives, they never forgot the importance of sisterhood.

Marianne and Kath shared the familial Wilson trait of female attractiveness. Both of them learned to appreciate that attribute and clearly understood its benefits. Their sisterhood kept them close, but they remained polar opposites on many issues. Marianne had always been a natural social butterfly, while Kath felt uncomfortable in crowds, remained introspectively quiet, detested small talk, and preferred one-on-one conversations. Kath followed in her father's fiscal footsteps, while Marianne tended to stray from that paternal path. As they grew older, Kath became the good girl in her father's eyes, but Kath refuted that moniker and said she just never got caught.

Youth

Kath learned to read at an early age and grew to be an educational sponge. She couldn't wait to go to school, but with a December birthday, she began a year earlier than most students, which always made her the youngest kid in the class. That created a difficult social milieu for a shy and easily frightened young girl. Kath's diffuse fear affected her to such a degree that she weaved a figure-eight path around and around the trees that lined her home street of Audubon and purposefully delayed her arrival to school. The painfully shy youngster recalled one afternoon in first grade when Robin Sherwood tried to kiss her and she ran all the way home.

Kath's years in Grosse Point Park offered a true *Leave It To Beaver* experience. The tree-lined streets formed a canopy of leaves with branches that created a giant Hobbit-like tunnel and exploded in color every autumn. The giant mounds of neatly-piled leaves from freshly-raked lawns sprang up by the curb every fall, and the neighborhood children raucously jumped into the fluffy mounds and redistributed the leaves back on the street.

Kath hibernated during the Michigan winters and passed those cold days reading even more than she normally did. Beatrix Potter became her favorite story. The personification of those characters so captivated her imagination that she incorporated those themes into her real-world life with a collection of the Beatrix Potter porcelain characters that she proudly displayed in the china cabinet. Her love for animals left her with zero tolerance for animal abuse, and cats always seemed to have a prominent place in her life.

The Michigan spring became everyone's favorite season...no matter how long it took to arrive. The ice floes on Lake St. Clair eventually gave way to open water, and Bob started to prepare his sixty-five-foot Cabin cruiser, the *RoMarJo,* for family summer excursions. The deciduous trees that lined the streets blossomed all at once and Philomine, the Wilson family housekeeper, planted the garden.

When Easter arrived, Carol dressed all the girls in their festive 1950s style outfits. Kath wore a large white hat with a pink ribbon around the sideband complete with a large red bow that secured some plastic daisies. Her outfit included a pink-lined white-lace skirt puffed out by a pettifor, with a matching blouse and white gloves. Her lacy anklet socks folded down above the ankle with a pair of patent leather Mary Jane shoes, and a small white handbag completed the look.

Kath loved Easter Holiday because the Easter Bunny filled her basket with a really big, solid chocolate bunny and lots of milk chocolate eggs. During one unusually warm Easter, the family visited Grandpa Ernie. Kath accidentally left her basket in the car and when the family returned, she found that all the chocolate had melted. Devastated at her loss, she failed to understand why her father refused to contact the Easter Bunny for a replacement.

Summertime walks to Windmill Park on the shores of Lake St. Clair offered a respite from the Michigan heat. Kath learned how to swim at that upscale park but not in the way most children did. The five-year-old stood at the edge of the large community pool in her frilly childlike swimsuit and unexpectedly jumped into the deep end, much to the horror of Carol and Marianne. She splashed and flayed her way to the side while her sister finally fished her out. Kath never professed to be an athlete and shunned physical workouts, but she had always been a good swimmer and never feared water.

This dramatic episode previewed how she managed future challenges. If Kath decided she wanted something she impulsively pursued it, often without a plan, but forever confident in her ability to work it out on the fly.

Kath developed a relationship with Grandpa Frank's sister, Lenore, which left an indelible mark on her young life. Bob frequently pointed out Lenore's admittedly "off-beat" behavior, but Carol regularly encouraged family visits with her aunt, much to the delight of young Kath, who roamed around Lenore's house studying her mysterious mystical objects.

Lenore explored the spiritual side of life, complete with astrological posters, crystal balls, Ouija boards, velvet cloaks, and sacred tiaras. She stacked esoteric books along the walls, and candles filled every shelf. Kath felt like she had been transported into a different land while Bob insisted that Lenore delved into the occult.

Kath couldn't have been more than eight years old when she tried her first séance. She made an altar, lit her candles, donned a makeshift cloak from the bedspread, absconded with her sister's tiara, and set about contacting spirits. For almost an hour, she faithfully did the chants and incantations that Lenore had secretly shared with her, but her attempts proved unsuccessful. Full of childhood rage, she stomped out of the house into the backyard, still wearing her tiara and cloak. She stood on the lawn, shook her little fist in the air, and loudly chastised the spirits that refused to be summoned, shouting, "If there's a God, give me a sign!"

Instantly, a huge crack of thunder split the crystal blue Michigan afternoon sky. Her jaw dropped, her fists opened up and fell to her side as her blue eyes widened to the size of silver dollars. Her feet turned around without her ever realizing it. She quickly ran back into the house, never losing her tiara or robe. It would be quite some time before she'd try that séance again.

In 1965, Kath became the youngest freshman in high school. She had already read every book on the syllabus for her English

Literature class and went on to read Jack Kerouac's *Dharma Bums, Wake Up: A Life of the Buddha,* Alan Watts's *Two Hands of God,* and Rachel Carson's *The Silent Spring.* She was hip to Timothy Leary, Ram Das, Padre Pio, and Gandhi. She developed an intense interest in reincarnation, karma, and the Dead Sea Scrolls. A lot of heavy stuff for a freshman. Kath's peers didn't understand, but Carol did.

Kath and Carol had many discussions on these topics while her mom quoted biblical passages that supported her young daughter's ideas. Like Psalm 46:10, *"Be still and know that I am God,"* and John 3:3, *"Except a man be born again he cannot see the kingdom of God."* Even Bob weighed in with some Christian Science beliefs that God is the sole reality and matter is but an illusion. Today this discourse would be referred to as New Age stuff. Bob never dismissed or discouraged Kath's ideas, which left his youngest daughter with a strong sense of respectful admiration for her father. But then an unexpected event made her regard for him grow even more.

Bob's door factory happened to be in a very rough part of Detroit on Strong Avenue near Mount Elliot. Bob believed he paid a fair wage at his factory, and his shop remained non-unionized in a quintessential union town. Most of the employees shared his non-unionized view at a time when the Detroit labor unions experienced increased labor unrest and the radicalization of workers. One day two men dressed in black suits, sporting fedoras and sunglasses, showed up on the shop grounds and tried to disrupt the work flow by intimidating the workers to sign on to their union. Bob came down from the office and literally chased them away with a large 2x4. Kath knew nothing of this when she noticed two men in a large black Cadillac parked in front of their house on Audubon. For seven days the car would arrive every night about 5 PM and leave around 9 PM. The young girl carefully listened to what her father said but never fully comprehended what her dad meant as he described his run-in with the union bosses. But she intuitively understood why her dad asked her to stay indoors on those days. This encounter forever changed how she saw her dad and helped her understand the courage it took to live in the world.

Kath's life seemed absolutely perfect. She felt protected, loved, and worthy of love, which gave her the confidence to be her own person as a sophomore at Grosse Pointe High. Her sisters taught her the world of fashion and the art of makeup, and she became very particular about her appearance, a trait that lasted a life time. These new-found attributes, along with her thin waist and incredible posture, guaranteed a steady supply of male admirers, which she never discouraged. Her friends and boyfriends hung out at the usual teenage places along Mack and did whatever teenagers did at the time. Although she chose not to compete with the "never wear the same outfit twice" rich kids, she felt comfortable with the person she had become, a hippie in the "Summer of Love."

The Move

A ll of this changed in 1967 when Bob bought the horse farm in Leonard, Michigan. He felt excited as a man could be as he stood on the threshold of fulfilling his lifelong dream, but Kath did not share his enthusiasm.

She felt blindsided. Moving to a small farm town in the middle years of high school would be traumatic for any teenager, but especially for a socially shy adolescent. But Kath's tearful pleas failed to sway Bob. Detroit had just experienced the worst civil unrest in history, and further social problems clearly brewed on the horizon. The inner city began to be uninhabitable, and the safety of a small town in the country made perfect sense to Bob. But Kath felt betrayed. No one asked for her opinion, and she resented not having any input in a decision that upended her life. Kath believed she deserved better. After all, her whole world was just about to end.

On her last day in the neighborhood Kath set about the task of emotionally hurting her father. Her thoughtful and introspective self took leave as she sought out Eric, her "longtime" boyfriend of six months, and acted out in a way that became a model for future dysfunctional coping skills. On that hot summer night she lost her virginity. Exactly how this sexual intrigue hurt Bob remained unclear, as she never discussed her sexuality with her father. But no one ever understood adolescent behavior, and Kath's proved to be no exception.

The family moved into the new house built to Bob's specifications on forty acres of rolling green pasture. The stunningly beautiful home had a view of Stoney Creek just outside the dining room window. The property had two large fenced-in pastures and a large modern-day barn that housed his horses. The farm felt isolated compared to the big city and Bob felt ecstatic. But as a teenager, Kath felt depressed.

Bob's young attractive daughter had nothing to do socially in this small farming town. The nearest neighbor lived a quarter mile away with a girl the same age as Kath, and the two would attend high school in the small town of Romeo, which clearly lacked the sophistication of Grosse Pointe Park. At sixteen, with no car, and being dependent on Mom, Dad, or Marianne for any kind of transportation, Kath's teenage world crashed in around her. But it didn't really matter because this hayseed town had nothing to offer her anyway.

Kath had no social life, no friends, no boyfriend and no one to call. Feeling lonely and alone, she began to withdraw and lost herself in books and music. Bob Dylan became "the" guy. Paul McCartney looked cute, but she had a thing for George Harrison while Jim Morrison became her favorite bad boy. She listened to music and smoked cigarettes that Marianne helped procure, but those activities failed to deter her fermenting rebellious state.

Kath occasionally joined Marianne and cruised the small town. Both girls were stunningly attractive, and boys naturally gravitated to them. Marianne had always been very social and quickly developed a network of friends. But as an introvert, Kath felt uncomfortable in Mari's world.

Roberta, her husband, Jay, and their first-born, Patty, lived on a parcel of Bob's property that he bequeathed to her. Given the proximity of their residence, Kath became their built-in babysitter. It not only kept her busy, but she also earned a few bucks. Unfortunately, she had nowhere to spend it. Being the youngest in her family, Kath now became a big sister to her niece. Patty admired

Kath in much the same way the youngest in the family often reveres the oldest sibling. Kath in turn viewed herself as Patty's protector and mentor and regularly bequeathed sagely advice to the amenable youngster. They developed a sister-like bond that grew ever stronger as they got older.

Kath always felt comfortable in Jay's company, until the family moved to Leonard. Was it her imagination or did he seem to find a way to stand next to her whenever the opportunity presented itself? Did she really see him study her from the corner of her eye in much the same way that young boys do who were on the make? Was he really a creep, or did she feel shame from her recent first sexual encounter? Nothing ever happened between the two, but she felt uneasy.

Joan had an intuitive, big sister way of keeping Kath out of self-destructive behavior. Her frequent visits to the farm and their long walks in the pastures probably did more for Kath than Joan ever realized. Kath spent a lot of time with Bob's horses, which ultimately proved therapeutic, but his prized thoroughbred, Abraxas, emotionally moved her more than anything else.

She traveled with her parents to various race tracks around the country where her father's horses competed and often won. Along the way, she learned about race horses, race tracks, and how to read the programs.

Bob busied himself with the demands of professional horse racing, which inadvertently distanced him from his wife. Carol began to share her thoughts, fears, and unfilled desires with Kath. Her mother had traded her aspirations of youth for the financial security Bob offered. Carol remained a product of the Great Depression, but Kath had become a product of her time, too. The sixties counterculture professed that happiness couldn't be bought, and Kath found herself unable to reconcile the idea that anyone would relinquish the dreams of their youth for material gain.

The adolescent girl saw her mom as a vulnerable person and viewed her parents' relationship through the lens of human feelings with insight into what a married relationship might be like, at least from the old school perspective. The sincere discernments her mother shared laid a strong foundation that would help Kath cope with the inevitable personal crisis every girl experiences at some point in her life. Carol hoped her words would somehow help her daughter weather the approaching adolescent storm.

Unlike Grosse Pointe High School, Romeo High had not been cursed with the affluence of money. Academically, the University of Michigan rarely considered any Romeo High School graduate for admission, regardless of GPA. This added to Kath's anger, and she began her junior year with a bit of an attitude.

On her first day of school Kath wore a pair of large, gold, hooped earrings that remained partially hidden by her long dark brown hair that flowed wistfully over her red cashmere sweater with a black floral design imprinted on the upper front half. A headband of thin braided hair wrapped neatly around her head with a small colorful plastic butterfly clip secured it in the back. A solid black macramé belt snugged up her tight-fitting low-cut hip hugger jeans, with her black boots partially obscured by moderately sized bell-bottoms. Her classic outfit would have been acceptable in Grosse Pointe but not so much in farm country. The initial ride on the school bus told the story of things to come. Her fellow students might have said she overdressed. She would have replied, "Comb the hay out of your hair and clean the manure from your shoes. You might smell better."

In the wealthy town of Grosse Pointe Park, she never really identified with the rich kids, but now she was the rich kid in a not-so-rich town. She never flaunted her father's wealth and didn't look down on those less fortunate, but she never understood why kids wore dirty clothes, smelled bad, and had bad hair days every single day. She knew this would not be an easy transition.

Meeting new friends never came easy for Kath, but she managed it. Greg Campbell, her new photographer boyfriend, made her feel special and at ease in front of a camera while her "Grace Slick" looks made her a perfect model. Years later his early photos of her found their way into his professional Ann Arbor exhibit.

Meticulous in her appearance, Kath always dressed fashionably correct for the school bus, even with gym as her first class of the day. Kath had never been interested in that type of organized exercise because the physical exertion wreaked havoc with her hair and makeup. During softball, she sat in right field and picked dandelions, while her one claim to the sports Hall of Fame came when she scored in a pick-up basketball game but in the wrong basket! Eventually, Carol came to her rescue and secured a permanent excuse from gym class.

Even though Kath was bored with the curriculum and had a 3.8 GPA, her teachers saw an underachiever with an innate ability to understand algebraic equations. Her counselors encouraged her to take calculus and higher mathematics, which would have made her the only female in the class. However, Kath's deep insecurity prevented her from following the path previously blazed by her sister Roberta, so she respectfully declined the offer. Kath spent her remaining high school days hanging out with her boyfriend and staying up late listening to music.

The newly created FM stations were all the craze and WABX became the avant-garde radio station of the day. Every evening she listened to "Dave the Night Tripper" on WABX, who played hip music from the beat generation. In 1968, for those who weren't there, this Detroit radio station set the standard for underground radio and proved to be ahead of its time.

On weekends, Kath drove with her boyfriend, Greg, to Detroit's Grande Ballroom to see the new musical acts of the day, which included Led Zeppelin, Janis Joplin, Bob Seger, Cream, and a local favorite, the MC5.

While in the city they traveled to East Grand Boulevard and visited Greg's mother, Caroline, but the neighborhood had changed since the days of Frank and Viola. Drug dealers became common sights, gangs roamed the streets, and Greg's mom was the only white person who lived on the block.

Caroline collected antiques and amassed a house full of Tiffany-style lamps with various expensive knickknacks that only collectors recognized as valuable. Caroline reinforced what Kath had previously learned from Aunt Bette about Tiffany lamps, the types of glass required for a quality lamp, and how to properly cane it. Once, Caroline awoke in the morning to find she had been burglarized and most of the lamps had been stolen. After her drug dealing neighbor heard about it on the street, the lamps mysteriously returned the next day and she never had another problem. Kath felt safe while visiting Caroline because the homies knew Kath's affiliations, and she felt especially cool because of it.

Kath lived vicariously through books and read about all the exotic places she wanted to visit but found it hard to be a junior in a very unhip high school in the not so cool farm town of Leonard, Michigan.

U of M

Kath completed all of her scholastic requirements for acceptance into the University of Michigan and mailed her application early. Ann Arbor remained the center for everything cool, and with her plan in place, what could possibly go wrong?

The University of Michigan denied her admission, and her life-long dream of roaming the academic halls of one of the most revered schools in the world laid in ruins. On the verge of complete despair, Joan intervened and motivated Kath to create a new plan. She could attend Eastern Michigan University and transfer to the U of M the following year. So, in the fall of 1969, she moved to Ypsilanti, just a few miles from Ann Arbor, and began her college life.

EMU did not have the stellar academic reputation the University of Michigan had, and studying proved difficult in the brand new, sexually segregated, Hill Tower dorm. Small colleges like Eastern Michigan became a haven for guys who used college deferments to avoid the Vietnam War draft, and the school seemed to have low admission standards. EMU had become known as a party school, and Kath's fellow students didn't always promote a scholarly atmosphere.

On one particular evening, a group of students repeatedly blared out a vinyl recording of Michael Jackson's *ABC*. After a dozen or so playings, Kath slammed her book closed, raged out her door, and stomped directly to the room where that ridiculous song kept playing. She pushed open the door and screamed at the top her lungs, "Turn that shit off," before slamming the door shut. When she returned to her room the song mysteriously stopped.

Determined not to let anything interfere with her dream of graduating from the U of M, she spent very little time in the dorm and studied in the campus library. It was there she met and became friends with Jean Valiere, who also shared the dream of transferring to U of M.

The weekends, however, proved to be a different story. Once, Kath's psychology instructor hosted a well-attended off campus party where everyone seemed high on booze, pot, and other drugs. The instructor became increasingly boisterous as the night wore on, and eventually chided Kath for not trying the various mind-altering substances readily available.

Egos ruled the night as student after student tried unsuccessfully to solve the puzzle of the Rubik's Cube. The instructor, who had a penchant for demeaning women, stared at Kath who sat quietly in the corner and challenged her to solve it. Staring right back him, she caught the cube that he tossed to her from across the room and after a few minutes threw the perfectly completed cube back to him.

Convinced she had cheated, the instructor became visibly upset and projected a loud verbal tirade directly at her. Kath got up from her chair and walked slowly toward him as his angry slurs diminished into silence. She stopped directly in front of him and purposely glared at his bloodshot, drugged-out eyes as he sat dumbfounded in his chair. He looked up at her as she twirled her middle finger in an upward motion followed by a big, but silent, "fuck you" smile. The room grew suddenly quiet as she stared at him long enough to let the moment sink in while others looked on. Then she turned around and walked away with a slight, but uncharacteristically, sultry sway of her hips. Kath looked over her shoulder at her nemesis, and their eyes connected for one last time. She saw the coward sink deeply into his chair, and he saw a confident woman who had beaten him badly at his own game. She waved a final goodbye then walked through a stunned crowd and closed the door behind her.

Kath didn't always feel that bold. She used her photographic memory and powerful intellect to overcompensate for her insecurities with people. Her choice of fashionable attire and good posture gave the appearance of extreme confidence, but deep down she felt emotionally insecure and feared rejection. At nineteen, who can claim otherwise?

The psychology instructor's comments about Kath's lack of drug use echoed a certain sense of irony as the new guy in her life, Scott McDonald, fancied himself as Ann Arbor's big-time drug dealer and the likely source of the professor's dope. She enjoyed being Scott's woman. The good girl persona that her father knew would never have dated a drug dealer, but the bad girl part he didn't know enjoyed the thrill of being with such a boy.

Kath always had one main boyfriend, but she always kept a second somewhere close in the background in case the first guy didn't work out. Scott seemed to have the whole package—a very popular, good looking guy from Ann Arbor with money in his pocket and a salesmen personality, but not a particularly good businessman. As a couple they looked dashing. He enjoyed the gorgeous girl who held onto his arm and thought of her as a dealer's dream.

Kath never smoked pot because it made her paranoid, while cocaine became her drug of choice, but she rarely used it. She never had a penchant for drugs, but she craved Scott's attention and the status that came with being his girl. But at nineteen, she didn't fully appreciate the risks.

Once, late at night on their way home to Leonard, the cops pulled Scott over for speeding in his 1969 Mustang. When the police made them exit the car, Kath quickly reached into the backseat and threw his stash of drugs through the open window and into the weeds off the side of the road. How the police missed it amazed her, but they never saw her throw it and he got away with a simple warning.

They drove away after the police left only to circle back to the spot where they had been stopped. Kath walked into the darkness of thick weeds and returned after only a few moments with the discarded stash clutched in her victoriously raised hand. The unlikely Bonnie and Clyde drove back home to Leonard with the windows down, their hair blowing in the warm summer wind, while the radio blasted out WABX's favorite tunes.

Kath spent the summer of 1970 at home in Leonard with Bob and Carol, while a constant stream of boys kept her company. As the father of four daughters, Bob had seen it all before. He remained the consummate gentleman and treated her friends with respect, no matter how long their hair was.

Although he still had some eccentricities, Bob never supported the Vietnam War, which always surprised her boyfriends. During World War II, he had received a deferment from the Defense Department. The OverHead Door Company installed the giant airplane hangar doors on the Willow Run bomber plant, which had been designated by the government as "mission critical," since only his company could quickly repair them should the doors fail. Bob had little interest in politics except when it came to business.

As an entrepreneur who had always made his own way, Bob never appreciated the increasing government regulation that had crept into small business, but he appreciated the tax breaks he got for his thoroughbreds. With all of his money, Bob never presented himself as a high roller guy. He had no debt and paid cash for everything. Kath learned a lot about her dad that summer and admired him even more when one of her boyfriend's mistook him for the gardener.

Kath never forgot the day when an official looking envelope arrived in the mail from the University of Michigan, and a relieved Kath read the acceptance letter to her proud parents. When the celebration subsided, Kath contacted Jean, who had also been accepted, and the two became roommates in an apartment house on Packard Street.

The excitement of academia intoxicated Kath, and she relished the Ann Arbor lifestyle. While many of her peers dressed in torn jeans and tie-dyed T-shirts, she always wore fashionable 5th-Avenue-style clothes and subtle makeup, which created a curious but almost out of step caricature in the 1970 hippie culture.

Kath lived in what she knew to be the Golden Age of music. George Harrison had just released *My Sweet Lord,* and the triple album *All Things Must Pass* resonated with her Eastern philosophies, while Bob Dylan released the *Nashville Skyline* album. Jimi Hendrix and Janis Joplin went on to meet their Maker, while bad boy Jim Morrison continued with his drunken escapades.

The politically active campus erupted with the news of U.S. troops in Cambodia followed by the Dawson Field hijackings, which later became known as Black September, perpetrated by the little-known popular front for the Liberation of Palestine. The energy of the times radicalized the student left wing, and demonstrations sprang up all over campus. Kath was right in the middle of a hullabaloo of political excitement.

Heads turned when Kath pedaled her green, three-speed Schwinn with silver fenders and a basket on the handle bars through the expansive campus to class. She rode through the campus diag in perfect posture with her miniskirt, leotards, black suede boots, and a dark suede jacket, as her long brown hair swirled in the wind. She confidently rode her bike past the demonstrations with an inner sense of achievement as she finally felt part of something cool.

Her wannabe hippie roommate, Jean, graduated from Regina High School on Detroit's east side, technically, Harper Woods, but Kath referred to that all-female school as "Vagina High." They became an unlikely pair, and their friendship lasted almost twenty years.

Jean spoke slowly and peppered her everyday conversation with big flowing words. She purposely changed the accent of a person's name for dramatic effect or created nicknames for those in her social circle. Kath became "BK."

Jean dressed in long, flowing capes with loose-fitting over-sized bell-bottom pants, and wore little or no makeup. She stood tall and lanky, with long dark, frizzy hair and a prominent nose that exaggerated her oval face. Her long, thin fingers matched her long, thin feet.

Kath came to find, as time went on, that Jean spent very little money on food and rarely cooked. Jean always ate Kath's leftovers and rarely did the dishes. Jean's habits never changed after Kath confronted her about these unacceptable behaviors. To resolve the issue, Kath bought food that Jean didn't like and ate off paper plates.

Personal styles, habits, and life choices are often influenced by the company we keep. Jean convinced Kath that birth control pills were the horror of horrors, with dangerous side effects that the drug companies covered up. She proclaimed IUD's to be safest way to go. So, Kath stopped taking the pill and had an IUD inserted at the U of M student clinic.

Consumed with her weekday studies, Kath revered the weekends at The Blind Pig and the Del Rio where she and Jean had become regulars. Scott occasionally accompanied Kath, as the area proved good for business, while Jean arrived with a steady stream of new boyfriends. But those relationships always ended badly as Jean's new found flames frequently hit on Kath, which embarrassed her and angered Jean.

Kath's college sophomore life exceeded her wildest dreams but screeched to a halt when her first health crisis occurred. It all seemed benign enough with nonspecific abdominal pain and persistent nausea, but she went to the U of M hospital emergency room after she vomited for no reason. She told the nurse she must be sick because, "I'd rather die than throw up."

The doctors viewed her subjective symptoms as nothing more than food poisoning and planned to send her home, but when she threw up all over the resident's white coat, a diagnosis of acute appendicitis suddenly appeared and off she went to the O.R. for an appendix that nearly burst. The day after surgery, Scott brought her a pastrami sandwich to celebrate her recovery, and he looked perplexed when she politely abstained.

She returned to the farm for two weeks of recuperation and the doting care that only parents can give. As a young girl Kath enjoyed her mother's French Toast nearly every morning for breakfast, and for two weeks she feasted on Carol's specialty. Kath found the serenity of the farm, the walks along the stream, and the beautiful horses to be the best medicine. Apparently, the small town of Leonard had changed.

One afternoon, Carol and Kath visited Grandpa Frank at the Masonic Temple nursing home where he had lived since Lucy died in her sleep some years earlier. When Kath first saw Frank, a cascade of pleasant memories flooded her mind's eye, but she let out an audible gasp when he shuffled closer. She saw the same mischievousness in Frank's blue eyes, but the skin around his face looked different. When he reached out his wrinkled arms to hug her, she thought, "*Wow, he's old!*"

She laughed out loud when the nurses revealed how Frank regularly snuck out the backdoor and frequented the local pub where he had become as well known as the nurses who retrieved him. Kath looked at her Grandpa Frank with unabashed admiration, as he still exuded a deep and genuine love for life even while it slowly ebbed away.

She also visited Grandpa Ernie while he recovered at home from throat cancer surgery and remained even more obnoxiously demanding than she'd ever remembered. Half of his neck and jaw had been surgically removed, which made eating or drinking difficult, but his incessant demands to smoke a cigar stunned her.

Her eyes struggled for a focal point when he pounded his cane on the floor and demanded the visitors comply with his wishes for a cigar. She wanted to look him in the eyes, but her eyes inevitably stared at the surgical scar, and that made Kath even more uncomfortable. Carol tried to please her father-in-law, which had always been impossible. But she tried anyway while Kath couldn't wait to leave.

The contrast between the two Grandpas presented Kath with a life lesson she never forgot. She witnessed how two people chose polar opposite paths as they navigated themselves through the final years of their lives. Kath promised herself that when her time came she hoped to be like Grandpa Frank, but swore she would never behave like Grandpa Ernie. His outbursts and hideous scar so upset her that she quit smoking cigarettes for nearly a week.

Kath made a full surgical recovery and excitedly returned to campus but never gave a second thought to the time bomb of post-surgical intra-abdominal scar tissue that eventually exploded upon her life decades later.

She immersed herself in Ann Arbor's collegial atmosphere, which excited her beyond belief, but the severity of her near catastrophic illness left her with a sense that she wanted more from life. She liked both of her boyfriends, but true love remained elusive to the ideological girl from Grosse Pointe Park.

Kath admitted to herself that Scott had been nothing more than an interesting boy-toy and would never be her intellectual equal. She knew that Greg truly loved her, but it remained an unrequited love that she had no control over, and she genuinely felt bad about it. She longed to feel the deep mutual love for a partner that would last a life time but so far had been absent in her young life. She admittedly looked for love in all the wrong places, but a chance encounter with a new bartender at the Del Rio changed all that.

The 6 Soulmate

Tom Saltzman stood just short of six feet tall, had straight brown, shoulder length hair, well-defined sideburns that melded with a two-day beard, and a bushy mustache. He didn't look exceptionally muscular, but his physique hinted that he exercised regularly. When he asked for her order, Kath fumbled for words and managed a feeble, "White wine, please." He responded with the house white and a smile which started a relationship that altered her life forever.

Tom did not act like the guys Kath had grown accustomed to. Greg fed her self-esteem by making her the principal subject in his photographic artwork. Their contemporary musical tastes spawned a history of memorable musical events that remained unrivaled, but their final date arrived on December 10, 1971, at the Crisler Arena on the U of M campus when they attended the "Free John Sinclair" concert.

A true hippie, John Sinclair headed the local Ann Arbor commune and became one of the original foundering members of the White Panther political party that supported Huey Newton and the Black Panthers. Their leftist manifesto unnerved the local authorities that convicted Sinclair for possession of two marijuana joints and sentenced him to ten years in prison.

Neither Kath or Greg cared much for the local politics of the White Panthers and remained apathetic about Sinclair's communes and the student gatherings that protested his "ten for two" jail sentence. They were just music freaks who went to see John Lennon headline a truly great musical venue. Although they shared a deep love for music, she didn't love Greg.

Scott lived life on the edge and, occasionally, on the run, which fed Kath's temerarious bad girl mien. His dangerous lifestyle intoxicated her but remained incongruous with her inner self. None of her friends understood why she stayed with him, but she said he made her laugh.

She enjoyed the adulation and attentiveness these two guys afforded her, but she always insisted that they meet her on her terms. Tom, by contrast, remained mysteriously aloof toward Kath, which attracted her to him much like a moth to a lightbulb.

By all measures Tom defined handsome and exuded the quiet confidence of a guy determined to pursue his life's plan. Raised in the affluent suburb of Birmingham, Michigan, he witnessed the benefits that wealth can bring and refused to squander the opportunity that an all-expense-paid U of M degree offered. The oldest of two sons, Tom revered his mother but had a turbulent relationship with his father, "The Big Salt."

Mr. Saltzman retired from a long and lucrative scotch liquor distributorship that he had created after World War II. He piloted fifty B-17 missions over Germany but carried survivors guilt the rest of life, which left him forever at a loss to understand why so many of his friends died and he didn't. Every Fourth of July he loaded-up several rounds of scotch and unloaded several shotgun shells into the night sky while the phonograph played, *Off We Go Into The Wild Blue Yonder*. He was tough to compete with, and Tom didn't even try.

"Toe-moss," as Jean called him, didn't care much for the boisterous antics of his father and learned to keep a tight lid on his emotions, but above all he refused to get angry. Raised Lutheran, Tom had no room for religion. Aloof and at times indifferent, his laugh came out more like a chuckle then a belly-laugh, and he never expressed the slightest hint of an impassioned public ardor. But Kath believed she saw through his detached demeanor. She saw a

42

sexually charged man under that buttoned-down veneer, who rocked her nights and fit neatly into the ideal astrological definition of a scorpionic male. Accustomed to unabashed affection from all of her previous lovers, Kath longed for his.

Before she realized it, Kath soon played by his rules. She acquiesced to his needs and became subservient to his will, which she justified in the name of love. But the sweetest fruit of reciprocal love remained just out of reach.

Their relationship continued unchanged for two more years. Kath continued intermittent contact with her previous flames but had convinced herself that she had finally found her astrological soulmate in Tom. But Tom remained clear about his nebulous, noncommittal relationship and never thought of Kath as an astrological soulmate. He thought about tomorrow's classes and the homework he hadn't quite finished or his next shift at the bar while he tried to make ends meet.

His roommates, the two Jewish Kauffman brothers, provided the couple with comic relief. Randy always feigned concern that his poor grades would jeopardize his family's funding for medical school and regularly joked that he'd willingly be a podiatrist if his family just kept the money coming. The Kauffmans had a penchant for sexual debauchery and regularly cavorted with the local hippie girls who believed in free love but had no morals.

One of Randy's girls had the tattoo of a snake coiled around the feet of a chained maiden imprinted on her back. She regularly got drunk, stripped naked, and danced around the living room while she performed for the group with an unreciprocated eye toward Tom. Randy had a very large snake that lived in an oversized glass aquarium that she used in a purported erotic display. This made Tom a bit queasy, but the brothers never seemed to mind.

The debauchery never made Kath uneasy, as she could write a few autobiographical chapters on that topic. But being an insecure jealous girl, she had no plans to sexually share her scorpionic boyfriend with anyone and clung even tighter to Tom.

And so it went until graduation, when everything changed. Bob felt as proud as a father could be of his youngest daughter, who graduated with honors from one of the finest schools in the land. As a graduation present he bought her a blue 1972 three-speed Lemans Coupe with a 400-cubic-inch V-8 engine.

Beneath his harsh exterior, Kath's father had a heart of gold. Whatever he gave one daughter he gave something of equal value to the other three. He purchased a car for each of his daughters on their college graduation except for Marianne, who never graduated from a four-year university. Instead, she received cash, which seemed to suit her better.

After graduation Kath packed her things and temporarily moved back home while Jean permanently moved to New Orleans. The Kaufmann brothers were both accepted into the U of M Medical School, while Tom prepared to move to Solana Beach, California.

Kath had no idea her astrological soulmate planned to move out west until he nonchalantly mentioned it at the Del Rio a few days before graduation. He painted a grandiose picture of life on the beach, endless surfing with lots of beach parties in perpetually good weather, and a new start for his career.

At first, she thought he was joking, as he had no family there and only a couple of "loser" friends who supposedly lived that quintessential lifestyle. Worse, he never invited her! There was no "us," only "him," and definitely not the starry-eyed narrative that she envisioned they would share together.

For two years, she convinced herself they would marry and start a family, but "Toe-moss" apparently had other ideas that he never shared. Kath became catatonically devastated when she realized she had been dumped by the love of her life!

Her anger grew as she paced alone in her room while her eyes fixated on the neatly framed picture of them she had recently placed on her dresser. The photo had been taken at the U of M Arboretum the previous autumn when the leaves blazed in color. The camera captured Kath throwing leaves in mid-air as they rained down on Tom's head.

Anyone who saw that picture witnessed a happy couple in a Kodak moment. Kath stopped pacing and stared at the picture for quite some time as she relived the memories of that captured moment and felt the faint tinge of a smile spread across her face. But then her sentimental joy quickly morphed into the instant rage of a woman scorned. She lunged for the picture and smashed it against the wall. Startled at her unexpected outburst, she looked at the shards of glass strewn across the floor and threw herself on the bed in unrelenting, fitful sobs that lasted all night.

Kath awoke the next morning with puffy eyes and a painful chest. She picked up the broken glass and carefully placed it in the trash along with the picture. She sat down on the bed with a hard thump, followed by a deep sigh and decided to attend that night's farewell party, not just to save face, but to show Tom the true cost of his unaccompanied travel plans. She spent most of the afternoon writing a poem that expressed how she felt about Tom's move to the West Coast and incorporated the titles of many Beach Boy songs within the verses that summed up her feelings. She planned to give it to him if he truly intended to leave her behind.

That evening she allotted extra time to precisely apply her makeup and carefully curl her long brown hair. Her tight jeans and revealing blouse would turn any man's head and as a full-blown woman, she wanted Tom to hear her roar.

Kath arrived fashionably late but stood outside the apartment for a brief moment before she drew a deep breath and opened the door to a crowded party. Inside, the eyes of the revelers silently followed her as she casually mingled about the room looking for Tom. Kath eventually found him on the balcony looking like he had already consumed a few beers. They shared a mutually awkward moment when their eyes met, but as she walked towards him she refused to have a teary-eyed emotional encounter, as she had already lost all of her tears the night before. She wanted him to always remember what he had intentionally left behind.

Though they were alone on the balcony, Tom never complimented Kath on her stunning looks. He asked if she planned on moving to Solana Beach, but the tone in his voice did not imply an invitation to live with him. She reiterated her love for Ann Arbor but coyly left the door open for any possibility. She spoke her words deliberately, without quivering and looked him right in the eye when she insisted on an explanation as to why he was parting ways. He shuffled his feet and manipulated the Stroh's beer can, before taking a long a swig that emptied the container. He spoke to the beer can as he said it wasn't about her but his new beginning, and he wished she would reconsider a move to the coast.

Kath thought his request sounded contrived, and his body language spoke volumes. She stared at him while he oscillated his gaze between her and the beer can. She wished him luck in California, kissed him on the cheek, and handed him the folded poem. Holding back tears, she returned to the party and proceeded to embrace the liquid spirits, probably more than she should have.

He looked at his empty beer as she walked away then set the can down. She purposefully maintained an unobstructed view of him while she stood across the room and watched as he unfolded the hand-written note. He held the paper with both hands and read the poem in the dim light.

46

Have *Fun, Fun, Fun* on your *Surfin' Safari*,
and I hope you *Catch a Wave*.
God Only Knows, When You Grow Up To Be A Man.
I could've been your *California Girl*, your *Little Surfer Girl*.
Wouldn't It Be Nice?
But *Don't Worry, Baby*, I won't be *In My Room*,
because *I Get Around* with my *Good Vibrations*.

They kept their distance for the remainder of the night. Tom stayed out on the deck for most of the party, but Kath made sure he heard her whenever she laughed with her friends and strategically maneuvered herself in such a way that he would see her when she danced with other guys.

Tom followed his plan to move to Solana Beach, and Kath returned to the family farm. She questioned the value of a four-year degree at the University of Michigan that landed her a full-time job answering phones at a student loan office near Oakland University for a crooked Pakistani, while her friends got married and started families as they pursued their careers. Everyone she knew chased their dreams while she answered phones and lived with her parents. The time had come for some serious introspection.

The north wind blew colorful leaves off the trees and seasonal change filled the air. Carol and Kath visited Grandpa Frank in the Intensive Care Unit of the local hospital. He recognized them but struggled to speak. His chest rattled and the oxygen mask made it difficult to hear his words, but they took turns putting their ear next to his mouth while they struggled to understand his message. On Kath's turn, he spoke so loud that she was a bit startled and lurched back. "Read to me," he said, causing mother and daughter to look at each other in a moment of surprise.

Kath found a Bible in the bedside stand and handed it to her mother. Carol knew exactly the passage to look for and thumbed through the pages until she found Ecclesiastes 3:1-8. When she read the passage, Frank slowed his breathing and appeared to relax. Kath became misty-eyed, as she watched her grandfather fade from this life. That moment defied words and made for a quiet ride home. Grandpa Frank died of congestive heart failure the following day.

Frank's Masonic brothers at the Royal Oak Lodge of Free and Accepted Masons #464 arranged his funeral. The ceremony had been well attended by the lodge brothers, but only a few family members showed up. The ritualistic detail of the Masonic service intrigued his young granddaughter and revived her memories of Frank's sister, Lenore.

There was an evergreen sprig on the casket, senior and junior warden columns, and a Bible that rested on a small stand that remained neatly opened to Ecclesiastes 12:1. A compass and a square had been purposely placed on top of the opened pages. The Masonic members wore their robes and aprons while they proceeded with the white-gloved hand gesticulations that signified some kind of secret code Kath did not understand. After the ceremony Frank came to his final resting place next to Lucy in the Royal Oak family burial plots previously purchased by Bob.

Grandpa Ernie remained obnoxiously cantankerous to the end, and when he heard that Frank had died he contemptuously mumbled, "That man never had a pot to piss in, and now that he's dead the only thing he's left his family is his debt."

The oral cancer surgery had left Ernie a hideous spectacle. His words became barely discernable, but his disparaging message remained clear. He declared Bob a disgrace and held him responsible for his deplorable living conditions. His condescending attitude and derogatory behavior had completely exasperated the

48

nursing home staff who asked him to leave on more than one occasion. But each time the administrator called Bob to discuss a transfer, Bob increased the monthly payment so they allowed him to stay.

On the last family visit, Grandpa Ernie continued to beat his cane on the floor, absent the commanding effect it once had. He became little more than a caricature of the person he had once been, which evoked pity from those who didn't know him and disgust from those who did. No one shed a tear when he died alone

Ernie had previously purchased his final resting place next to Viola when she passed, but he had no religious affiliation and certainly hadn't professed any Christian Science views. Bob had no affiliation with any organized church either, so Carol arranged for the liturgical services at the Romeo Lutheran Church, where she sang in the choir. The solemnities were well-attended by family and friends, but the eulogy was delivered by a vicar who clearly didn't know Ernie. Bob felt relieved after the graveside service, but found himself completely devoid of the melancholic emotions that he experienced when Viola passed.

Bob did his duty as he made the social rounds at the catered repast and offered the survivors consoling small talk on Ernie's extended suffering. At the end of the day, he prepared himself for his responsibilities as executor of Ernie's financial affairs, but as its architect, he already knew its allocations and made sure everyone received equal shares of the estate. The grandchildren each received $10,000 in 1973 money, and Kath had a pretty good idea of what to do with it.

Kath learned two themes from her diametrically opposed grandfathers. Frank taught her that money can't buy happiness, but Ernie taught her that it's a lot harder to find happiness without it. She became convinced that her destiny intertwined with that young man who had just moved out west. Nothing in the occasional letter Tom sent her remotely suggested he pined for her, but she became compulsively obsessed with the notion that her astrological, scorpionic soulmate wanted her to join him in California. Visions of romance, marriage, and the start of a new family danced in her head, as she now had the means to move out west.

Bob never discouraged his daughters from travel, as he took frequent business trips on the train from coast to coast for the OverHead Door Company. For his honeymoon, long before freeways existed, he drove his 1938 Packard from Grosse Pointe Park to Goldfield, Nevada, and Cameron, Arizona, to visit Ernie's brothers and sisters.

Bob tried to be supportive of his daughter, but he subtly discouraged Kath from taking the long, solo trip to California, not because of the inherent dangers of a young woman traveling alone but because he knew why she wanted to go.

As the father of four daughters he knew better than to let his distrust of Tom enter into their conversation. Instead, he voiced his concerns in a logical, fatherly way, carefully pointing out the fallacy of chasing a boy that had purposely left her behind, while trying to impress upon his youngest daughter that Tom lost more than she did. He even sweetened the pot by offering her an all-expense paid post-graduate education at her alma mate, but he found himself on the losing end of that offer.

In short order, Kath loaded up her blue LeMans and headed west on I-94. She only stopped for gas, coffee, and fast food, and slept only when her eyes would no longer stay open. The southerly route took her through Indianapolis, St Louis, Oklahoma City, and Albuquerque. In Arizona she turned south on 89A at Flagstaff and traveled for the first time through Oak Creek Canyon.

The deep gorge of Oak Creek and towering red rock walls provided a stunning sight for a girl from the flat green lands of the Midwest. Enthralled with its energy, she took an unexpected overnight break at L'Auberge de Sedona to savor the sights and sounds of Sedona.

With the Red Rocks of Oak Creek Canyon in her rearview mirror, she promised herself that she would return some day as she drove south to Phoenix and turned west for the final stretch to California. She arrived unannounced at Tom's Solana Beach house completely convinced that she'd be greeted as a long-lost lover. She wasn't. With the ring of a doorbell that didn't work, followed by a hard knock on the door, the 2,500-mile romantic adventure came to an abrupt end. Tom opened the door with a faintly discernible look of surprise.

After an uncomfortably awkward hug, he welcomed her in, not as a former lover, but as someone who might have been the sister of his best friend. He could have accommodated her some-where in the rented, one-bedroom house, but he made alternative arrangements with a group of women he knew needed a roommate.

Kath moved into a two-bedroom flophouse near the beach and shared a bedroom with an unemployed stoner hippie. With no furniture and few clothes, she quickly realized the cost of linens, towels, and other staples would rapidly deplete her recently acquired working capital, so she quickly landed a job as a cocktail waitress at a bar where Greta, one of her housemates, worked.

Although she had no experience waitressing, her short skirt and tight blouse rewarded her with good tips. Midway through her first shift, the owner told her all the tips were pooled and shared, but she could retain a higher percentage of the receipts if she agreed to give him regular blow jobs in his office.

Staring at his ogling, drooling face she said, "Excuse me, do I look that desperate to you? No, forgive me, you're right. I'd love to suck your brains out, if you had any. You may think you're 'Long Dong Silver,' but from what the other girls tell me, you're more like 'Shorty Rides Again.'" She took her money, flipped him off and drove back to the beach house. Kath never worked as a waitress again.

She reeled with indignation as she charged through the front door of her new rental and directed her anger at Greta, who failed to understand Kath's indignation. After all, she made good money. Kath flailed her arms and struggled for words but found herself staring into a pair of blank eyes, when she suddenly realized why Greta didn't seem upset.

She abruptly halted the tirade in mid-sentence, lowered her arms, and loudly proclaimed, "Oh my God, Greta, you're such a bimbo," then stomped off to her room. Kath began to foster serious doubts about this whole California thing and wondered why she had chased a guy who used her for sex and treated her like crap, as her dad's warning echoed in her ears. A deepening sense of disgust gradually coalesced within her when she realized she had more in common with Greta than she had previously thought.

Bewildered by her life's quandaries and fed up with moronic males, Kath left town and found herself driving to see her sister Roberta, who had moved to Barstow years earlier. The two-and-a-half-hour drive from Solana Beach gave her some quiet time to breathe, but she may have jumped from the frying pan into the fire. Arriving just before sunset, she felt the warmth of her family when they came out to greet her with ten-year-old Patty leading the pack, but her heart sank when she saw her brother-in-law, Jay.

She instantly felt herself transported back to an earlier time, when she believed Jay stood just a little too close, and his kiss lingered a little too long on her cheek. Now she wanted to recoil, but she couldn't move. Suddenly she felt guilty and confused because he really hadn't done anything. Did she over react? Did she misread his intent? She couldn't be sure about anything except the need for a hot shower.

The dinner table included an extra helping of advice from the elders. They helped her understand that she could buy the house she was in now with her inheritance and rent the rooms out to cover the monthly payments. Plus, her sister would cosign the loan. With the right deal, she might even generate a small income.

When Jay asked what she planned to do for employment, she recounted the success of her short-lived waitressing job but left out some of the details. As a hospital administrator, he pointed out the advantages of a nursing career and the low cost of education for California residents. It surprised Kath that she hadn't thought of those things herself.

If she pursued those plans it meant remaining in Southern California with no resolution to her preoccupation with Tom or his lack of reciprocity. Her perceived romantic dilemma and possible solutions remained foremost on her mind when she drove Jay's 1972 Volkswagen "Thing" into the Mohave Desert, with Patty riding shotgun, giggling the whole time. As the miles wore on, her problems slowly evaporated into the arid expanse. Her mind slowed down as she began to appreciate the beauty of the not so empty barren desert landscape, and an abrupt epiphany regarding her life choice suddenly became clear. The solution to her problem suddenly became obvious and shattered the solitude of the desert.

Back in Solana Beach, she had researched nursing requirements and closely studied the housing market. Her findings convinced her that Jay's plan could work, and she traveled to Barstow a few more times for updates and encouragement. She felt less apprehensive about Jay and came to view him as a big brother.

She still met up with Tom at the bar and went on long beach walks, but a curious thing happened when he realized she planned to buy a house and go to nursing school. He began cozying up to her. Did he do it because she had money, or did her new-found motivation genuinely intrigue him? When Kath noticed that change she became less clingy but more suspicious.

When she was a young girl Kath's father often said, "They're only interested in my money," which she had dismissed as the rantings of a paranoid man. Now it seemed to have an air of authenticity. With that in mind, she became cool and aloof toward Tom but punctuated it with periods of affection. She played him and felt empowered for the first time in years.

The holiday season fast approached. The day before Thanksgiving her roommates got stoned and decided to camp at the Grand Canyon. Kath happened to be the only one with a car and agreed to drive them, but she insisted they pay for the gas. She had also been the only one in the group who had been to Arizona and reiterated the inverse correlation between altitude and temperature. Her roommates naively insisted that Arizona is a desert and is always hot.

The morning temperature reached a pleasant 60 degrees when they left San Diego and increased as they traveled east through the desert. Kath thought the four of them must have been quite a sight in that LeMans, wearing sunglasses, smoking cigarettes with the windows down, while the radio blasted their Rock and Roll and their long hair blew in the wind.

When they passed Black Canyon City, between Phoenix and Sedona, the weather changed with the elevation gain. A cold front moved through and the wind picked up, with a noticeable drop in temperature. The windows went up as they drove through Oak Creek Canyon, and she turned the heater on.

No one spoke as they traveled further up the Canyon and snow began to fall. Without sounding like an "I told you so," Kath began to query the beach bunnies as to their camping equipment. Their inventory included old sleeping bags but no tent and no cooking utensils. They all wore sandals, shorts and tie-dyed T-shirts, while Kath wore jeans, suede boots, a sweater, and a warm leather jacket. None of the others had brought hats, though Kath had a knit cap. Reluctant to state the obvious, they were ill-prepared for the Grand Canyon in November. As the snow continued to build, Kath decided to turn the car around and no one protested. They spent Thanksgiving, 1973, in a Sedona motel and woke up in the morning to blue sky and snow-covered Red Rock Mountains. That picturesque scene left the girl from Leonard, Michigan, in awe of the natural beauty she inadvertently found herself in, and she kept that feeling close to her heart. The next day the wayward campers returned to Solana Beach.

That misadventure and the upcoming Christmas season made Kath reassess her strategic plans. The holidays are historically a poor time for real estate deals, and she longed for Ann Arbor. Even Leonard, Michigan, appealed to her. Although an impartial observer would have had difficulty recognizing it, Tom finally showed some romantic interest in Kath. She convinced herself that money had nothing to do with it, but she had decided to leave and no longer cared what he did.

Once again, she loaded up the LeMans, took the southern route, and headed east. Just west of the Rockies she picked up a hitchhiker, but when he announced his final destination as Columbus, she nearly threw him out of the car. She still felt angry with Ohio State but shared with him the cause of her discontent, which had everything to do with football rivalry.

During her first year at the U of M campus on the Friday afternoon before the Big Game between Michigan and Ohio State, Kath walked along Packard Avenue to the campus library when a car full of drunken visiting Buckeyes slowed down and threw beer on her, which ruined her new suede jacket. Dripping in beer and shaking her fist, she screamed words that couldn't be found in the Bible. She hated OSU more than she hated football.

Christmas went well at the Wilson house and her parents could not have been happier to have their daughter home for the Holidays. Roberta called from Barstow to wish Carol a Happy Birthday and offered her regrets for not being there, but the remaining three daughters enjoyed a splendid prime rib dinner with all the trimmings. The table talk flowed as freely as the wine and soon everyone got up to date on everyone's business.

After dinner the family retired to the living room, where the ten-foot Douglas fir had been trimmed to the hilt. The fireplace roared and the stockings on the mantle sagged from the weight of gifts. Mari played all the Christmas standards on the piano while Carol sang along, and Kath remembered the evening as a Norman Rockwell moment.

Two days later, in the early evening, Kath answered a knock at the door to find Tom standing there looking very cold. He had just returned to Michigan and offered to buy her a birthday dinner in Ann Arbor. He had completely surprised her, but she refused to show it. She purposely let him stand out in the cold for a few moments before she invited him in, and deliberately delayed an answer to his invitation. She knew from the moment he asked that she planned to go and eventually said so in a nonchalant way. This was the moment she had been waiting for.

Living the Dream

In January, Kath and Tom rented an apartment on Fuller Street in Ann Arbor and lived there for more than two years. She picked up a job at the Ann Arbor vision center answering phones and scheduling appointments, and Tom managed to get his old job back at the Del Rio. Together, they busily connected with old friends and made new ones, which included a black cat named Alex and an orange tabby named Max.

In 1975, they both left their full-time jobs and started a stained-glass business. They sold small hand-made terrariums, Tiffany-style lamps, and window inserts plus any custom orders they could find. Kath's knowledge of Tiffany glass and the special technique of caning she had learned from Caroline, Greg Campbell's mother, set her work apart from the rest.

Without a storefront, they utilized Tom's 1972 Chevy Vega to frequent local street fairs, with the Ann Arbor Fair being their largest event. Tom fared better as a salesman than Kath, who grew irritated if the customer praised the piece but preferred a different but unavailable color. Overall, revenue barely exceeded cost, but the fun they had proved priceless. They continued this lifestyle for a year until the financial realities finally set in.

In 1976, Tom took a job with an accounting firm in Ypsilanti that paid more than the glass business and included benefits, but Kath recognized that her degree in Psychology with a minor in Sociology proved useless in the labor market.

Kath finally acted on her brother-in-law Jay's advice and enrolled in a one-year Licensed Practical Nursing program at Washtenaw Community College, which she paid for with the last of her inheritance. She knew nothing about nursing but believed she could always find a job with that profession.

Kath reveled in academia, but even with her demanding schedule she always tried to be home in time to take her turn cooking dinner. They moved from Ann Arbor into a three bedroom house in a family neighborhood on Sheffield Street in Ypsilanti, which happened to be closer to Tom's office.

Hanging out at the Del Rio became a thing of the past. Instead, the new pastime included staying at home and entertaining married friends who had kids. During school, Kath's student nurse friends talked of their children or their plans to have them. At twenty-five, she started to daydream about kids and starting a family, but being a practical person, she spoke little about that dream and waited until after graduation. Besides, neither of them had even discussed marriage let alone starting a family.

When they worked together in the glass works, Kath and Tom were constantly in each other's company, loving, laughing, and living life, but after the glass works closed Kath felt a subtle change in their relationship. Tom seemed to slip back into his aloof and more distant self. His newfound belly laughs had been supplanted with somber solemnity and a forced chuckle. She asked her friends if they thought Tom had fallen out of love with her, but they saw nothing different and convinced her that she had imagined the whole thing. She tried to put that uneasy feeling out of her head and graduated from nursing school with honors.

In September of that year, Kath married her astrological soulmate in a small wedding at the family farm. Marianne agreed to be her maid of honor, and Jean flew in from New Orleans to be her attendant. By all accounts it was a happy gathering of two families who united and supported the new couple.

They honeymooned in New Orleans and Jean gave them an insiders' tour of the town with a front row seat in a small bar where the Neville Brothers and Dr. John played several sets into the early morning hours. After the show the group was walking down Saint Peters Street in the midst of an inebriated crowd when a man who happened to be walking next to Kath suddenly fell down an open man hole. Not believing what had just happened, they all stared in disbelief as the man climbed up out of the sewer and continued on as if nothing had happened.

In October, Kath started a new job as an office nurse for a large medical practice in Ypsilanti. The three internal medicine doctors, Banks, Banks, and Lyon, serviced a community of auto workers with UAW health insurance that paid a very high reimbursement rate. Her duties consisted of registering the patients, escorting them to the exam rooms, obtaining the vital signs, and helping with any procedures.

Their two full-time incomes dramatically improved the family savings rate, but what they saved for remained a point of contention. As DINKS, (Dual Income No Kids), Tom searched for any available tax break he could find. Buying a house would have helped enormously, but they lacked sufficient funds for an adequate down payment. In those days, mortgage rates were at just under nine percent interest for a thirty-year loan. At their current savings rate, it would take a few more years to even qualify for a mortgage.

Kath grew impatient with Tom's financial conservatism and reminded him of others with far less income who started families. "Kids area tax deduction, too" she argued, but Tom had a stubbornly clear vision for family planning.

The Holidays brought more stress into the young couple's lives, as they juggled extended family dinner dates and tried not offend anyone. They preferred staying home, but that's not what the Holiday Season is about. These gatherings birthed the inevitable question of family planning and always progressed along gender specific lines. The men debated the cost of raising children, while the women discussed the maternalistic joys of creating a family.

Early in the new year, the family planning discussion frequently found its way to their dinner table but with no hint of compromise. Eventually, they avoided the topic all together, which cast a long, dark shadow on their relationship. As Kath's frustration mounted, their communication began to suffer. Their dinners at home were no longer what they used to be, and the fun times of cooking and sharing a meal seemed to be a thing of the past.

Kath began to take emotional refuge in her job. The doctors held a regular Friday night office meeting at various expensive restaurants and invited Kath to attend. At first she felt hesitant, not knowing what Tom would think, but the doctors persisted and soon she became a Friday night regular. When Kath introduced her sister to Dr. Lyon, Marianne became a regular, too, and the sisters began to look forward to the end of the work-week outings.

Family planning continued to be a dinner table conversation and their views remained unchanged, but the intensity of their arguments certainly persisted. Clearly frustrated, Tom spoke in a restrained voice. "If you want kids, fine, then go ahead, but you'll have to raise them on your own. Don't count on me!" Those words remained seared into her memory forever.

The couple remained seated at the dinner table completely surprised at how quickly the events of the evening spiraled out of control, but neither attempted to sooth the bruised feelings the other one felt. The room grew uncomfortably quiet until Kath suddenly pushed away from the table, stomped into the bedroom, and locked the door behind her. Tom slept on the couch that night.

A distinct chill filled the morning air as they sat uncomfortably at the breakfast table and silently stared at the steam that swirled from their coffee cups. Tom tried to make small talk, but Kath refused to partake in any conversation and left early for work. She had always been slow to anger, but once that threshold had been crossed she carried a grudge for a long time.

The office schedule happened to be exceptionally heavy that day, and Kath struggled to keep up. Dr. Lyon thought she appeared tired, but when he inquired about her obvious fatigue she forced a smile and simply acknowledged his insight with an affirmative nod. He replied with a sympathetic smile, but simply chalked it up to a youthful late night.

As the hours dragged on, the previous night's altercation echoed in her head and further exacerbated her anger until she had completely convinced herself that she had no choice but to retaliate against her husband. By lunchtime she knew Tom's ultimatum could not go unanswered.

When the day had finally ended and everyone had left the office Kath remained behind to lock up after Dr. Banks saw his last patient. She stood silently in the exam room but felt distracted as her anger fulminated out of control, and she struggled to formulate a retaliatory response against Tom. The patient sat precariously on the edge of the table in a paper gown, but Kath noticed the doctor's misplaced attention as he periodically glanced her way while he conducted the examination. She initially thought that once again she wrongly imagined a guy coming on to her, like she had with her brother-in-law. She immediately felt guilty until their eyes met.

Kath had seen that look before at the Friday night meetings after he'd had a few drinks. He always managed to sit next to her and regularly brushed his hand across her thigh but made it seem unintentional. Once, she caught him eyeing her cleavage, and he responded with a sheepish grin but never looked away. She chose to ignore his suggestive behavior and vowed not to be paranoid. Besides, they were both married.

He finished the exam and the patient remained seated on the table as Kath buttoned up his shirt. Dr. Banks stood directly behind Kath, which obstructed the patient's view of him while he discussed his findings.

As he talked to the patient, the doctor slowly and deliberately caressed her behind with one hand while he held the bulky medical chart in the other. Kath's tired eyes popped wide open in shocked surprise. She struggled not to reveal her sudden astonishment while lightning bolts of sexual energy shot up her spine and traveled down her legs all the way to her toes. When he had finished his discussion, the doctor walked toward the patient and shook his hand goodbye before he asked Kath to schedule a return appointment. Then he left the room. She didn't know what to do except to say, "Yes, Doctor," and escort the patient out.

Kath returned to the exam room and was cleaning up when she heard Dr. Banks enter the room. She pretended not to notice when he stood behind her. Without saying a word, she stopped cleaning and rested her hands on the exam table. Her head dropped down in disbelief because she knew what would happen next. After a brief moment, Kath felt his hands glide up her bare arms, but instead of pushing them away her palms remained glued to the table. His breath quickened while he massaged her neck, and to her surprise, she didn't move except to lower her head even further. She felt his hand reach for the zipper on the back of her white nurse's dress and heard it slowly unzip.

Frozen in that position, she felt the dress slip from her shoulders and allowed it to fall to the floor. The rest became a blur as the two engaged in adulterous passion right there on the exam table. When he finished what he had set out to do, Kath remained on the table while she watched him get dressed.

Tears filled her eyes as she felt the early stages of remorse and the initial ramifications of her actions began to take hold. When he tried to speak, she shouted, "Shut up, just shut up." Then she slid off the table. She fumbled for her clothes and hurriedly dressed, unsure if she had put them on correctly. She left the building without saying a word, leaving him to lock up.

Kath returned to a disturbingly quiet home and walked past Tom but never responded to his conciliatory greeting. She went directly into the bedroom and locked the door, then sat on the bed and buried her face in her hands, carefully stifling her emotional sighs while she relived all that had happened.

She leapt from the bed and frantically threw her clothes into a haphazard pile before she ran into the bathroom. The mirror reflected her naked image, and in a subdued but sorrowful voice, she asked the reflection why she had done what she did. The hot shower lasted a long time, as she compulsively scrubbed her body in a futile attempt to wash off the disgust that oozed out of every pore.

Dressed in her pajamas, she dried her hair and quietly opened the bedroom door but returned to bed without a word. Tom eventually joined her. They laid on opposite sides of the bed but never spoke. Kath stared into the darkness of the empty room and thought maybe her father had been right about Tom as she searched for any reason to justify her earlier actions.

Unable to sleep, Kath crawled out of bed in the early morning hours and sipped her coffee at the breakfast table while she tried to convince herself the sexual liaison had never happened. Tom eventually joined her, but the uncomfortable absence of any conversation about future children and the willful reluctance to acknowledge her unknown affair drowned out the short but civil discourse they had before she left for work.

The staff greeted her in their usual upbeat fashion when she walked into the office, but she paid close attention to her coworkers for any hint that the previous night's torrid affair had become water cooler gossip. She went about her normal routine but nervously paused for an anxious moment in the doorway of that now infamous room. When she finally stepped in, the flood of memories nearly overwhelmed her.

Never in her life had she experienced the sexually charged adrenalin rush that shuddered through her body the moment she consciously surrendered to her carnal desires and allowed herself to become a complicit victim. The residual feeling from that sexual fire remained a smoldering ember that she hoped would be extinguished over time, but she lived in mortified fear that one day it would unexpectedly be reignited.

All of that changed when Dr. Banks arrived at the office and the two philanderers met for the first time since their sexual dalliance. He greeted her as he normally did but with a subtle grin that she perceived as something more than a well-meaning gesture, even though no one else noticed.

As the hours passed, a deep animosity toward her carnal cohort violently simmered beneath her calm demeanor while his adolescent attempts at seductive glances angered her even more. The accidental lovers readily expressed a keen desire for a quick end to a long day but not for the same reasons.

When the last patient had finally left the office and the two stood alone in the exam room, Kath felt his hand gently rub her behind. His amorous smile turned to utter shock when the full measure of her self loathing poured over him like a raging torrent of water from a failed dam.

She slapped his hand away as she turned toward him and purposefully stopped just inches away from his nose. "Stop that!" she shouted. He stood frozen in place with his eyes wide open before he shushed her into silence out of fear the office staff might hear the commotion. At first she didn't care if the whole world knew about their loud confrontation, but as she glared at his befuddled face, she realized the precariousness of the social quandary she suddenly found herself in and continued to speak in a subdued voice

She blamed him for the whole tawdry affair and insisted that he purposely used his position of authority to take advantage of her for his own salacious gain. She admitted her minor indiscretion had been a major mistake and promised to make things right with her husband. But when she asked her adulterous lover if he planned to tell his wife about their affair he responded with cold silence.

She let that silence fill the room for added effect before she said, "Once I tell my husband everything that has happened, his anger will know no bounds. He will seek you out and kick your ass." A streak of fear flashed across his face because he knew that Tom carried a black belt in taekwondo, and she seized on that fleeting moment of manly weakness to escalate her demands. She insisted that he stay far away from her and threatened to tell his wife the whole story if he continued his bawdry pursuits. They stared at each other for what seemed like an eternity before she pushed him out of the way and left for home.

As she drove through the busy narrow streets of the city she formulated her plan of how to tell Tom all that had transpired. When she walked through the front door at her usual time a strong scent of Italian marinara greeted her. Tom stood in front of a pot of bubbling spaghetti sauce and a colander filled with steaming noodles. The dinner table had been set. She placed her purse on the kitchen counter as they exchanged a cautious greeting before she sat down.

Tom lifted the lid from the pot of bubbling sauce and sniffed the scented cloud of Italian spices that filled the air, which reassured him he had gotten the mixture just right. His obvious attempt to bring peace to the household caught Kath by surprise. She nervously walked toward him, gently placed her hand over his, and slowly guided the lid back onto the pot. He felt confused when she reached around him to shut off the burner, and he turned to look at her with a puzzled face when she asked him to sit down for a minute.

Kath anxiously paced around the kitchen as she frantically searched for the well-rehearsed words to start her confession, but her emotional dam suddenly burst and a torrent of words just poured out.

He patiently listened to her agitated tale without a hint of emotion, while tears of shame streamed down her face. When she finished her story, they stared at each other in utter silence except for the muffled sobs that she tried to stifle before he asked, in a matter of fact way, "Do you love the guy?" With desperate emotion, she replied, "No, I love you!" After a long pause, he asked her why she did it. She looked at him with a blank face that he sensed hid an important piece of the story before she replied with a silent shrug of her shoulders.

They remained seated at the table in complete silence for an uncomfortably long time before he listed his conditions for reconciliation in a dispassionate and controlled voice.

She must end the illicit affair immediately, which she claimed to have already done. She agreed to quit her job and promised to never to be unfaithful again. He looked at her puffy eyes and the streaks of tears that streamed down her face before he added in a convincingly sympathetic tone, "Everyone makes mistakes."

Their appetite for dinner had long since disappeared, and she quietly retreated to the bedroom while he repackaged the untouched meal for leftovers. They laid in confusion on opposite sides of the bed as Tom tried to process all he had heard, while she questioned the lack of anger in his response.

She had grown up in a house where men ruled the day and angrily spoke their minds if they had been unjustly wronged. Kath believed the louder their outbursts the more they cared, but Tom's muted response left her puzzled. Did he not want to confront the man who raped his wife and defend her honor? What kind of man would leave such an egregious insult unanswered? She slept very little that night and silently questioned whether he cared for her at all.

She returned to work the next day and submitted her two week's notice much to the surprise of everyone including Dr. Banks. She stood in his office with the door open and reiterated the end of their affair in very clear terms, but Dr. Banks refused to let go. He promised her all the usual things a philanderer promises his mistress, but she wanted no part of it. Once again she threatened him with her husband's revenge and promised to detail their affair to his wife if he continued his carnal pursuit of her. She left the office with a smile, knowing that in two weeks she would be rid of that sexual predator for good.

Kath experienced a certain degree of relief when she submitted her employment applications to the many local healthcare facilities in the area and felt excited when some of them called for an interview.

At home, Tom believed they had left this tawdry business behind them, but he remained cordially aloof. He had always shied away from the overt emotions of either anger or love, but Kath knew him as a kind man. He too had been raised with a bellicose father who enjoyed loud arguments, but he decided early in his youth to never become like his dad.

Kath longed for passionate male attention. Not the harlequin novel type, but a romantically intimate affection that could be felt across a crowded room. She believed Tom to be that man, but he had always been emotionally reserved. She wanted him to change and fulfill her emotional needs, but she soon convinced herself that she was the only one who made any changes while he remained the same, which once again stirred the pot of angry resentment.

On her last day at work, the Friday night members gathered at the usual restaurant for an official goodbye dinner. All of the office staff attended, including Dr. Banks, but Kath sat next to Marianne and stayed far away from her ex-lover.

The drunken laughter and boisterous voices grew even louder as drinks flowed freely. That may have been an unsavory distraction for the other diners in the restaurant, but no one at the party table even noticed.

Dr. Banks mingled very little and uncharacteristically kept to himself before he announced an early departure from the raucous party. He kept his distance when he wished Kath luck in her new adventure and left without so much as a hug. His sudden change of behavior confused Kath as she watched him walk out the door.

Before long the obviously inebriated partygoers shared drunken hugs and goodbyes. Kath and Marianne walked to the parking lot together before Kath proceeded to her car alone.

By happenstance, or devious planning, Dr. Banks had parked his 1977 Lincoln Town Car next to Kath's. He waited there with his keys in his hand until she walked toward her car. She never saw him in the darkness as she stumbled awkwardly toward her vehicle. But when she fumbled for the keys in her overstuffed purse, she sensed a presence and looked up to see Dr. Banks in the shadow of a street light.

She stumbled against the car more out of surprise than a drunken misstep but kept her distance when he asked if she felt okay? He continued to talk, but his conversation quickly became background noise. She became preoccupied with the continuous internal debate she'd had with herself about her husband's persistent aloofness, and that drowned out everything else.

The alcohol fueled an anger toward her husband that spewed out of control, as she completely convinced herself that Tom's emotional distance meant he didn't care about her. She became so self-absorbed with her internal delusions that she never heard a word Dr. Banks said. Her surge of animosity soon swelled into spousal retaliation as she felt herself move a step closer to her unwanted suitor. After an awkward moment he opened his car door and she slid into the spacious backseat.

She drove home very inebriated and became increasingly angry with herself even though she blamed Tom for her repeated transgressions and broken promises. When she opened the front door, he stood quietly on the other side, and his silence spoke volumes.

She swayed a bit as she stood in front of him with misaligned buttons on her blouse, slightly smudged lipstick, and hair that needed to be brushed. Tom recognized what would be obvious to a blind man but said nothing while the shame of her actions became too much for her drunken self to bear. Mortified by her behavior and filled with self-contempt, she blamed him.

"What kind of man stands there and says nothing knowing full well that his wife just had an affair?" she screamed, "What does it take to get a reaction out of you?" She ran toward him and hysterically pounded on his chest with her closed fists. Tom tried to back up, but she kept coming. He continued to retreat backwards across the room and instinctively utilized a taekwondo technique that gently redirected her momentum away from him but unintentionally sent her to the floor. Her face accidentally struck the edge of the coffee table.

The impact temporarily sobered her up while the blood from her upper lip elicited an immediate fear in both of them. Tom looked down totally mortified at what had happened, as Kath lay on the floor in blood and tears. She sat alone on the floor and cried, not because of the pain or blood, but because she knew her selfish actions had just ended their marriage.

The small cut required two sutures from the local emergency room. The next morning, with little fanfare, Tom gave her yesterday's mail, which included an official letter that formally offered her a position at Ypsilanti State Hospital.

A New Beginning

In less than a week, Kath found herself in a dissolved marriage, living by herself in a new apartment, and starting a new job.

Ypsilanti State Hospital was a psychiatric facility with a nine-hole golf course built on the outskirts of Ypsilanti, Michigan, in 1930. It housed over 4,000 patients of all ages and had dormitories straight out of *One Flew Over The Cuckoo's Nest*. Many of the original patients who arrived as children lived their entire lives within those hospital walls. Kath took a job in the eerie back wards of a classic institutional facility the world had purposely ignored and no one cared to remember.

After three months of employment, the locked doors that restricted access to the patient care areas became a routine part of Kath's work environment, but she never acclimated to the olfactory scent from decades worth of dried urine that permeated the air.

On a cold December day in 1979, the hospital staffing office temporarily reassigned Kath to another work area for the day. She never complained about these reassignments, but this particular unit housed a few exceptionally disturbed young adults with violent histories of unpredictable behavior toward unfamiliar faces. They had all physically harmed staff members in the past.

The distinct tinny sound of keys that jiggled on Kath's large keyring filtered through the locked entrance door of her newly assigned unit and quickly attracted the attention of Bette Mays, who regularly hovered just on the other side, a mere dozen yards from the door. Bette waited with eerie anticipation for the metallic click of a turned lock and carefully watched as the door creaked opened.

Kath walked across the threshold and quickly pushed the door closed as she inserted the key that flipped the heavy dead bolt that locked the only exit from the unit. She took a few steps from the door but abruptly stopped when she saw that Bette stood only a few yards away with a menacing glare that warranted caution.

The five-foot-eight autistic African American young girl had a psychotic reputation that included a long history of unprovoked violence that struck fear in the hearts of all who knew her. The scleral whites of Bette's eyes opened dangerously wide and stood in stark contrast to her black skin, as she remained laser-focused on the unfamiliar visitor. She slowly raised her arm and pointed her index finger directly at Kath. "Who is that?" she shouted in an uncharacteristically clear voice.

The close proximity of the entrance door to my office allowed me to overhear Bette's commotion, and when I stepped into the hallway I nearly bumped into her outstretched arm, which still pointed at her target. That's when I saw Kath for the first time.

The new replacement nurse stood perfectly still in front of the locked door but never appeared frightened or upset and calmly waited to see what the voices told Bette to do next. I bribed Bette back into the office with the promise of a cigarette and waived for our visitor to follow. Kath followed us with all the confidence of a runway model. Her incredibly erect posture had a spine so straight that a book could be balanced on top of her head and telegraphed an enormous sense of poise. Her precisely curled shoulder-length, light brown hair complimented her oval face, while her eye makeup accentuated a pair of stunning blue eyes. Bette sat next to me, and Kath purposely sat on the opposite side of the table, as Bette smoked her cigarette and softly conversed with her unheard voices.

"They sent me to help because someone called in sick," Kath said. "Great," I responded. I retrieved two cups of coffee from the nearby coffee maker, but Bette gave me a "where's mine" look and I quickly returned with a third. Kath politely declined the cigarette I offered, but she retrieved the same brand from her purse. The three of us sat around the table as Kath and I completed our formal introduction. Bette continued smoking her cigarettes and talking with her voices.

When our conversation drifted to our personal histories, Kath and I discovered that we shared more in common than our cigarette brand. We had both attended Eastern Michigan University and graduated with degrees in Psychology and minors in Sociology. I rented a house on Sheffield, the same street Kath had lived on until her recent divorce. She smiled a barely contained pompous snicker when she discovered that my birthdate made me a Cancer while her birthday, which happened to be in three days, made her a Capricorn. She proclaimed that our opposite astrological signs suggested any relationship we might find ourselves in would either be very successful or completely disastrous, with no middle ground. I countered that opposites attract and therefore our prospects looked pretty good.

A fair amount of conversational time passed before Kath asked, "Doesn't your staff need help out there?"

"Heck no." I said, "They have it covered. If they need help, they'll ask for it."

But Kath insisted on an assignment and refused to let others work while she smoked cigarettes and drank coffee. Bette continued to converse with her voices and remained in the office while I introduced Kath to the staff, who guided her for the rest of the day.

At the end of the shift Bette and I escorted Kath off the unit and I casually inquired as to her birthday plans. She replied that she had none. I stood dumbfounded and couldn't believe that such a beautiful woman would have no plans for her twenty-eighth birthday.

I had no idea this seemingly strong and attractive woman was desperately crawling out from under the rubble of her life. Nor did I know anything about the events in her past that sculptured the person who stood in the doorway of a crazy-house acting as if everything was normal. Hopeful that the astrological alignments were in my favor, I invited her for a birthday dinner date and, to my astonishment, she accepted.

I planned a pasta dinner with cake and ice cream for dessert, plus a new stethoscope for a birthday gift. When I arrived at Kath's apartment, my persistent knock on her door went unanswered for an uncomfortable amount of time. Then the door finally opened, she greeted me with, "Oh good, it's you."

"Who were you expecting?" I asked.

"Never mind," she answered, "I'll tell you in the car."

I waited on the couch while she collected her things and noticed the high-quality furnishings in her apartment, but I found the lack of any Christmas sentiments or family photos very curious.

Our light conversation flowed smoothly until we approached my car and her small talk was subtly replaced with a silent chuckle that quickly escalated into a full belly laugh when she realized I drove a 1972 Gremlin. She howled hysterically at the huge round dent on the hood of my car, while I tried to explain how a moose in Nova Scotia had landed on it. That made her laugh even harder as tears streamed down her face. It took awhile before we regained our composure.

During the fifteen-minute-drive to my house, she explained her hesitancy to open her apartment door. Since her recent divorce, Dr. Banks had repeatedly pestered her to resume their relationship, but she tried to avoid him. She even threatened to call the police, but he continued to show up at unpredictable times. She wanted to make sure it wasn't him before she opened the door.

When she saw the candles on the cake and smelled the aroma of dinner, her eyes teared up and she thanked me for my efforts to celebrate her day. As the dinner progressed, I began to understand why she felt so alone on her birthday. She blamed herself for the dissolution of her marriage and felt unworthy of any love or attention. In her mind, she continuously replayed the saga of all she had lost and accepted perpetual guilt as a just penance. I witnessed firsthand the burden of her anguish and felt the weight of her sadness that no one should feel on their birthday.

After dinner we sipped the last of the wine and discovered we shared a common desire to relocate as far away from Michigan as possible with little regard for the final destination. When I spoke of my plan to tour the country as a travel nurse, she smiled her approval and acknowledged that the idea had merit. Her mood brightened as we spoke of our common need to leave our old ways behind and start a new life.

The success of that dinner date lead to many more, but as the months passed those travel plans receded into the background and the momentum of life propelled us along a stagnant trajectory. The habit of living kept us in our routine while we danced around the edges of a deeper personal relationship. In the meantime, our disparate lifestyles began to emerge.

As frequently happens in divorce, mutual friends struggle with a divided loyalty. Her family stood by her, but few friends wanted to stand by a scarlet woman. That collateral loss propelled her into a misanthropic world, and she immersed herself in the solitudinous company of the literary classics.

Kath believed the practical and logical nature of her Capricorn sign stood in sharp contrast to my astrological Cancer's laissez faire attitude toward life, but I gave little credence to horoscopes and star charts. I still lived with roommates, as I had in college, and inhabited a house awash with social activity. Friends came and went, as we smoked pot, discussed Tolkien, drank beer, played Euchre, and watched *M.A.S.H.* reruns.

Kath found that lifestyle intellectually stifling and boring. Once, while several of us sat in the living room stoned out of our minds while another rerun of *M.A.S.H.* blared on the television, she stood in front of the screen and in a patronizing voice asked, "How many times have you seen this episode? Don't you have anything more interesting to do?" We all bobbed our heads left and right in a comical synchronistic but unconscious effort to see the screen while everyone remained completely oblivious to the question.

In silent frustration, she collected her purse and left. As I caught up to her outside, she turned around and said, "Hey, if you want to sit there with those zombies and watch that show for the umpteenth time go ahead, but don't count on me to sit there."

"You're right," I said, and we continued our conversation over dinner at the local Big Boys.

Aware that Kath abhorred intellectual stagnation, I sought out creative avenues we could explore as a couple. We visited photographic exhibits, took walks at the U of M Arboretum, and spent many hours chatting on the banks of the Huron River. In the early fall, we went on a seafaring trip down the Detroit River.

The boating season had long since passed, and Kath felt a bit nervous as we motored alone on the huge river in my small 1958 wooden Lyman fishing boat, which did not compare with her dad's cabin cruiser. She recalled the pleasant childhood memories of her father skippering the family boat back in a time when her life felt secure and her dad took care of everything. We sat next to each other as we cruised the smooth waters of that large river and shared a sense of beauty and peace which made it a most memorable event.

Another adventure included a trip to New Orleans for Jean's wedding. Her old roommate invited Kath to be her attendant and planned to romantically match up Kath with one of the single ushers. Kath fully expected me to decline when she invited me to accompany her, and she didn't know how to respond when I accepted. My unexpected attendance severely complicated Jean's matchmaking plans.

On the night of the rehearsal dinner, I stayed in the room to give Kath some space, and that turned out to be a good thing. Her other date happened to be a handsome guy who had a great deal of cocaine. Kath always enjoyed the white powder, but when he hinted at sexual favors in return for the drug, she dumped him and called me to join them at a local bar, where we laughed and danced the night away to a live performance from *The Stray Cats*. She felt grateful I rescued her from the clutches of yet another guy who simply wanted to get laid. We hit it off quite well on that trip, much to the chagrin of the bride.

In Ann Arbor, we explored the entertainment scene and regularly danced to live music. One night at a local bar, while Kath demonstrated her mastery of eight-ball, the resident drunk tried to vie for her affection. At first, she ignored him and encouraged me to do the same, but that approach ultimately failed. I asked him to stop his unwanted attention toward Kath, but in his drunken stupor he clearly stated that he had no plans to quit and asked me what I planned to do about it. A conflict seemed inevitable as I quickly removed my leather jacket and tossed it to Kath.

He laughed and asked me if I was pretending to be Superman. Without a word, I grabbed his arm, spun him around, and launched him across the room. The bar became quiet as he sailed through the air, bounced off the pool table, and landed on the floor. I scampered toward him and thumped his head several times against the floor before the bartender intervened. The crowd watched in silence as the bartender and I picked this dazed fellow up and, just like in the movies, threw him out the front door. He landed with a thud on the sidewalk, and the chatter resumed in the busy bar as the unfazed patrons returned to their drinks. Years later Kath confided to me how that particular episode became the turning point in her affection toward me. She said, "No one had ever done that for me before."

The casual observer would never have noticed Kath's subtle sense of low self-esteem which stemmed from a strong belief that she ruined what she once believed to be a true love story. Angry about the mistakes she had made, but careful to hide her perceived self-imperfections from others, she over compensated with a dispassionate sense of supreme intellectualism and a distant, non-committal approach to intimate friendship. The many protective layers she wrapped around her inner core served as a strong shield against future relationship disasters, but her catastrophic history with romance never dampened her deep-seated need to have at least one man in her life. She looked at me and thought, *"Why not him?"*

The irretrievable loss of what she perceived to be the "once in a lifetime perfect love" with Tom cast a long, dark shadow of doubt on the success of any future relationships she might have. She totally convinced herself that every new suitor would be forever second best.

Her emotional-self continued clinging to an unrealistic hope that she could somehow repair the damage she had done. But her intellectual self recognized the obvious flaw in that approach and realized that if she wanted a better future she had to move as far away from Ann Arbor as physically possible. She had no particular end destination in mind and didn't really care. Her previous attempt to relocate alone resulted in complete failure, so she decided she would not repeat that same mistake again.

She discreetly asked our Ypsi-State coworkers about the suitability of my character and found that everyone unanimously encouraged her to take the emotional risk. She felt good about our budding romance but had concerns about the opposite nature of our astrological signs.

Kath's Capricorn attributes were diametrically opposite to my Cancer ones. She preferred cats to my dogs. I smoked pot, she like alcohol. She preferred wine to my beer. I had no sisters and came from a blue-collar family. She had no brothers and enjoyed the comforts of the upper class. She had gone to U of M, I hadn't. All of these differences ultimately proved to be irrelevant because we shared a common desire to move away from Ann Arbor, and timing proved to be everything.

Our relationship continued to evolve. The personal revelations we shared in the name of truth slowly peeled back the multiple layers of our complex individual natures, but each new exposure carried with it the potential to destroy the very thing we wished to build. Kath surprised herself with the speed at which she rose from the ashes of her failed marriage into a new relationship, but her strong subliminal need to be associated with a man who promised to accompany her to a new promised land and help her leave her troubles behind overrode all of her reservations

Kath agreed we should live together when her twelve month lease ended and planned to move into my rental until we relocated out of state. One week before she moved in, we shared a dinner at the house and had emptied a bottle of wine when the conversation turned to sexual history. She wouldn't talk about the affair that ended her marriage but mentioned, almost in passing, that she'd had a drunken sexual encounter with another a woman and discovered she preferred the eroticism of men over women. I spoke of how a gay experience in my distant past also convinced me of my heterosexual preference, but she nearly stopped breathing at my comment and silently stared at me for a long time. Kath said nothing as she pushed herself away from the table. She grabbed her purse and said, "I can't be with you," then walked out the door.

All communication suddenly stopped. I never knew she had returned to live at the family farm, picked up a job in a nursing home, and registered in the pre-nursing curriculum for the winter semester at Oakland University.

We remained estranged until after the New Year, when she unexpectedly contacted me and expressed an interest in resuming our relationship. She respected my openness about our deep, closely guarded secrets, but made it clear that gay activity had no place in our shared life, while I made it clear that I fully agreed with her.

During a break in her busy scholastic calendar, Kath traveled to Ann Arbor and attended a party at the house where she had once planned to live. The beer and wine flowed freely among the crowd, but I squirreled away a few bottles of champagne for Kath to enjoy. The music grew loud as did the crowd while everyone danced with drinks in their hands.

Gail, a platonic friend from my nursing school days, swayed with the crowd while the stereo blasted. Her six-foot stature cast a commanding figure. Her large Italian bone structure might be easily mistaken for being overweight, and she styled her thick, long jet-black hair in such a way that it added to her perceived height. A polite and mild-mannered person, Gail's size presented an imposing figure among the dancers. As Gail swayed to the music, she danced her way through the crowd and moved closer to me, while the partiers continually jostled about. Kath took notice of Gail's proximity and danced even closer to me, and the two women became aware of the others intentions.

The tempo of the music increased while the dancers gyrated to the pounding beat when Kath literally kicked up her heals as part of a dance move and discreetly booted Gail in the butt, then nonchalantly moved away. Gail acknowledged that something had tapped her behind but assumed it to be an innocent bump and continued to dance.

Kath nonchalantly moved under the cover of the blaring music to be near her perceived antagonist and once again kicked her in the behind. This time Gail knew who did it but chose to ignore it. When Kath kicked her a third time, an infuriated Gail stopped her dance, took an aggressive stance in front of Kath, and screamed various threats while Kath deceptively played the innocent. I moved between them and deescalated the confrontation, and Gail thankfully walked away. Tempers cooled and the threats subsided, while the dancers continued to sway uninterrupted to the music.

Kath and I quickly left the crowded party, stood alone in the driveway, and made faces at each other over her outrageous antics that nearly got her punched in the face. Music filled the outside air as we swayed to its beat, being careful not to spill our drinks while the amorous intoxication that flooded the moment led us to the back seat of a car parked in the garage.

Our plans to leave Ann Arbor continued to solidify. The furniture sold at fire sale prices to anyone who wanted it and the proceeds from the sale of the Gremlin went toward the purchase of a new car for the cross-country trip. All of the household possessions had been disposed of, as we planned to travel light with only our clothes packed into our two cars. The success of our coordinated efforts strengthened our relationship, and we soon thought of ourselves as a couple rather than two people going on a trip.

Somewhere along the relationship continuum we crossed that blurred line when marriage subtly crept into the conversation and matrimony became the expected end point. That unexpected revelation surprised Kath, but her willingness to pursue it surprised her even more. She feared the stigma of another failed marriage, but her planned exit from Ann Arbor to rebuild her life with a male companion proved too enticing to ignore, and she would do whatever it took to make sure that dream happened. The ink on the divorce decree had barely dried when she unexpectedly found herself immersed in the detailed plans of a marriage ceremony.

We traveled to Detroit to buy an engagement ring, but the friend who recommended the jeweler failed to mention the shabbiness of the poorly-lit neighborhood ghetto that we found ourselves in. We stared in disbelief at the dilapidated stores that lined the block. A well-lit street number identified the address that stood above a single, large windowless black door with small white lettering that spelled out the owner's name, but nothing advertised it as a jewelry store. We parked as close to the entrance as possible and quickly walked to the door which had multiple security cameras strategically placed around the entrance. After we rang the bell, the electronic buzzer unlocked the heavy bomb-proof security door. We entered a dark narrow stairway that reeked with a dank moldy aroma that made us question our judgement. A single, low wattage lightbulb dangled from the ceiling on a crooked wire that barely lit the area, and the solid thud of the steel door that closed behind us echoed up the staircase. As we climbed the stairs, Kath nonchalantly mentioned that inexpensive jewelry made of cheap alloy metal gave her a bad rash.

At the top of the stairs we pushed hard against the large, black metal door that opened with an obligatory creak, but the bright light that shined inside the mysterious room temporarily blinded us. When our eyes finally adjusted to the light, we found ourselves in a huge, windowless showroom filled with dozens of brilliantly lit glass display cases that held every imaginable type of jewelry. A frail old man with a jeweler magnifying glass on his forehead greeted us as he sat on a stool behind one of those huge glass counters.

Kath spoke the language of high-end jewelers and effectively conveyed our needs to the old man, who described the technical points of the various pieces she had picked out. She chose a two-piece interlocking white-gold engagement ring with a large ruby stone in the center surrounded by numerous small diamonds. Her face glowed when I slid the ring on her finger, and the old man grinned his approval.

Not getting married became our first official decision as an engaged couple. The exploratory costs of a local wedding spiraled well beyond any reasonable budget, and if fully implemented would indefinitely delay our plans to permanently relocate. Some family members and friends failed to understand why we abruptly canceled the wedding plans, while others cheered our anticipated move to parts unknown.

This Is the Place?

The embarkation date finally arrived. As we squeezed the last of the belongings into our cars, a nest of newly hatched robins chirped away in the morning twilight and caught our attention. We peered into their home and stood in awe as their tiny heads bobbed around with their tightly-closed newborn eyes and their beaks wide open, while they waited for their momma to bring them breakfast. The birth of the new feathered family had deep symbolic meaning for a young couple intent on starting their own brood in a distant land. We perceived the young hatchlings to be a prophetically good omen.

Kath took one last look around before she took a deep breath and slid behind the wheel to begin the adventure of a lifetime. The two-car caravan headed west. We only had each other to rely on, and our mutual trust set in place building blocks for a strong interpersonal relationship that lasted a lifetime.

On the fourth day of travel, the sun was setting as we crossed Parleys Summit on I-80 in Utah and marveled at the twinkling lights of Salt Lake City that unfolded in the valley below. Once we entered the city limits, we pulled off the freeway and found a phone booth where we searched the white pages for the number of an old college roommate who had moved to Salt Lake years earlier. Fortunately, Dan answered the phone and allowed us to stay the night in his nearby bungalow home. In the morning we walked the neighborhood and couldn't believe the beauty of the East Bench area of the city.

The barren Qquirrh (pronounced Oaker) Mountains stood tall on the distant west side of the high desert valley, but Dan lived on the east side in the foothills of the forest-covered Wasatch

Mountain Range that towered 11,000 feet over the valley floor. The unpolluted city air felt crisp, and old deciduous trees offered a canopy of green over extra wide streets lined with beautiful bungalow homes that seemed filled with nostalgic family stories while the nearby University of Utah Medical Center offered numerous job opportunities for a couple of unemployed nurses. This enchanted land felt like the right place to be at that time in our lives, and we decided to stay awhile.

We began our new life in Salt Lake City financially broke, with all of our credit cards maxed out. We quickly acquired jobs at the University of Utah Medical Center and started to dig out from the financial hole we found ourselves in. Kath's frugal nature helped keep our expenditures in check, and we followed a simple rule: debits never exceeded credits. The individual veto power we each possessed over any decision in our combined lives greatly contributed toward our improved bank account, but the swing shift jobs at the medical center offered much more than income. It afforded us the opportunity to sit on our rented bungalow porch and talk until sunrise announced our bedtime.

Kath frequently spoke of her desire to start a family and recalled with fondness her babysitting days with Patty, Roberta's first born, but the new emphasis on family planning necessitated a resumption of our marriage plans.

We decided on a small ceremony at my brother's house in San Jose, California, on September 4, 1981, with Kath's sister Marianne once again as her Maid of Honor. Bob Wilson refused to fly, but he and Carol took the cross-country train ride from Ann Arbor, very reminiscent of their days gone by, to attend the wedding. Keenly aware of her not so recent marital problems, Kath felt truly blessed knowing that her family cared enough to support her decision and stand by her side.

Kath liked the Episcopalian minister who officiated the wedding, as they connected on the virtues of children and family. She felt emotionally prepared to move ahead with the perceived joys of motherhood and looked forward to the beauty of a family. She believed that her life choices and the astrological stars had finally aligned with her wishes.

Two days after the wedding, we loaded all the gifts into the car and said goodbye to family and friends for the return trip to Salt Lake City via the less traveled Lincoln Highway through Nevada. Much to our delight, one of the many gifts we received happened to be a two-gram packet of pharmaceutical grade cocaine that we enjoyed at various secluded spots along the way home.

Salt Lake City far exceeded any of our expectations. The post card beauty of Utah's southern desert complimented the forested northern mountainous ski areas of Salt Lake City, but Kath never considered herself a rugged individual and had little interest in carrying a heavy backpack on a mountain trail.

Kath preferred car camping with hot showers and electrical outlets that allowed her to properly dry and curl her hair. She remained more of a city girl who dabbled in the pseudo rustic world of the wild west while enjoying the amenities of a good salon and fine dining. She bought a gym membership, but attended yoga classes far more than she utilized the weight machines or the aerobic classes, and maintained her figure with her dietary habits rather than any heavy physical exercise.

Above all she wanted to be a mom, and for the first time in her life, she began to nest. The basal body temperature chart became a daily routine. We ate healthier, stopped drinking alcohol, and quit smoking. We even planned the nursery. The anticipated joy we shared while we pursued the baby-making-path slowly gave way to concern when the results proved unsuccessful.

We lived in the baby capital of the world and received a great deal of unsolicited advice from well-meaning friends, but the best advice came from the ever-practical Kath when she suggested an infertility work-up.

Salt Lake City offered access to numerous highly experienced infertility specialists, and after a huge battery of tests, the preliminary studies suggested a blockage of her fallopian tubes. This was confirmed by a hysterosalpingogram that proved quite painful, but the final gynecological consultation proved to be eerily prophetic.

Major abdominal adhesions (strings of scar tissue much like rubber bands) completely obstructed one of her fallopian tubes and partially blocked the other. The doctor said the appendectomy she'd had years ago played a role in the blockage, but her history of pelvic inflammatory disease from either a sexually transmitted disease or her previous I.U.D may be equally culpable for the damage. He counseled that pregnancy could still be possible but was very unlikely and recommended exploratory surgery in an attempt to repair the tubes.

Ironically, the surgery he suggested could further scar the very tubes he hoped to repair. As the doctor reviewed the consent for surgery, he unexpectedly hinted the tubular damage could be so severe that a prophylactic total hysterectomy might be warranted to reduce the possibility of future cancer, but he wouldn't know for certain until he surgically explored her abdomen.

That particular comment greatly disturbed Kath. She had gone to the doctor to get pregnant, but now he wanted to do a sterilization procedure and talked of cancer? After an uncomfortable moment of silence, she declined to sign the consent and said, "I need to think about this. I'll call you with my decision."

We started that day as happy newlyweds lost in the romantic belief that the infertility specialist would resolve the pregnancy problem but finished the day as a disheartened couple with more problems than we had started with.

The ride home remained unnaturally quiet as Kath silently stewed. Without warning her emotional dam suddenly burst, and she spewed forth an angry tirade. "That damn Tom had untreated chlamydia, and he kept reinfecting me. That fucker didn't want any kids and now because of him I can't have any."

"Well, wait a minute," I said. "What about that I.U.D.?"

Kath shot back, "That asshole roommate Jean talked me into that. She said I should stop taking birth control pills, which she convinced me were dangerous, and switch to the safer I.U.D." Now I'm pissed at myself because I followed her asinine advice. Why did I ever listen to that idiot?"

It took a few days, but her anger eventually subsided. We stopped visiting doctors and returned to the basal body temperature chart. As months went by the specialist's advice became a distant memory, and the dire prediction of a deadly cancer remained unspoken but never forgotten.

One day Kath had been unusually quiet until she suddenly burst from the bathroom with a wild look of excitement and announced that she was about two months pregnant. She had performed the pregnancy test on two different occasions and felt confident in the results. Her blue eyes danced with delight as we literally jumped for joy. We cried rivers of happy tears and embraced each other for a long time, while we basked in the glow of a new family.

Several days later Kath sobbed uncontrollably in the bedroom, and laid curled up on the bed in a fetal position as tears streamed down her face. In between sobs she hesitatingly blurted out that she had lost the baby.

The spontaneous abortion began with significant cramps followed by bleeding, and then she passed a very tiny fetus. She cried so hard that I could barely understand her words, as she described how she stared at that tiny lump of cells for a long time as it lay lifeless on the floor before she could bring herself to flush it down the toilet. Devastated beyond belief and completely inconsolable we simply laid on the bed together and didn't move for a long time.

The basal body temperature chart seemed to disappear along with her outdoor interests. She lost herself in various books, her cat, and music, as George Harrison and Eric Clapton echoed throughout the house. Although we still conversed and lived life as a couple she preferred to be alone, but showed all the subtle danger signs of postpartum depression that no one recognized.

I received an abrupt reality check when I returned home from work and found her unconscious on the bed with an empty bottle of valium on the night stand and no idea how many pills she had taken. She lay there lifeless and failed to respond to all of my attempts to awaken her. She breathed regular but shallow breaths with no signs of anoxia or any evidence of aspirated emesis. I never called for emergency help because I didn't want an attempted suicide to be part of her permanent medical record. So I sat next to her while I monitored her breathing and kept her safe.

In the morning she slowly stirred and looked at me through sleepy eyes. She sat on the side of the bed for a moment before she realized that she remained fully dressed, and the magnitude of her previous day's actions crashed over her. In less than a second her emotions ranged from half asleep, to complete fear, to stern determination. My questions went unanswered as she moved to the bathroom, closed the door, and remained there for a very long time.

I heard the flush of the toilet followed by a prolonged shower. After a few moments, the hair drier blow for an extended period of time followed by the sounds of makeup bottles as they clanked against the glass vanity. Kath reemerged in her robe, and I followed her into the bedroom where she proceeded to get dressed. Finally, she broke her silence and said, "I'm sorry for what I did, and I'll never do that again. I'm going shopping now. I'll be back in a few hours." She left without any further discussion.

She returned home as predicted, but during our thirty years together she never again spoke about that suicide attempt and completely ignored any inquiry about it. Eventually our relationship returned to normal, and Kath renewed her interest in a family, but through the possibility of adoption.

Kath did all the research on the adoption process before she made the first call, as she considered us to be excellent, low-risk adoptive candidates.

We dressed in business attire for our first interview with the adoption agency and hand carried our many documents in a large secure folder. We arrived early and sat quietly in a small but cluttered waiting room with no check-in procedure. Thirty minutes past our appointment time a gravelly voice that originated from behind a half open door unceremoniously summoned us. We gathered our materials and entered the mysterious office.

The small room had one old but sturdy desk with two very worn and scratched armless wooden chairs in front of it. Behind the desk sat a middle-aged, heavy-set, but not obese female with a braided leather eyewear strap looped around her neck tied to small reading glasses that rested comfortably on her large saggy breasts. Without looking up, she positioned her glasses on her nose and searched for our file from the many that covered her desk. Just as we were ready to sit in the old chairs, she found our file, peered at us over her glasses, and introduced herself without a handshake. After she felt satisfied we were the couple her file identified us to be, she began her inquiry in a monotonous and business-like tone.

We handed her the paperwork that confirmed our employment and financial status. When we presented the lease agreement, she asked us to explain why we had moved from Michigan. When she asked the reason for Kath's divorce we looked at each other in silence before Kath simply said, "Irreconcilable differences." When she asked about our emotional well-being and if we had a professional psychological profile, we paused before we simultaneously answered, "No." When asked if there were any misdemeanor or felony arrests in our past, we began to feel put upon. We simultaneously answered with a stern, "No!"

She proceeded to discuss the fees involved and identified the long list of people who collected that money, which totaled well over ten thousand dollars.

For over forty minutes the interrogator continued her barrage of questions, then lowered her glasses to their original resting place and asked if we had any questions. We wanted to ask, "Why are so many people involved in this process and who decided their fees?" But instead we just said, "No questions," thanked her for her time, and excused ourselves. Our car echoed with derogatory comments about the adoption system for the entire ride home and well into the next day. The adoption process had left us very uncomfortable, and we never pursued it again.

Kath stood at the center of an epic personal quandary and struggled to redefine herself as a motherless wife in a childless marriage, while she silently convinced herself that she had failed as both a female and a spouse. In the months that followed, she lived a rudderless existence, and our relationship became stuck in an eddy on the river of life.

We left the Medical Center for better pay at a dayshift job in a local nursing home with identical work schedules that afforded us an opportunity to be together all the time, both at work and at home. Soon it felt odd to be apart.

The music and laughter once again reverberated through the house, and we rediscovered the reciprocal joy of a happy couple. We busied ourselves with outdoor activities and found a common interest in snow skiing. Kath had never been athletically inclined and historically frowned upon participating in any sport, but she took a shine to downhill skiing and in short order learned to parallel ski.

As part of the new benefit package from work, we booked two free nights at the company condo at a ski resort in Park City. We arrived in time for a champagne dinner and then hit the slopes for a unique venue of night skiing.

Kath seemed happy as we rode the chairlift up. She sang *I Feel Pretty* from West Side Story at the top of her lungs as we skied back to the base. When the lifts finally closed, we returned to the condo where she relaxed in her thermal underwear, donned her sunglasses, and wore a round, weaved basket for a hat as we smoked cigars, drank champagne, and laughed the night away.

Kath mastered her slalom skills on that trip and over the course of the season improved her technique enough to cautiously ski most of the blue diamond runs at any of the resorts around Salt Lake City.

Disaster struck near the end of the season at the Alta Ski Resort when she tore her right knee in a slow, twisting fall, and the ski patrol sledded her down the hill in a basket. An orthopedic surgeon performed an ACL repair.

After the surgery, when I exited the elevator on the orthopedic floor I heard an agonizingly painful scream, followed by a flurry of profanity that would embarrass a sailor as it echoed through the hall. I initially found the rant to be humorous, until I realized the identity of the screamer and saw firsthand the wild-eyed look that greeted me when I entered Kath's room.

She clutched the overhead trapeze bar with both hands to steady herself as she sat up in the bed and screamed for the surgeon. My eardrums rattled as she screeched, "That son of bitch never said anything about this pain. Where are those nurses? I need some fucking pain meds."

Momentarily embarrassed, I retreated to the nurse's stations and returned with a nurse who administered another dose of morphine, which seemed to help. When the surgeon visited later that afternoon, Kath ripped into him for not being upfront about the full extent of the pain. He apologized, fully explained the surgery, the reason for the pain, and the anticipated recovery time. But she only heard the words, "This repair should last twenty years." "Great," she said. "I'll call ya in 2005." Then she nodded off to sleep. She eventually made a full recovery but never skied or hiked again.

As winter turned to spring, our social activity turned to drinking and dancing at the private clubs made famous by the weird Utah liquor laws. We became binge drinkers and alcohol played an increasingly central role in all of our social events. Periodically we supplemented those drunken nights with an occasional trip to the border town of Wendover, Nevada, where we partied all night to near passed-out conditions.

Kath looked forward to the occasional weekend bender at the desert oasis, but on one such excursion, for no apparent reason, she became angrily withdrawn during the one-hour drive and disappeared within the casino shortly after we arrived.

Nearly two hours passed as I stood alone in the center of the gambling hall and anxiously scanned the crowd for any sign of her. At the distant end of a long walkway lined with flashing slot machines that incessantly chimed, Kath drunkenly sauntered toward me accompanied by young long-haired man. His arm rested comfortably around her shoulders with his hand deeply inserted into her blouse. He gleefully fondled her breast as they strode in step together. She stared directly at me with an inebriated sneering smile as they continued to parade in my direction and stopped directly in front of me. Her facial expression remained unchanged, and she never uttered a word while her companion blithely smiled as he continued to fondle her breast. Then suddenly he realized the uncomfortable position he found himself in. We were standing within inches of each other when he slowly removed his hand from inside her blouse and quickly exited. Kath ignored my repeated requests to explain her behavior and never once attempted to defend her actions, but with a slight stagger simply walked to the bar for more drinks.

The unfettered alcohol use ended abruptly when Kath received a D.U.I after an all-day champagne party at a friend's house. Fortunately for her, the police reduced the charge to careless driving and fined her two hundred dollars with a mandatory two-day drunk-driving class. At first glance, this appeared to be a disaster but the drunk-driving school changed her life.

Kath always paid attention in every class she ever took, and this one proved to be no exception. She carefully listened to the discussion about alcohol and what she heard troubled her. The excuses offered by her fellow classmates made her angry, and when she discovered that some of them drove to the class drunk, her outrage boiled over.

"Look at all of you," she said in a quivering voice as the chatter in the room momentarily ceased, "making excuses as to why you're here. We all know why we're here, but most of us won't admit that we have an alcohol problem." The chatter resumed as no one cared to listen, but she cared about the undesirable path her life had taken and decided to do something about it.

She immediately stopped drinking, quit smoking, returned to the gym, and became a vegetarian, while spiritual books of all persuasions littered her bedside stand. She tried to understand why alcohol had played such a dominant role in her life, and that led to the inevitable search for the meaning of life and her place in it.

The undisputed Mormon presence in the area we lived in created a unique cultural atmosphere for spiritual discussion, which indirectly promoted deliberate spiritual discourse in coffee shops, restaurants, or even gyms. Every SLC citizen in some way or another declared their spiritual stand even if meant advocating atheism, and that dynamic spiritual atmosphere offered her numerous opportunities to study the diverse theologies of the world.

With books stacked all over the house, Kath became well-read on all the major religions and drew a strong personal distinction between religion and spirituality. With her excellent memory and self-proclaimed MENSA status, she presented a powerful force forrebuttal when the Mormon Missionaries rang our doorbell. The history of Catholicism interested her the most, and as with anything Kath did, she completely immersed herself it.

She studied at the Cathedral of the Madeleine with Father Merisman. A World War II bomber pilot and not your average priest, Father Merisman privately schooled her in the doctrines of the Catholic Church. She learned the names of historical figures who favored certain writings that eventually became included in the modern-day Bible, but she also studied other ancient legitimate writings that had been purposely excluded from the good Christian book and nearly forgotten.

She read all of those rejected writings and soon found that she favored the forgotten Gnostic Gospels. She preferred reading about non-mainstream spiritualists like Padre Pio, Thomas Merton, Siddhārtha, Paramahansa Yogananda, and many other great spiritual thinkers. She studied the teachings of Joseph Campbell, which defined how the ancient art of astrology and mythology influenced the religions of the world.

She often lost track of time when she discussed these philosophies and their relationship to the current Church doctrine with Father Merisman. They had formed a unique bond and Kath had never been happier as she incorporated those unconventional beliefs in her search for God. Her studies culminated with her baptism by Father Merisman, which happened to coincide with the Harmonic Convergence, the world's first globally synchronized meditation event organized by José Argüelles.

Her intense spiritual immersion reawakened her desire to help others. She returned to school and completed her associate's degree in nursing. Kathy Wilson R.N. had finally found her purpose, and her depression quickly lifted.

She pursued her interests in spirituality, yoga, and astrology while alcohol became a thing of the past. After she read *Autobiography of Yogi* she signed up for mail order lessons from the Self Realization Fellowship center in L.A. and meditated a couple of hours a day.

Kath believed Eastern philosophy dovetailed nicely with Catholicism, and she actively pursued Yogananda's scientific method of finding God. After many months of private SRF practice, she traveled by train to the SRF center in Encinitas, California, for a multi-day silent retreat. She returned more relaxed and meditated even longer, while she practiced the various SRF energization exercises and embraced their quasi Hindu like philosophy. Kath continued her SRF practice and privately prayed a daily affirmation that an opportunity to move to San Diego would soon present itself.

A few months later, she left for a second silent retreat in Encinitas with specific instructions not to be called except for a dire emergency. Two days after she left, I received a job offer in San Diego, but it was contingent upon a prompt reply. I called the SRF Hermitage in Encinitas, and when they finally tracked her down, she greeted me with a whispered, "Why are you calling me? What's wrong?" I told her about the job offer and asked for her opinion. The phone went suddenly silent before she whispered, "I have to tell you something."

In a barely audible voice, she described how she had meditated for hours seated on a bench at the edge of a three-hundred-foot bluff that overlooked the Pacific Ocean and asked the spirit of Yogananda to facilitate a move to San Diego. When she finally opened her eyes, she watched a dolphin surf a large swell before the wave crashed on the beach below her. A hummingbird suddenly buzzed her head and hovered just a few inches from her face, as it stared at her for a full minute before it finally flew off. She took these events as a sign of good things to come, and when I asked her again if I should accept the job she answered with a loud, "Yes."

In 1988, we moved to the North County area of San Diego. Kath worked as a nurse in a nearby urgent care clinic, and our dual income helped us settle into the California lifestyle. Sunday services at the SRF temple in Encinitas became a regular event, and its Eastern philosophies became a cornerstone in her spiritual world.

One Sunday afternoon, as she reflected on her life's journey, Kath took me to the neighboring town of Solana Beach and showed me the house she had once lived in years ago when she pursued Tom. She rarely spoke of that difficult time, but when she stood in front of that house as a successful California girl, she realized her journey had finally come full circle.

Kath grew very comfortable with the San Diego lifestyle. She liked the beauty of the beach and the quasi upper crust lifestyle that surrounded her. She fancied herself as a cross between a Buddhist and a financially conservative Grosse Pointe Girl.

As a Buddha girl she visited the temple at least once a week, and her daily meditations lasted for hours. She attended the annual SRF convocation at the Bonaventure Hotel in L.A a few times and occasionally took a weekend trip to the Mother Center on Mount Washington just to hang out. She considered Paramahansa Yogananda her guru and loved everything about SRF, but she never thought of herself as a Guru groupie.

As a Grosse Pointe girl she enjoyed the various clothing outlets in Southern California but always bought her apparel on sale. Her hairstyle and color changed with the times, but she never paid top dollar. She cut out coupons for the groceries and scoured the newspapers for weekly sales. She detested those who flaunted their affluence but liked to think of herself as a bit of an aristocrat. Kath enjoyed the perks that money could buy but, the conservative money management she had learned from her father served her well.

The Fall of Family Icons

Kath valued the Wilson family dynamics of her formative years and juxtaposed them with the life she created in San Diego. In an odd way she emulated her mother, who had a great affinity for Sunday services at the local Lutheran church. As an ex-Sunday school teacher, Carol enjoyed the scholastic rewards of biblical studies. Kath learned a healthy skepticism of fraudulent theocracies from her father, who remained purposefully distant from anything religious, as his compelled Christian Science upbringing by his evangelical mother left him jaded toward anything ecumenical.

Kath's family roots remained strong, and she always maintained a close rapport with her mother. They spoke for hours on the phone at least once a week, and she regularly flew back to Michigan for a yearly visit. But her last phone conversation with Carol alarmed her.

Bob had begun to show signs of paranoid dementia. He regularly walked around the house with a loaded revolver stuffed in his pants pocket and propped a double-barreled shot gun against the wall by the front door.

Bob had always been a bit eccentric and once had fired his gun through a second story bedroom window at a perceived burglar, but this time the whole situation seemed different. We flew back to the family farm for Thanksgiving dinner and clandestinely assessed the situation.

Both of Kath's parents appeared to be in good physical shape, and Bob no longer carried the revolver in his pocket, but the shotgun remained propped next to the door. Kath convinced her dad to store the gun in a safe place, and it disappeared before Marianne and her husband, Chuck, arrived for dinner.

The sisters worked in the kitchen as Carol supervised the activity, while the guys gathered around the TV to watch the obligatory football game. Everything appeared normal until the kitchen drain plugged up. Bob stood over the sink and assessed the problem before concluding the clog appeared to be further down the drain line, which meant an excursion into the crawl space under the house.

Bob knew every inch of the home he had built and gathered his supplies to venture into the large crawl space. Kath asked me to follow him.

Armed with a couple of flashlights, we went into the large crawl space that resembled an unfinished basement to investigate the drain line. As we shined the flashlights on the pipes and debated the next course of action, Bob said, "You know, the Mafia is behind this." With a poker straight face to cover my complete surprise I answered, "What?"

"Yes," he said. "The Mafia, they're behind this problem."

I looked at him in stunned silence while the flashlights lit up our faces, and then I said, "Let me get this straight. You're telling me the mafia gave up watching a football game on a Thanksgiving afternoon, drove to your house, snuck into this crawl space, and plugged up your kitchen drain? Is that right?" He looked at me with a moment of pondering clarity followed by a wry smile and said, "No, I guess not." With that we returned to the kitchen and found a plumber who rescued the day.

In light of her father's diminished reasoning and all the glaring signs of deterioration, Kath knew it would be just a matter of time before she returned to Michigan to help her father. In less than a year Bob had become completely paranoid and walked around the house with his guns at the ready while Carol feared for her life.

Although Marianne worked hard to get him placed in the appropriate medical setting, Bob resisted all attempts to leave his home. Finally, with police intervention, he left his beloved farm for the last time. Kath bore witness to the cruelty of life as the once powerful Robert C. Wilson refused to eat as he lay on the nursing home bed and, in a humiliated fashion, willed himself to die.

Although Carol mourned his passing, she also felt relief. For years she had been subjected to his delusional ways and at times feared for her life. But that fear had died with him and now she felt reborn. That new perspective gave her the courage to face the rest of her days without Bob and to comfort her four daughters, who gathered around her to grieve their father's loss in their own way.

Like most families not everyone got along, but everyone acted respectful and courteous when they gathered for the service. But silent undertones of family discourse discretely bubbled just beneath the surface. Kath never understood Joan's animosity toward Carol and felt protective of her mother, but in the midst of the wake's emotions the two sisters rekindled their bond.

Bob had broken with protocol in the estate's legal aftermath and designated his youngest daughter as co-executor of the Wilson Family Trust along with her mother. While that appointment raised some eyebrows, all involved respected his choice because Bob knew, as did everyone else, that Kath could be trusted to do the right thing. And she possessed the courage to do it.

While she regularly consulted with Carol on the estate's financial matters, Kath also encouraged her to move to an independent living center. Carol recognized the need to downsize, which meant the farm had to be sold, but she had no experience in real estate affairs and relied on Bob's old connections for proper guidance in that matter. Kath felt proud of her father's accomplishments, as she remembered how he had lived his dream, taken a risk, and built the farm. She always felt safe there regardless of her adolescent troubles, and it would always be home.

For months Marianne searched to find a suitable place for Carol to live, but when word came that Joan had been diagnosed with some form of abdominal cancer, the search abruptly stopped. As a very private person, Joan never fully revealed the extent of her condition to any of the family members, but with the little information they did receive, it sounded grim.

Joan had finally sought medical treatment for an abdominal discomfort she had minimized since before Bob's death. She underwent urgent surgery, and the outcome came as a shock to everyone when the surgeon acknowledged that her abdomen was full of cancer. He said any attempt to surgically remove the tumor would not be helpful and simply closed her up. Kath never understood why her sister pursued chemotherapy after such a dire discovery.

Devastated by the news, Kath recalled her previous visit three months ago when her fifty-four-year-old sister gleefully chased her six-year-old daughter through the house. At the time, Joan looked fine with no hint of trouble, and Kath convinced herself that Joan's latest condition had been blown out of proportion. Surely her husband, Pete, a radiologist, had some insight into this disease and had already recruited the best doctors in the Detroit area to treat her. The family updated Kath as often they could, and everyone felt encouraged by the news that Joan would attend her eldest son's wedding. With that information, Kath took a wait and see approach before she returned to Michigan. After all, how bad could she be? But shortly after the wedding, Joan became progressively worse, and Kath took the next flight to Michigan to see for herself.

During that four-hour flight, her mind flew faster than the plane. How could this have happened to Joan, her sisterly mentor? Did her late in life pregnancy have a role to play? Did she take hormones to promote conception, which may have inadvertently fueled the cancer? Could this disease be hereditary? Kath had many questions but would find few answers at Joan's upscale Birmingham home.

A somber family greeted Kath as Joan's daughter played in the living room oblivious to the drama that unfolded upstairs in her mother's bedroom. Her husband, Pete, informed the family of Joan's poor condition and politely relayed her personal request for no bedside visitors. But at Joan's behest, he escorted Kath up to the room.

What Kath saw shocked her. Her once vibrant sister had been reduced to a bloated skeleton with sunken and dimmed eyes. Her arms were thinner than the scraggly hair on her head. Her fluid-filled abdomen had grown to the size of a pregnant women, and her legs were thin as rails. Her skin had a flat ashen grey color to it, and she barely spoke above a whisper.

At a loss for what to do, Kath fluffed the pillows in a futile attempt to make her comfortable. Devastated, Kath fought back tears as the sisters engaged in a long, personal, but physically difficult talk. Joan spoke barley above an audible whisper when she requested that Kath keep her company, but she also wanted Kath to act as a gate keeper and limit access from any well-wishers.

Joan's approved visitor list remained incredibly small and failed to include Carol, which made Kath uncomfortable. Kath knew that Joan would die soon, but the thought of her mother's emotional pain at being excluded from her daughter's deathbed bothered Kath. With teary eyes, she pleaded with Joan to allow their mother to visit, and after some cajoling, Joan finally agreed to meet with her. Carol entered the room in silence while Kath waited outside. Although Kath never knew the content of their conversation, that small triumph made her feel good in the midst of all the misery.

As Joan's health quickly deteriorated, the home health nurse arranged for hospice care at the local hospital. The family watched in helpless horror as the paramedics navigated the occupied gurney down the stairs and out the front door for the last time.

Shortly after she arrived in her new room, Joan lost consciousness. Kath and the family settled in for a lonely bedside vigil. The pleasantries of everyday conversations disappeared, and silent, sad looks that evoked teary-eyed but nervous smiles became a common sight. In silent unison, the family stepped away from the bed whenever the nurse entered the room and watched in awkward silence when she injected the IV morphine. Everyone wondered how this could have happened to someone so young, which left Kath with many questions, but Pete gave few answers. After a long mournful night, the family watched in unbridled sadness as Joan took her last breath and finally found peace.

Alone with her thoughts on the long flight home, Kath resolved to aggressively pursue her own cancer screening in an attempt to avoid all she had just witnessed. Two weeks later, she had her first appointment with an internal medicine doctor.

11
I Have What?

Doctor Mongio's business attire consisted of a flowing, dark colored, ankle-length skirt with a white blouse and a beige colored waist-length jacket with black embroidered flowers over a white blouse. Her ever present stethoscope dangled around her neck, and her large glasses with thick lenses enlarged her eyes to comical proportions. Her short, black frizzy hair with long thick bangs definitely turned heads, and without eyeliner or makeup she looked older than her fifty-one years.

Dr. Mongio listened while Kath described a diffuse dull ache in her lower left back, just below the belt line. She showed feigned interest when Kath detailed her contraceptive history and her sister's untimely demise. After a PAP smear and gynecological exam, the doctor announced her findings as lower back pain from improperly lifting patients. Her treatment plan included muscle relaxants, a review of proper lifting techniques, and liberal use of a heating pad.

As a yoga fanatic who twisted her body into unimaginable positions, Kath listened in disbelief to these medical conclusions before she thanked the doctor for her services and left for home. Kath believed these findings to be not only wrong but out right laughable. She decided to pursue a second opinion from an OB/GYN doctor.

Dr. Winter's short, lean stature and white hair presented a grandfatherly appearance that made him look professional in his white lab coat. Kath relayed the same information she had previously given to Dr. Mongio, but she felt confident a different conclusion would be reached.

The physical exam proved to be very involved, and when the ultrasound machine entered the room, she knew the doctor had found something suspicious. However, he offered no hint as to what it might be. After the exam, he handed her a prescription for a long list of blood work and X-rays with a follow-up appointment in two weeks to review all of the results and wished her well.

Kath completed the tests in short order but became so obsessed with her pending appointment that she barely reacted when I told her my employer insisted I attend an all-expense paid annual company meeting in Cancun, Mexico, and they would also pay for her flight.

Nurses rarely have an opportunity to go anywhere on the company dime, let alone Cancun, but I stood speechless when she declined the invitation.

"Why not?" I asked.

She replied, "I know those test results will show something and whatever it is, I want it out of me."

"But," I said, "you're not sick and totally healthy. What difference would a week make? How can you pass up this opportunity over a problem that you might not even have?"

"I wouldn't have any fun," she said. "Besides, I don't even like Mexico." I reminded her of our Mazatlán trip years earlier, and she acknowledged that memory with a coy smile but refused to change her mind.

"Well, don't make any hasty decisions," I said. "When the results come up negative, you may kick yourself."

She recalled with uneasy emotion the horrid memory of Joan's tortured and bloated face when she died and promised herself that her sister's death would not be in vain. She firmly believed that if she had cancer, anything that delayed its removal or treatment would be unacceptable. "You don't mess around with cancer," she said, and a trip to Cancun would be a waste of time until she knew the test results.

Her adamant refusal angered me, but the company left me no choice, I had to go. I failed to understand why she refused a "once in a lifetime trip" that simply delayed a dubious medical workup by one week, based on an undiagnosed suspicion, and completely unsupported by any facts other than her own "paranoid" intuition. If she believed she had terminal cancer why not live it up while she still felt good and looked totally healthy? My underlying anger continued to simmer over such an unreasonable decision, and I felt convinced she had inherited her father's hypochondriacal genes.

Kath spoke very little when she discussed the results with Dr. Winter on the phone, but after a lengthy one-sided conversation she sat in the chair by the kitchen table and silently stared out the window. She turned to look at me and without any spoken words, her teary eyes said that Dr. Winter's lab results failed to support Dr. Mongio's findings.

Her mind flashed back to her days in Utah when she refused to accept the infertility specialist's inference that a total hysterectomy might be necessary to prevent cancer in the future and became angry with herself about her abject denial. Dr. Winter discovered an ovarian cyst and recommended an ultrasound guided biopsy to test for cancer. It was scheduled the day before I left for Cancun. She refused to postpone the test until I returned, and said, "The sooner I know the better off I'll be."

I felt a little guilty as I waited in the outpatient area when she returned from her biopsy in a wheelchair two hours later. She reached for my hands, and with a forced smile, she reassured me that everything would be okay. But a deep silent sigh betrayed her overt sense of calm. As we drove home she explained that the biopsy results wouldn't be available for nearly two weeks, but she felt confident in the outcome and didn't want anything to interfere with my trip to Cancun. With mixed feelings, I flew out the next day.

While at the corporate rah-rah meeting on my second day in Cancun, a hotel representative interrupted the event and informed me that I had an urgent phone call at the front desk. While I hurried to the phone I tried to prepare myself for some tragic family news, as my mind raced through various possible scenarios.

When I answered the phone, I heard Kath's subdued but anxious voice describe how she had developed a significant vaginal bleed and didn't know what to do. I reminded her that I couldn't do much from three thousand miles away, but if she felt the need, she should drive to the ER or call 911.

She had casually mentioned earlier in our conversation that she had cleaned the entire house just before the onset of bleeding, and I suggested that she cease her activity for a few hours to see if the bleeding would stop. She laid on the bed while I leaned against the front desk, and we talked for almost an hour. I felt frustrated in an odd sort of way because this event may have been avoided if she had delayed the biopsy for just a few days. I wondered if her father's paranoia had once again expressed itself in his daughter's behavior, but I quickly reminded myself that hypochondriacs don't actively bleed.

When I called her back a few hours later, she said the bleeding had stopped and apologized for the previous call. "No apologies," I said. "It's scary when you're by yourself and bleeding. If that were me, I would have been scared to death. Just promise me you'll stop cleaning and put the vacuum away." She laughed and promised she would.

Alone at home, Kath felt completely overwhelmed with a sense of impending doom. She accepted as truth her assumption that Joan's inescapable path would be her path, and it frightened her. Alone in Cancun, I denied any similarities with her sister and refused to accept the possibility of cancer. Instead, I felt angry that a perfectly good romantic getaway had been ruined by lousy timing.

When I returned home, Kath appeared to be her old self. Any worry about cancer had been replaced with the blissful distractions of everyday life that continued until her follow-up doctor's appointment one week later.

I believed the biopsy would amount to nothing and went about my normal work routine, but when I returned home late in the evening, Kath didn't greet me as usual. Instead, she remained seated at the kitchen table and silently stared out the window while she gently petted Natasha, our Siamese cat who sat on her perch next to Kath. I stood at the kitchen entrance for a few moments before she slowly turned her head and greeted me with tear-filled silence that revealed the test results.

With halted words she struggled to reiterate Dr. Winter's information, which confirmed her earlier suspicion that she did have cancer, only now it had a name, Borderline Serous Tumor with Low Malignant Potential, a long name for a type of slow growing ovarian cancer.

I held her hand as we looked into each other's eyes and saw that terror ruled the moment because we knew nothing of what the diagnosis truly meant. Her fear chose to focus on the first part of the cancer's name while my denial focused on the last part. The doctor explained how all cancers are not the same, and this particular cancer comprised less than twenty percent of all known ovarian cancers. But it differed from the deadliest strains of cancer because a complete abdominal hysterectomy offered a near guaranteed success rate. He said, "If you're unfortunate enough to develop ovarian cancer this would be the one to have."

The emotional shock didn't handicap Kath for long, as she quickly developed an action plan. She scheduled surgery for the earliest possible date, and three days later I accompanied her to the local hospital for the recommended procedure.

The five-hour operation lasted much longer than the predicted ninety minutes, and Kath seemed uncomfortable after the surgery while she slept in the hospital bed with mechanical sounds of the various monitoring equipment humming in the background. When Dr. Winter arrived later in the evening, he seemed delighted with the success of the surgery and nodded approvingly to everyone in the room when he confidently announced that all the cancer had been removed.

Kath half opened her sleepy eyes and offered a satisfied smile while we shared a gentle hug of happy jubilation. The doctor reiterated the extensiveness of the surgery when he pointed out her large horizontal abdominal suture line and sternly cautioned her about the post-operative hazards of pain or fever. He specifically instructed her to avoid heavy lifting for six weeks.

We listened in happy disbelief when he described the surgical success rate for this unique form of ovarian cancer, which carried an incredibly high cure rate. He reassured her that chemotherapy would never be needed, and her longevity would no longer be threatened by that cancer.

He lingered at the bedside for a brief moment while he surveyed his successful work. Then he literally patted Kath on the head and said, "Have a good life." Then he smiled as he left the room. Two days later she returned home with a long list of post-op instructions that curiously lacked any information on the effects of surgical menopause, which always occurs after a complete surgical hysterectomy.

Kath suddenly lacked the organic ability to manufacture the female hormones of estrogen and progesterone, which precipitously dropped immediately after the procedure. Any post-menopausal female could relate to the consequences of a rapid change in hormones, as could any mature male. Kath mistakenly believed the hormone replacement therapy she had started in the hospital would make up for the abrupt-loss, but post-menopausal symptoms soon reared their ugly head.

Her dry skin soaked up all of her favorite body lotions. Her sleep cycle became disturbed, and she slept at odd hours. Her extremely dry eyes precluded any use of her contacts, which compelled her to wear glasses. The hot flashes flamed up at unpredictable times, and at night she often found herself in sweat-soaked bed sheets. I finally noticed these symptoms when she angrily snapped at me for no particular reason, and her face looked distraught with hauntingly dispirited eyes.

Her emotions suddenly poured out like a torrential rain, as her words haltingly flowed between the tears and sobs. She felt paralyzed with fear from a cancer that she believed might yet prove fatal, and the thought that she too would die her sister's death intruded upon her every waking moment. Her voice rose in disgust as she went on to describe her lack of self-worth. She viewed herself as a hollowed out, incomplete female, who would never bear children, and an absolute failure as a sexually compatible spouse.

I struggled to say something that would console her, but she remained inconsolable. A strong embrace provided the degree of comfort that only a human touch could offer while her wail of mournful words became muffled in my shoulder. The hormonal replacement therapy took another three weeks before the menopausal symptoms abated, just in time for Kath to travel to Michigan to help Carol sell the farm and move into a new assisted living center.

Reflections

Carol stood impatiently at the top of the long gravel driveway and joyously waved her arms as Kath slowed the rental car to a stop in front of their home. While Kath reminiscently gazed at the green rolling hills, she realized the alchemy of the farm still impressed her. She had pleasantly drifted off into a flood of fond adolescent memories when the sound of her mother's voice abruptly broke the spell, and she awoke to find Carol's faced pressed against the driver's side window. Kath chuckled at the scene, as she slowly exited the car being careful not to bump her eighty-three-year-old mother with the door.

Arm-in-arm they retreated to the house where they sat in the spacious sunken den with the huge picture windows that overlooked Stoney Creek and caught up on all that had happened in their lives since they last met. Carol sat in stunned silence as she carefully listened to every detail of Kath's cancer story. When Kath talked about the surgical cure, Carol cried out, "Thank God," and immediately shuffled toward Kath with outstretched arms. She embraced her daughter as only a mother could, ecstatically confident she would not lose a second one to cancer.

Their conversations lasted well into the evening, and they made plans to visit the family graves in the morning. Sleep did not come easy for Kath as her mind swirled with logistics of the move and memories of her past.

Joan's ashes resided in an urn on the corner of the fireplace mantle at her home in Birmingham, but a memorial plaque in her memory had been placed on the outside wall of her church in the company of other plaques that overlooked a beautiful garden with benches families used to reflect on the departed.

One thought stuck in Kath's mind as they drove in silence. Why had her sister allowed such an advanced state of cancer to go undetected for so long? As they stood in front of the plaque, Kath broke the silence with an angry rhetorical question. "Joanie, how could you have let that happen?" Unfazed Carol whispered, "But her death saved you." Through misty eyes, they looked at each other with a quiet realization that Carol spoke the truth. After a short prayer, they silently returned to the car for the second leg of the journey.

The scenery around Bob's grave stood in stark contrast to Joan's small city garden. Bob had purchased multiple family plots under the shade of a huge oak tree on a small rolling hill with manicured lawns at Oakview Cemetery in Royal Oak, Michigan. Burial plots had been reserved for each of his daughters plus their spouses for eternal rest.

Kath and her mom walked arm-in-arm toward the four-foot-tall rose-colored granite headstone that proclaimed "Wilson" in large engraved letters. It identified the only inhabitant of the family plot, and a smaller granite stone placed at the head of the grave contained biographical details of her father.

Kath remarked on the splendor of the giant oak tree that protected the family site, much like her father who she remembered as being a larger than life figure who stood strong against the storms of life. After a few moments Carol said a short prayer, and when she concluded, Kath said, "I wonder when I'll be buried next to him?" Carol reached her arm around her daughter's shoulder and quietly answered, "Not today." As they turned to leave, Kath looked back one last time and quietly pondered her unanswered question.

As they drove home, Carol filled the conversation with the joyous expectations of her new adventure in independent living, while Kath tried to imagine how in less than a week she could empty a house that took thirty years to fill.

Marianne and Kath worked tirelessly for days before the three of them stood together in the empty house and stared silently out the giant picture window that overlooked the creek. They quietly recalled their own special memories before saying their final good-byes to the farm.

How One Thing **13** Led to Another

B ack in San Diego, Kath reflected on all that had happened in the six weeks since her surgery. She felt proud that her father had chosen her as the co-executor of the estate and relieved that Carol seemed happy in her new residence. Kath believed she had lived up to her father's expectations. That boosted her self-confidence, but as those family distractions dissipated, the reality of her diagnosis slowly crept back into her consciousness.

She aggressively researched medical journals in an effort to understand the origins of this unusual cancer. As the nebulous information slowly coalesced, she discovered that Dr. Winter had correctly linked her history of pelvic inflammatory disease to her infertility, the spontaneous abortion, and the cancer. Her bewilderment quickly turned to anger when she remembered being treated for chlamydia almost twenty years before, which most likely set the stage for pelvic inflammatory disease.

At forty-four years old, Kath struggled physically, emotionally, and spiritually with the choices she had made twenty years prior that directly caused this mess. Her hormone replacement therapy remained an inexact science, as mood swings ruled the night. Although her surgical pain had substantially subsided, she purposely avoided the use of pain medications because she did not want the additional complication of opioid dependency. While she had successfully managed to navigate through the physical realities of the surgery, she clearly struggled with the emotional aspects.

Elisabeth Kubler-Ross, an expert on death and dying, identified five stages of grief that included denial, anger, bargaining, depression, and acceptance. Dr. Winter helped Kath minimize the denial stage when he confidently proclaimed the cancer would not return. Although that swaggered assurance made it easier for her to celebrate its departure, she secretly feared the unwanted guest would return, and that worry always remained in the back of her mind. Forever on guard, she worried that any ache or pain might indicate the cancer's return, but soon she felt like a hypochondriac and kept those thoughts to herself as the emotional strain insidiously escalated.

Dr. Winter's proclamation tempered her anger toward the non-existent cancer, but she held a silent rage at both Tom and Jean and felt angry at herself for the foolish choices she had made in her youth. Emotionally tormented by her inability to conceive a child, and with no hope of raising a family, Kath had plenty of fuel for the angry fire that burned inside her. But she recognized the destructive energy of that anger and refused to be its victim.

Instead, she redirected that negative energy into a positive force and used Self Realization Fellowship as her guide. For years she had studied the SRF doctrine, but her recent brush with mortality breathed new life into her meditative practice, and she viewed her initiation into SRF's Kriya Yoga technique as a huge metaphysical leap.

SRF, founded by Yogananda, resonated with Kath on many different levels. She felt the allure of the Golden Lotus Temple in Encinitas years ago when she lived in Solana Beach, but since Tom showed little interest in those ethereal beliefs she never pursued it.

Her life had dramatically changed over the years. The metaphysical rituals she practiced in her prepubescent life and her recent study of Catholicism created a synergy that led to an enlightened appreciation of how Krishna's Eastern Hindu philosophy melded neatly with Christianity, while SRF combined those beliefs into a single avenue that promised to satisfy her longstanding desire to see God. She felt spiritually awakened as she diligently studied the SRF teachings and truly believed in Yogananda's promise that the earnest Kriya Yoga practitioner would see God.

Aerobic workouts were never her style, but her passion for yoga dovetailed nicely with her Kriya practice. With an uncanny ability to focus her mind in deep meditation, she finally experienced the inner calm she had long sought.

Kath wanted to walk down that enlightenment path with a spiritual partner who shared her euphoric enthusiasm for mystical rituals, but I could never be a guru groupie or meditate for hours at a time. As omnist partners, we shared a common ethereal belief and attended the SRF Sunday morning service for years. Afterwards we enjoyed a late morning brunch at Saint Germaine's Cafe that lasted well into the afternoon. We always finished the day with a long walk on the Encinitas beach and discussed the individuality of our spiritual integrity.

Kath found happiness in the rituals of religion and the supernal experience of spirituality, but she struggled to find it in everyday life. She felt the satisfaction of deep compassion for animals and the patients she took care of as a nurse, but the joy of long-term social relationships escaped her.

She cherished the bond with her mother and respected Carol's counsel but always maintained a comfortable emotional distance from her sisters. She never kept in touch with her high school friends or attended any reunions, while her only college friend, Jean, rebuffed any communicative attempts with little explanation.

Of the two friends she made in Salt Lake City, Theresa fell off the radar when her marriage dissolved, and Kath rarely contacted Kesty, the person she went to nursing school with. In San Diego, she sporadically socialized with two of the nurses she worked with at the urgent care clinic, but that fraternization never matured into an intimate friendship.

She never viewed her SRF involvement as a social experiment but a private, personal experience, and while she attended the various services for years, she never made any friends there, either. Socially isolated, Kath ultimately choose an ascetic life, not because of her misanthropic leanings but from deep seated shame.

Kath's low self-esteem convinced her that no one would befriend her if they knew of her hidden indigenous conflicts that she regularly waged with herself over her unforgivable faults she mistakenly believed were unique to her.

Of her many self-debated conflicts, she struggled most with the Cinderella image she created in her mind of her betrothed soulmate from her failed marriage. She convinced herself the loss of what she perceived as a once in a lifetime love affair could never be replicated. She longed to live in a Shakespearean love story that she believed remained sadly absent in her second marriage. She somberly realized the soul mate she destroyed years before would never be resurrected, and she suddenly felt trapped in a perceived loveless marriage. She belatedly recognized as true what Marianne had brazenly stated when she first heard of Kath's second engagement, that "she could have done better."

Depressed about her less than idyllic marriage, Kath felt she had followed in her mother's acquiescent marital footsteps and frequently sought her counsel for that same problem. Although Carol listened sympathetically, she subtly reminded her youngest daughter that she had been married for fifty years under far worse conditions. She encouraged her to look for the good while her rhetorical advice remained unchanged, "Are you better off with him or without him?" The negative ramifications of a second divorce encouraged her to follow her mother's advice. She focused on the good in what she perceived to be a troubled marriage and pursued activities that made her happy. She regularly practiced yoga at a nearby gym, signed up for night classes at a community college, doubled her meditative efforts with SRF, and read more books on the esoteric philosophies of consciousness. She felt her life had finally turned around, as the reality of cancer faded into a distant memory. But then a dramatic dream suddenly delivered an unexpected message.

Kath dreamt that she sat alone in a small, windowless patient exam room while the chill of the air-conditioned breeze wafted through the thin paper gown she wore. The door slowly opened as a somber-faced doctor, dressed in a white lab coat with a stethoscope around his neck quietly entered the room. He began his exam with an informal nod of acknowledgement, as she felt the cold stethoscope on her chest and the pressure of his hands on her abdomen. He peered over his glasses while he scribbled notes in the chart and declared that she had fully recovered from the surgery. He went on to say she would be cancer free for ten years but suggested she use those years wisely because he couldn't predict what the future would hold after that. Confused, she pleaded for more information, but his sad eyes said nothing as the dream abruptly ended and she woke up alone in a cold sweat.

The morning coffee trembled in her hands as she stared past the ripples that danced across the cup and stroked her cat while she pondered the dream's mysterious message. Her left brain recited Dr. Winter's positive proclamation, but her right brain felt an ominous foreboding as she struggled to reconcile the dream. In less time than it took to finish her coffee, she suddenly felt a vibrant awareness previously found only in her deep meditation. The cat's fur suddenly felt like mink as Natasha's purr roared like the universal Om and vibrated with each thunderous breath. In a moment of clarity, her consciousness melded with her spirit as she glimpsed into another world and intuitively understood the illusion of death but reluctantly accepted the painful demise of her bodily vessel as part of life's deal.

As she floated in her transcendental state, she felt the unconditional love from a universal source and no longer feared death, just the process. She suddenly awoke to a quiet house, but her sense of calm remained as she stared into an empty cup and pondered what had just happened. That feeling lingered well into the afternoon, but she kept the memory to herself and never shared that moment with anyone.

Over the next few years, the regular physical exams and lab work became routine. Initially she went quarterly, then twice a year, then annually. Her anxiety increased with every visit, but with no sign of tumor growth and negative CA-125 results (the ovarian cancer tumor marker in the blood). Dr. Winter's prophecy continued to hold true. As the fear factor faded, she felt she had been given a second chance and embraced life with gusto.

With her well-being no longer threatened, Kath no longer interpreted any new aches or pains as the start of a new tumor. Music once again filled the house as she engaged with life and did what she did best.

She studied for and qualified as a Reiki Master. She graduated from an Encinitas massage school and became a licensed masseuse. She resurrected her interest in astrology and created free charts for those who might be interested. She studied the history of all the Spanish Missions along the El Camino Real and traveled the entire California Coastline to light votive candles in each one. She regularly visited her mother in Ann Arbor and once joined Carol and Marianne on a four-hour train trip to Chicago for a weekend stay. She finally found happiness in her troubled life.

More Lessons in Loss

Shortly after she returned from Ann Arbor, Kath received word that Patti, her thirty-three-year-old-niece, who had never smoked a cigarette in her life, had been diagnosed with lung cancer. After months of regular phone contact, she felt compelled to be at her niece's side in Patty's Bakersfield, California, home. Kath stayed for almost two weeks, but what she found greatly disturbed her.

Sick and emotionally overwhelmed, Patty remained in deep denial about her illness as she attempted to live the life she had before chemo. Patti's malnourished state caused significant weight loss, but she insisted on a vegetarian, almost vegan diet, even though very little stayed in her stomach.

Patti's husband, a California Highway Patrol motorcycle cop, had difficulty with the degree of emotional support his wife required and felt nauseous every time she vomited. Kath felt with a few more hugs and tender moments from her husband, Patti would have found greater peace in the midst of a very troubled time, but those intimacies remained absent. The cancer forced a public display of their private grief and devastation for all to see and tested the limits of everyone's endurance.

Roberta, Patty's mother, brought her alcoholism to Bakersfield, with empty vodka bottles hidden in her room, and became more of a liability than an asset.

When Kath accompanied her niece to the chemotherapy center, she asked the East Indian doctor why Patty received the caustic intravenous chemotherapy through a small needle in the arm rather than through a standard chemo port surgically placed in a large vein near the collar bone. He quickly changed the subject without an answer and became visibly annoyed when Kath questioned why the therapy remained unchanged when the disease had significantly progressed.

In the midst of all this dysfunction, she witnessed how Patti's immediate family tried to live a normal life in the midst of such unbelievable angst. On the return trip to San Diego, Kath reflected on her niece's life journey and their shared moments of youth. The Bakersfield experience rattled her because for the first time she realized cancer is not a solo act. Kath prayed that if she was unlucky enough to have the cancer return, I would be emotionally engaged.

Her experience in Bakersfield helped Kath recognize the happiness in her own life and comfort in her marriage. We trusted each other financially and never doubted our fidelity, which created a mutual respect that formed a bond that never broke. Along the way, we became good friends with regular dinner dates and sunsets at the beach.

In her youth, Kath viewed Valentine's Day as a commercialized celebration. For many years she avoided its romantic touches, but eventually she decided to highlight the intimate sexual aspects of that Holiday. That type of deep personal expression had always remained elusive in her life, but she arranged for a Valentine's Night at a beach front hotel in San Juan Capistrano. After a candlelight romantic dinner, complete with a sunset walk on the beach, Kath modeled a new negligee that could have been on the cover of Victoria Secret.

For twelve years we enjoyed the Southern California lifestyle, but so did millions of other people. Traffic congestion dramatically increased the commute time to our favorite places, but when Lego Land decided to build on the Carlsbad flower fields near our backyard, we decided to move.

When others questioned our sanity, Kath understood what they did not. The swanky pulse of the Southern California lifestyle stood in sharp contrast with her ethereal beliefs, and she chose spiritual health over physical wealth. She had celebrated a second chance at life when the medical community proclaimed her cancer free. She recalled her prophetic vision of good health for ten years but privately struggled to convince herself the cancer would never return. As the question of longevity silently screamed in the background of her mind, her thoughts of relocation dominated the conversation. She didn't know where to move but trusted that the universe would provide the answer if she simply verbalized to the Cosmic void her specific request for a small town with no traffic and clean air.

I'm Moving 15 Where?

K ath's answer arrived in an unexpected manner as she lay on the floor and practiced alternative healing techniques with a number of large quartz crystals placed strategically on the electromagnetic lay lines of her abdomen in an attempt to realign her body's surgically damaged energy flow. As she meditated on her splenic chakra, and her abdominal muscles finally relaxed, she drifted into a deep inner calm when her mind inexplicably visualized Cathedral Rock in Sedona, Arizona. She had never seen that geologic formation in her life, but the accompanying voice subtly whispered its name. The crystals suddenly crashed to the floor when she abruptly sat up and realized the universe had answered her question.

While my choice to move to San Diego had proved financially beneficial, her choice to move to Sedona proved a bit controversial. We had been to Sedona many times before and felt drawn to its picturesque landscape, but the lack of high paying employment opportunities and the absence of oncological services made it a poor choice. Undeterred, she felt convinced the universe would find a way, and she made up her mind to move to the high desert. The decision came with a sense of irony because Kath really disliked hot weather.

Kath felt validated when the San Diego house promptly sold, but the sudden need to find a Sedona replacement in sixty days dampened that brief moment of elation. The enormity of the task heightened her sense of urgency and left no time to ponder her cancerous past.

We took multiple trips to Sedona and scoured the local newspaper for homes to buy. Luckily, with only two days left in our last visit we found a single-story house at the end of Frisco Trail. As we walked the property, Kath gave an audible gasp when we saw the view of Cathedral Rock from the backyard. As we stood on the deck she whispered in my ear, "This is the place."

We closed the deal that day and finalized financing of the house with a letter of "intent to hire" from a local nursing home. Neither of us expected to work there, but we used the letter as collateral for a loan. We couldn't believe our luck when the bank actually gave us the money and we closed the deal. The six months of savings we had in the bank afforded us a comfortable window to get to know the neighborhood and find good paying jobs.

We returned to San Diego to pack up the house and load the moving van. Kath left our beautiful Southern California home without melancholy or regret and never looked back. Relocation to Kath meant an opportunity for personal growth, as she left her negative emotional baggage behind and gave away material possessions that no longer had utility. She felt a bit uneasy when the time came to quit her job, and she falsely promised to stay in contact with the few friends she had met there.

We started the eight-hour drive to Sedona at sunrise, and in our excitement barely noticed our two cats who howled through the entire trip. We traversed large swaths of empty desert landscape, and the sparsely populated Verde Valley reminded us that we were no longer in California.

Our furniture remained in transit as we celebrated our first dinner in the new house with fast food from the local deli, served on paper plates, with a Coleman cooler as a table. The cackle of Gambel's quail broke the quiet of the neighborhood. The night slowly replaced the day as the Milky Way gradually revealed its galactic splendor in the clear Sedona sky. We stood in the driveway as Kath struggled to find the astrological sign of Leo in the midst of a gazillion stars, and she talked about the Grand Cross, which appeared in the sky that August night for the first time since 1910.

She described that cosmic alignment in astrological jargon with words like conjunction, square and opposition, but the layman definition proved more insightful. The Grand Cross is a cosmic alignment of many stars, planets, moons, and asteroids that rarely shared an astronomical space. But whenever this unusual alignment occurred it defined a specific point in time when the momentum of events shifted and things changed.

The Grand Cross always appeared at the peak of a "life" cycle. Whatever had been a dominant force on the climb up, that cycle would be replaced with something else on its slide down. This event could be interpreted macroscopically on a global scale or played out microscopically in a smaller, personal one. Either way it made for a major astrological event that predicted radical change.

When she pointed out that this particular astronomical event occurred in the astrological "fixed mode," which corresponded to the Vedic tamas guna, she found a blank stare on my face. But when she explained the Hindu definition of tamas as death, destruction, or transformation, we both got really quiet and decided to go to bed.

Exhausted from the day's journey, we curled up in our sleeping bags and quickly fell asleep in the empty bedroom with no window coverings or lamps. We suddenly awoke to the sound of ominous scratching that originated under the bedroom floorboards. The cats were in full chase mode, as they raced around the bedroom and searched for the source of the eerie noise. We had no idea what it could be, but it grew progressively louder and sleep became impossible. Between the cats running around and the loud scratching, we moved our bedding into the living room and finished the night there.

The house had been built on the slope of a red rock hill, and entirely supported by concrete columns. While the front had a six-foot walk space underneath the joists, the clearance gradually diminished as the hill rose to meet the back of the house where the frame finally met the red rock. The sliding bedroom door stood directly above that point.

As I inspected the bottom of the house, I discovered the noise originated from pack rats who lived between the floor joists of our 1,300-square-foot-home. The previous home owner had placed sheets of insulation under the entire house and had effectively sealed off the subfloor joists from the elements. However, the pack rats easily gnawed through the styrofoam insulation and created many portals of entry into the empty space between the floor joists. But the largest entrance happened to be under the bedroom door, which provided a grand gateway to the luxurious rat hotel for all their nocturnal activity.

After I had successfully sealed off the entrance to the rat hotel and solved the rodent problem, Kath received word that her niece, Patti, had died. We felt the sadness of shattered lives that were left behind when we attended the funeral services, and the long ride home became uncomfortably quiet.

We returned to our life in Sedona, but being overrun by rats under the sign of the Grand Cross in the Tamas Guna, and the heart-break of Patti's death signaled an inauspicious start to our new ad-venture. We were strangers in a strange land without any emergency contacts or a friendly set of strong hands to move heavy furniture. But we relied on each other for everything as we had done in San Diego and Salt Lake City, and that strengthened an already strong personal bond. For the next month we enjoyed lazy mornings and long evenings as the boxes slowly emptied into an organized home. We savored our temporary retirement lifestyle and enjoyed the leisurely pace of "Slowdona." But eventually, the time came to find work in a small town with limited nursing opportunities.

Kath landed a dayshift job with Dr. Reynolds, a local physician in West Sedona, who catered to the quartz crystal and alternative medicine crowd, while I found work at a hospital in nearby Flagstaff. However, the new job left me with little time at home, and after six months, Kath felt the California rat race had simply changed addresses. I soon transferred to a closer hospital in the neighboring town of Cottonwood, which offered us more time together, and we pursued our life as the couple we originally intended to be.

We chatted through Friday night dinners and awoke every Saturday to the sleepy silence of the morning sun as it peeked through the bedroom curtains, but one morning we awoke to the clanking of a hammer against metal. As we peered through the curtains, we saw our neighbor silhouetted against the bright morning sun armed with a hacksaw. We watched in disbelief as he started to remove the chain link fence that obstructed an otherwise pristine view of the Red Rock landscape. "I don't know who this guy is," I said, "but he's my new best friend." This ultimately proved to be true, as we worked together and removed that eye sore.

Mel and Mary had recently moved to Sedona from Phoenix after their son died in a motorcycle accident. Neither their degrees in Divinity, nor Mel's time as a young pastor in a small town in the Upper Peninsula of Michigan had prepared them for that loss.

The removal of a chain-link fence led to neighborly visits that started heartfelt discussions about life after death and included the views of legitimate authors such as Carl Jung, David Hawkins, Eckhart Tolle, and Yogananda. What may have started out as a group discussion between two couples ended up as dialogue between Kath and Mel, as they quoted Biblical or Bhagavad-Gita passages that supported their shared views on mediation and reincarnation. *Psalm 46:10: "Be still and know that I am God,"* or John 3:3: *"Truly, truly, I say to you, unless one is born again he cannot see the kingdom of God,"* or B.G 2:13: *"As the embodied soul continuously passes in this body, from boyhood to youth to old age, the soul similarly passes into another body at death. A self-realized soul is not bewildered by such a change,"* or B.G. verse 2:22: *"As a person puts on new garments, giving up old ones, the soul similarly accepts new material bodies, giving up the old and useless ones."*

Kath had finally met a spiritually-grounded intellectual in the land of spurious Sedona "woo-woo's." The two shared an Eastern metaphysical logic that proved synergistic with her years of spiritual study. Kath relished this new-found connection with her like-minded friend. It melted away her introverted self and helped her blossom into the existential conversationalist she longed to be.

Kath also met another friend that shared similar interests after a cat sauntered into our backyard where mountain lions, bobcats, and coyotes frequently roamed. The cat's arrival triggered a distant painful memory of a coyote that had fatally attacked her previous cat, Boris. She had chased that coyote down a San Diego street in a vain attempt to save her cat, but watched in horror as the predator taunted her with his speed as he dangled the lifeless prey securely in his jaws. Concerned for the visiting feline's safety, she brought her wayward friend into the security of our home and called the number on its ID tag.

Carla, who lived one street over, promptly arrived with her husband, Rick, and reclaimed Ebanno, whose feigned attempt as a lost kitty initiated a bond between its human counterparts that lasted a lifetime. Childless and a few years younger than Kath, Carla, with her Native American heritage, felt the universe had purposely guided her cat into our yard only to be "rescued" at just the right moment. That set into motion the necessary forces for a lasting friendship. As the strangers became acquainted, they discussed shamanism, astrology, tarot cards, and all those alternative beliefs readily found in Sedona society, and Kath inwardly glowed at the opportunity to discuss some of her favorite topics.

The neighborhood social club expanded to include Glenn, Janet, Candy, and Tom, two couples on our street who were of similar age and marital duration but also without children. As childless couples in a world populated with kids, we all experienced the tactless comments from thoughtless parents who offered their offspring to us, if only for a day. While none of us chose infertility, we all felt the uncomfortable need to explain the absence of kids, but in this social milieu, parents were the odd ones out. In the past, Kath struggled with her infecundity, but with her newfound friends, she no longer felt like an anomaly of nature.

For over a year the group hosted monthly informal dinners with martinis served in elegant, broad-rimmed, clear crystal glasses. The conversations flowed as freely as the intoxicants, and occasionally a member or two of the triumvirate became forgivably tipsy. But since all lived within a minute stagger from home, the respective spouses served as the homing pigeon.

One evening, Kath felt particularly mischievous toward an unfriendly neighbor who had adorned his lawn with dozens of miniature ornaments. She felt the miniature ceramic squirrel that stood in the center of the yard needed a hat, and when Kath saw Candy's tequila bottle with the large sombrero cap she couldn't resist. After she separated the hat from the clear bottle, she lifted the open container and tilted her head back for a quick drink of courage before she handed the bottle to Candy, who repeated the ritual. Filled with liquid audacity, the two of them ran out the front door with the little hat, and their giggles faded into the night. Minutes later, they returned in a fit of laughter but without the sombrero.

We continued to attend the monthly dinner parties, but Kath felt the distilled spirits impeded her ability to consciously interact with the world and decided to make a lifestyle change. Alcohol had once again insidiously crept back into her life, and once again she decided to give it up.

She resumed a daily meditative practice and sat for hours in pursuit of inner peace. She joined a yoga class and demonstrated a flexibility that awed her instructors. She immersed herself in literature and read so many books that our office ran out of shelf space. She expanded her knowledge of astrology with online courses and completed in-depth charts for all of her friends. She became so enthralled with Marion Zimmer Bradley's *Mists of Avalon* that she vigorously studied WICCA and became an expert in Celtic history. But when she read *The Power of Myth* by Joseph Campbell, all of her metaphysical studies coalesced in her mind, as she incorporated those divergent beliefs into her spiritual understanding of the world. At the same time, she felt annoyed when she couldn't find a mainstream religion that accounted for all the various aspects of the "New Age thought" she had come to believe. Instead, she fancied herself a solo practitioner in a spiritual quest surrounded by friends who accepted those eclectic beliefs while she passionately pursued the topics that inspired her.

When Kath was very young, Carol began sharing her religious views with her youngest daughter and encouraged Kath's spiritual pursuits. Kath greatly admired her mother and subconsciously modeled herself after her. If you knew Kath you saw Carol. Both preferred to see the best in others but were not easily fooled. They dressed fashionably but never in poor taste and appreciated the finer things in life though never flaunted it. Although both struggled with their marriages, the depression era flapper shared her insights from fifty years of matrimony. That helped Kath see the success in all areas of her life and made her feel happy, and in that joy, she discovered that she had married her best friend. Happy with her chosen path, Kath focused her energy on her husband, her mother, and the pursuit of a higher power.

Where Ya Going? 16

As the years progressed, Kath remained in the sweet spot of a storybook life. Buoyed by good reports from quarterly cancer check-ups and a consistently negative CA-125, the shock of that dismal diagnosis had faded over time. Dr. Sandra DeMarco, Kath's Sedona oncologist, felt so strongly the cancer had been defeated that she discontinued the CA-125 testing and closed her case file.

For years, Kath had constantly worried that the cancer demon would raise its metastatic head from the protoplasmic depths and cast a deadly shadow over her well-being. Now Kath took advantage of her second chance to live the life she had always imagined. She felt the unmistakable emotional connection of a twenty-year marriage and sought to strengthen that bond with increased intimacy. Unfortunately, her libido had dried up years before when she stopped hormone replacement therapy out of concern for an increased cancer risk. Excited that Dr. DeMarco blessed "all-natural hormonal replacement therapy" prescribed by Dr. Reynolds, Kath made the pharmacy her first stop.

Declared free from cancer, Kath felt she had been bathed in the Pool of Siloam and viewed the absence of cancer as a miracle. Like the New Testament man born blind but made to see, she devoted herself to the higher power she believed had intervened.

She quit her job at Dr. Reynolds', volunteered at the Sedona Library surrounded by all the books she could ever read, and pursued on-line courses at home with topics that appealed to her eclectic tastes. She busied herself with household duties and always had dinner on the table when her man returned home from work.

Freed from the emotional baggage of her first marriage, she happily celebrated her twentieth wedding anniversary amongst the early autumn colors of New England only to be on top of Mount Washington when 9-11 hit. For the years that followed, all who knew Kath saw a happy and contented person...until one Saturday afternoon in 2005, when she left home without notice.

The morning started out like any other, but the muted conversation over breakfast felt even quieter without the usual soft music in the background. Although we exchanged no harsh words or any hint of marital discontent, an uncomfortable stillness lingered in the air like the calm before a storm. But Kath denied that any such cataclysm loomed on the horizon. While not totally convinced, I readied myself for spring yard work, as she sipped her coffee alone at the kitchen table, still dressed in her pajamas.

Armed with tools of the trade, I was gathering the fallen leaves into numerous organized piles when I glimpsed her through the bedroom window and watched as she peered out through the glass. I leaned on the rake and acknowledged her presence with a smile, but she looked right through me as she sipped her coffee. Then she disappeared from view.

With the leaves properly bagged, I returned to the house through the garage door only to find her packed suitcase sitting in the hall. Unable to process the scene, I stared at the luggage as she briskly walked toward me fully dressed with her purse slung over her shoulder and the car keys in her hand. Her pace never slowed as she snagged the suitcase, pushed by me into the garage, and announced her need to get away for a while.

As I stood at the doorway covered in sweat and dust, she hastily said, "I'll call you later," then tossed her suitcase into the backseat. I shouted over the engine noise asking her intended destination, but she silently turned her head, looked out the rear window, and backed down the driveway. I waved my arms, as I followed her out of the garage, but I stopped when she reached the street as she simply drove off and never looked back.

Unsure of what had just happened, I stood alone in the deafening quiet of the neighborhood. The sound of the car faded into the distance as I shuffled back into the house and closed the door.

Two full days passed before she called from the Sedona Hampton Inn and announced her intention to return home the next day. But she politely refused to discuss any aspect of her sudden sabbatical. She arrived home as quickly as she had left, suitcase in hand, and unapologetically reiterated her need to get away. She ignored my questions and calmly went about her business as if nothing had happened, then simply said she had no further plans to leave.

It took some time before our relationship returned to some semblance of normal, and she finally shared her reason for her abrupt departure. Her recent visit with a non-oncological nurse practitioner left her emotionally apprehensive as she nervously awaited the results of the CA-125, which hadn't been drawn since Dr. DeMarco closed her oncological file years ago.

A decade had passed since her vision at the kitchen table in San Diego predicted ten years of a healthy life, but the uncertainty of the eleventh year resurrected the prospect of a cancer resurgence and an acute awareness of her own mortality. She ran away to ponder her fate when the ten-year anniversary of that prognostication left her emotionally overwhelmed. But she eventually concluded that quality of life trumped longevity, and she vowed to make the best of whatever time remained.

As it turned out, Kath did have something to worry about. When she returned home from the nurse practitioner's office her face revealed the unfortunate answer long before any questions were asked. The cancer had returned.

She remembered how it had felt ten years ago when she first heard of a borderline serous tumor with low malignant potential. Once again she experienced that fear as it crashed down on her like an avalanche. An overwhelming sense of cataclysmic doom alternated with hopeful denial as she struggled to hold on to what had been a normal life. She felt the fear that her sister and niece must have felt when they first received news of their cancerous predicaments.

Kath slumped into the kitchen chair with a deep sigh while her emotions painted a frighteningly vivid view of the future. With misty eyes, she looked at me across the table as she silently pondered her oncological fate. Her spine slowly straightened as her somber sense of the inevitable morphed into a flicker of hope. She resolutely resolved to vanquish the cancer by all means necessary.

She immediately scheduled a CT Scan and hoped it contradicted the notoriously unreliable CA-125 results. But as the radiologist reviewed the study with us, he pointed out the many diffuse abdominal calcifications scattered throughout her entire abdomen. With a calm sense of urgency, he recommended a visit with Dr. George Goodman, a skilled abdominal surgeon.

As we drove to Flagstaff for that hastily scheduled appointment, Kath felt unsure about her future and a sense of melancholy filled our conversation. With a fated sense of doom, she silently listened as the surgeon bleakly detailed the CT results, which left little doubt the cancer had vigorously returned. But Dr. Goodman felt he lacked the necessary skills for a successful surgery and shattered any hope that his magical scalpel would ride to her rescue.

Everything moved in slow motion as the implications cut Kath to the core, and she circled her emotional wagons in an attempt to process the unexpected information. She saw Dr. Goodman's lips move but didn't hear him speak, as he described the complex surgical details that carried a high risk of complications from the meticulous dissection of the omentum from the rest of the abdomen. Nearly paralyzed with fear, Kath struggled to return her attention to Dr. Goodman, when he suggested she would be better served by Dr. Freeman, a gynecological oncological surgeon in Phoenix with extensive ovarian cancer experience. Dr. Goodman recognized Kath's emotional turmoil and offered words of encouragement. But he failed to recognize Kath's sudden loss of confidence in all medical professionals and their prognostications. Dr. Winter's rosy prediction for a long life had proved to be dead wrong, and the life she had envisioned just days before changed in an instant.

From the sanctuary of our home, Kath struggled to understand her medical history in light of recent information, and as those details emerged, her allegiance toward Dr. Winter waned. The procedure he planned ten years ago originally involved more than a complete hysterectomy. It included the removal of the omentum for which she had signed legal consent.

The omentum, positioned just behind the skin of the abdomen, spread out like a fatty blanket. It covered all the abdominal organs and clung like velcro to their surfaces. Mother nature intended the fatty mass to catch and destroy foreign microbes, but it also served as a collection plate that provided an ideal environment for cancer cells to grow.

Kath had read numerous medical studies for borderline serous tumor with low malignant potential that supported Dr. Winter's prediction for a long and healthy life, but that success depended upon the removal of the omentum. Kath felt confused as she pondered Dr. Goodman's discussion about the risks of an omentectomy and experienced a chilling moment of angry clarity when she realized that Dr. Winter never removed it.

Before Kath's original surgery, Dr. Winter had understood that her abdomen would be surgically complex and most likely required a higher level of skill than he possessed as a basic GYN surgeon. In preparation for the surgery, he recognized his limitations and prearranged for a second surgeon to assist if needed. Unfortunately, he never summoned him and never dissected the fatty layers of omentum away from the intricate web of Kath's abdominal contents. Instead, he simply left the omentum behind.

The animosity she felt toward Dr. Winter tested her Eastern philosophical beliefs, but the current oncological predicament diminished that anger, as her logical mind desperately sought answers to a number of rhetorical questions. If the omentum had been removed would she be in this quandary? Did the natural hormones she had been taking awaken the long dormant cancerous beast? Why would this surgery be any more successful than the last one? These and many other questions were discussed as we traveled the two-hour drive to Dr. Freeman's Phoenix office.

Several chairs in the small waiting area were occupied as Kath walked through the center of the room to the open office window where the receptionist talked on the phone. Kath quietly leaned against the counter and waited for the secretary to finish the call. She acknowledged Kath's presence with a smile as her left shoulder snuggly tucked the phone against her chin. She handed Kath the "sign in" clipboard and gestured for her to complete the appropriate areas.

Kath promptly returned the finished form and stood at the window for further instructions, while the receptionist remained on the phone and reviewed the clipboard for accuracy. Kath heard frustration in the receptionist's voice as she urged the person on the other end of the phone to keep a scheduled chemotherapy appointment. But from that window, Kath had a good view of the busy chemo-room directly behind the office.

The occupants of those recliner chairs were predominately elderly females. None of them looked particularly healthy, and one appeared ready to vomit. "I would rather die than throw up," Kath said to no one in particular and turned to find an empty chair in the waiting room.

Middle aged to elderly female patients who desperately tried to conceal their apprehension from their daughters, granddaughters, and an occasional husband, sat all around us. Some of them looked nervously around the room and engaged in small talk, while others busied themselves with magazines. All that muffled clamor suddenly ceased whenever the office door creaked open, and a nurse summoned another name from the long list on her clipboard then escorted the winner to the doctor's office.

Once again the door creaked opened and the nurse loudly announced, "Barbara Wilson." With startled apprehension we momentarily looked at each other. Kath acknowledged the summons with a deep sigh, and we followed the nurse through the door with great trepidation. As we entered the unoccupied office the nurse plopped a large manila folder on an old, but well-polished cherrywood desk and beckoned us to sit in the soft cushy chairs on the customer side of the desk. "The doctor will be right in," she announced as she exited and closed the door behind her.

The doctor's large office had its usual complements of framed degrees and certifications adorning most of the walls along with scattered pictures of presumed family. The desktop remained free of clutter except for the previously placed folder, a keyboard, a mouse, and a computer monitor. A lone box of Kleenex sat on our side of the desk.

As short time later Dr. Freeman entered the room and introduced himself with a firm handshake, then sat down in his oversized desk chair. He looked professional in his dark suit and white shirt. His full head of white hair parted on the left, and his thick white eye brows portrayed him as a kindly grandfather, while his soft but confident voice immediately put Kath at ease as he read from the papers in the manila folder.

After he finished reading he turned the monitor toward us, and we both leaned forward as he showed us the detailed results of the CT Scan. He reiterated all that Dr. Goodman had said and went on to explain exactly what needed to be done. He pointed out that borderline serous tumors grew slowly but often recurred ten years after the initial surgery. Ignoring it could be one option since it had a slow growth history. If left untreated, Kath could possibly live uneventfully for another several years without symptoms. However, on rare occasions this type of cancer could mutate into adenocarcinoma, which would quickly shorten the time frame for complications, often with fatal results. He recommended immediate laparotomy with surgical debulking (open the abdomen and remove the tumor), followed by chemotherapy after the incision healed.

Speechless, we both leaned back in our chairs. The room remained quiet for what seemed like an eternity before Kath leaned forward and quietly asked how this tumor could be so detrimental when she felt fine. Dr. Freeman cited an absence of symptoms as the main reason for the grim statistics of ovarian cancer, but explained that since this tumor may have been caught early, surgical intervention remained her best option.

Kath sat back in her chair and tears welled up in her eyes. She quickly beat them back and asked if she would be in this predicament if the omentum had been removed ten years earlier. Dr. Freeman showed a reluctance to answer then said, "Science has done a poor job in detecting ovarian cancer. The CA-125," he said, "is the only blood test that screens for it, but fifty per cent of women tested in the earliest stages of cancer, and twenty percent of women tested in the later stages of cancer get false negative results. That leads them to mistakenly believe they are cancer free only to be fatally surprised some years later. The symptoms are diffuse and can be attributed to just about anything, which usually delays any cancer screening. But once the cancer is detected, surgery followed by chemo is the only option."

Nothing in Kath's life had prepared her for this moment. She stood at the beginning of a very long journey and was fully aware of the unfavorable odds. Inwardly, she bargained for any possible alternative, but she knew only two options existed. Do nothing while the cancer surreptitiously snuffed out her life in a very unflattering way, or roll the dice on a surgery that she already knew had a painful recovery. She held my hand as she looked at me, not for a solution to this unsolvable dilemma but to be reassured of my commitment to stand with her in this moment of terror. In a clear and unwavering voice, she told Dr. Freeman to schedule the surgery.

As we returned to Sedona, Kath felt overwhelmed by the gravity of the situation and unsure if she had made the right decision. In a rhetorical monologue, Kath spoke of the pros and cons of all the possible treatment options and tried to convince herself that she had made the correct choice. I simply listened, but we both knew the obvious answer.

We returned to Phoenix one week later and for a moment sat quietly in the parking lot of a large city hospital as Kath silently gazed out the windshield while she gathered her courage, much like a soldier before he charges into battle. After a deep breath she awoke from her trance, got out of the car, and beckoned me to hurry along.

We walked hand-in-hand toward the entrance of the hospital. Just before the sliding glass doors opened, she suddenly stopped and, with my hand held tightly in hers, abruptly pulled me back from my forward stride. Somewhat surprised at how well she had anchored herself, as I recoiled backwards toward her, I heard her say in a low but somber voice, "Once I walk through that door, my life will never be the same." She abruptly resumed her march with a controlled but frightened look of courage as the hospital doors opened and we walked side-by-side into the medical equivalent of Mordor.

We stood in the lobby like clueless tourists, unsure of where to go, with no guides or signs pointing the way. We followed a narrow path through the construction zone of the lobby that led to a small open area by an elevator. As I squinted to read the sign that directed us to the second-floor registration department, we heard the hurried pace of high heels clacking toward us.

I attempted to ask the hastily approaching hospital administrator for directions, but she literally pushed by us with her clipboard and entered the open elevator just before the doors closed. We stared at the silver doors in utter disbelief before Kath said, "That's a bad omen, I think we should leave." But we didn't leave. When the elevator returned we went up to the registration area.

From there we were given directions to the pre-op area. After a few missed turns in maze-like corridors, we found ourselves in front of a small, dimly lit room. Inside were several hospital gurneys parked in neat rows. A young nurse dressed in blue scrubs, spun around on her swivel stool when she heard us at the door, and said, "Barbara Wilson?" Kath nodded yes, and the nurse beckoned her to sit on a gurney.

When the nurse finished the paperwork, she handed Kath the infamous "one-size-fits-all" hospital gown. By it's very design, the gown exposed areas better left unexposed and immediately stripped away the last remnants of Kath's personal dignity as the nurse pulled the privacy curtain. That gown made her feel cold in an already chilly room, and the thin sheet that covered her while she lay on the gurney offered little warmth.

As the effervescent nurse prepared to start an IV, Kath warned that her veins always disappeared whenever she became cold (which made cannulation, inserting an IV needle difficult).

But the self-confident nurse ignored Kath's suggestion of applying a warm compress to her arm prior to starting the IV. Beads of sweat formed on the nurse's brow as she became visibly flustered after a failed third attempt. With a bruised ego, she reluctantly agreed to Kath's request that another nurse should finish the job. Unfortunately, when the second nurse failed after her second try, I intervened and asked them to summon the anesthesiologist. He promptly arrived and offered to place a "central line" (a large bore IV catheter usually placed in the internal jugular vein on the right side of the neck) once Kath arrived in the operating room. Kath's eyes grew large, but when she glanced at the multiple band aides on her arms, she looked at me with sad eyes and accepted his offer.

Dressed in his surgical attire with the obligatory, blue hair net, Dr. Freeman entered the room and stood beside Kath's gurney. Her anxiety surged as she searched his eyes for any clue that he wouldn't be another Dr. Winter.

He noticed the barely bridled emotion behind Kath's forced smile and responded with a human touch and a soft voice that revealed the humanity behind his professional demeanor. Her tears welled up when she kissed me a silent goodbye and with a deep breath rolled away on the gurney toward the OR to meet her fate.

The surgery took two hours longer than the sixty minutes Dr. Freeman had anticipated. When he arrived in the surgical waiting room to give me an update, his poker face proved difficult to read, but I felt troubled about the information he relayed.

He first had to cut through an excessive amount of abdominal and pelvic adhesions (lysis of adhesions). These tough pieces of scar tissue stretch like rubber bands around the intestines and anchored themselves into the abdominal wall or organs, but are aberrantly formed in response to previous abdominal surgeries or any pelvic inflammation.

Once he navigated through that maze of tissue, he tediously worked to free the velcro-like omentum entangled around the intestines. Carefully avoiding any perforation of the bowel, he finally removed a tumor about the size of a small loaf of bread that consisted of hundreds of small B-B sized cancerous growths that had found a home within the omentum. After he meticulously removed the unwanted tissue, he painstakingly searched for any cancer that remained and scraped it away.

I expected to find a nearly dead spouse as I walked into the recovery room, but Kath greeted me with sleepy eyes and a warm smile as she sat up in the bed half-awake with a nasogastric tube taped to her nose. (A nasogastric tube is a thick hollow tube that is placed through the nose and into the stomach to drain the gastric contents into a plastic container.) With a raspy voice, she reassured me that she felt fine. She squeezed my hand in gratitude but fell asleep in mid-sentence.

As her husband I felt helpless as a myriad of potential complications danced in my head. But as an experienced intensive care nurse I scrutinized every breath, body movement, and vital sign as if she were my own patient.

Kath grimaced with every abdominal movement, which limited her ability to take a deep breath, but she felt more comfortable after the nurse reluctantly complied with my request for more pain medicine. The IMED (a programable IV pump that delivers intravenous fluid at a desired rate) flowed at the expected dosage through a well-placed, intravenous catheter in the right side of her neck without any sign of an unintended pneumothorax (collapsed lung), but no x-ray had been ordered to confirmed the lung had avoided an accidental puncture. I borrowed the nurse's stethoscope and listened to the breath sounds of Kath's lungs to convince myself that her lungs had not been damaged.

The urine drained from the "Foley catheter" (a tube placed in the bladder that collected and measured urine output) appeared normal in quality and quantity. The NG Tube appeared well-placed, but I noticed a very old-school practice referred to as "drain to gravity," which siphoned the gastric fluids into the collection bag placed on the floor. To me this meant Dr. Freeman didn't believe in "modern" mechanical intermittent suction that automatically drained the stomach contents. He obviously remained stubbornly set in his traditional old-school ways. Although she remained sleepily sedated, Kath appeared to be in no distress and had stable vital signs. The nurse prepared to transfer her to the oncological floor.

Kath arrived at her private room very late in the evening. Ellie, a young nurse, announced herself as "Barbara's" nurse for the night, and two nurses transferred her from the gurney to the bed. Although both nurses were careful, Kath grimaced in pain as she landed on the bed but felt relieved to be off that hard stretcher.

Ellie spoke softly to Kath while she assessed her condition. She remained by her side for some time until she felt confident about Kath's status.

The dimly-lit room appeared old and in need of a paint job, like the rest of the hospital. The bed had the old-styled round, chrome guardrails, and the gears groaned when the head of the bed moved up or down. The equipment on the wall appeared well used but functional, and the yellowed white ceiling tile had collected some stains over the years. The bathroom appeared clean, but the shower smelled of mildew. I sat close to Kath in an old recliner that no longer reclined and dozed off to the sounds of the medical devices, as they chimed and beeped their way through their mechanical duties.

At one thirty in the morning, I sleepily scanned the automated blood pressure machine and found it had recorded an unusually low BP. That result should have provoked an audible alarm but it didn't. My heart pounded me awake as I abruptly jumped out of the chair and leaned over the rail of Kath's bed. I sensed trouble when I saw Kath's glassy eyes in the dimly-lit room and felt her quick shallow breaths on my face. Beads of sweat had built up on her brow. I held her cold hand and asked how she felt. "A little lightheaded from the anesthesia," she said. I pushed the button that recycled the BP machine, but it unfortunately confirmed an even lower one. Kath went on to say she hadn't felt right for a while but didn't want to awaken me, as she thought it would pass. When I recycled the BP a third time, it resulted in an even lower reading. Kath whispered that she felt bad and struggled to keep her eyes opened while I vociferously insisted that we maintain eye contact and turned on the nurse's call-light.

Although it seemed like forever, Ellie responded rather promptly. But as she stood at the bedside Kath called out in a weak voice and said, "I'm going out! You better do something, I'm going out." With a panicked look, Ellie said, "I have to call the doctor."

"But," I said, "what are you going to do now? Can't you see she's in trouble?"

Ellie emphatically reiterated her "call the doctor" refrain.

"Are you crazy?" I screamed. "Fix her blood pressure first then call the doctor. Give her some volume!" (When a person has a symptomatic low blood pressure episode, frequently the correct procedure is to give IV normal saline, in increments of 500 cc's as fast as it can be delivered). "I can't do that without calling the doctor first," Ellie shot back. "Either you bolus her with saline or I will," I insisted.

Ellie hesitated momentarily but set the IV pump for 500cc's to be delivered in thirty minutes. Before she left the room, she flashed a collaborative smile and said, "I need to talk to the doctor." She quickly returned with a third-year resident, who reviewed Kath's current predicament and ordered a blood transfusion, to my satisfaction.

The phlebotomist arrived to draw the necessary blood sample from Kath's arm. I stopped the technician as she prepared to insert the needle into her vein and summoned Ellie, who painlessly obtained the required blood sample from Kath's "IJ" catheter in her neck, thus avoiding an unnecessary needle stick.

The saline infusion had successfully stabilized her blood pressure, but the hematocrit level (the blood count that determines the need for blood transfusions) had dropped dramatically and indicated the need for multiple blood transfusions, which were completed by the morning.

Kath felt stronger the next day, but her contorted face silently chronicled her pain when two nurses helped her into a chair. Kath knew physical movement would hasten her recovery, but her surgically incised muscles screamed bloody murder whenever she changed position. By evening, with the help of some morphine, she walked around the room and ignored the pain. The next morning, she slid herself out of bed and lumbered toward the bedside chair, then carefully lowered herself into the recliner. After the pain subsided, she opened a small mirror in the bedside stand and gave an audible gasp, not from physical pain but from the image that reflected back.

Kath always maintained her outward appearance even under the worst conditions. Years before, when we had camped in the 110-degree-summer-heat in the Moab, Utah, desert she had kept her hair curled and her make-up intact. While vanity may have played a small roll, she learned at an early age that her outward appearance reflected her inner self. She refused to be defined by cancer and instead let her physical presentation become her narrative. So, it came as no surprise that she found her way to a mirror and pursued that task so soon after surgery.

When Dr. Freeman entered the room, he saw her in front of the mirror with lipstick in her hand. He smiled apologetically then he politely asked if she wanted to finish before he removed the obnoxious nasogastric tube that protruded from her nose. She looked over the mirror with her rose petal lip gloss partially applied, and without a word smiled, as she pretended to pull out the NG. After he removed the tube, he gave her a cup of ice, which she munched on with great delight as he sat next to her and spoke with a melodious voice about further treatment options for ovarian cancer.

He immediately excluded radiation as a possibility, but focused on chemotherapy, specifically intravenous Taxol with Cisplatin that would be given over three hours once every three weeks for a total of four doses. He referred to it as the first line of defense against ovarian cancer.

When he discussed the side effects of this therapy, Dr. Freeman talked in specific numbers. Ninety percent of people experienced neutropenia and leukopenia (loss of white blood cells which fight infection). Ninety percent had alopecia (hair loss). Eighty percent dropped their red blood cell count and over half had neuropathy (phantom pain usually on the legs, feet, or hands from damaged nerves). When Kath asked about the cure rate, he remained curiously vague except to say he'd had a lot of success with those two drugs.

He rebuffed my inquiry about intraperitoneal chemotherapy as a treatment option (the delivery of chemotherapy through a catheter directly into the abdominal space), and cited the inability of that treatment to deliver a precise dosage of Taxol, which often led to a toxic overdose from that very poisonous drug. And he became visibly irritated when I quoted studies that suggested increased survival rates from that therapy.

He also remained elusive when I asked about the tumor pathology report, and he avoided eye contact when he said those results were not yet finalized. He then spoke to the urgency of chemotherapy, as he unabashedly promoted his office program along with the experienced chemo-nurse who managed it. But when he sensed Kath's angst, he saved the full recruitment pitch for another time.

The reality of the surgical trauma made it painfully clear to Kath that her life's trajectory had dramatically changed, and in midst of her emotional turmoil she saw the questionable outcomes of the many unknowns. This created a tectonic emotional shift that frightened her to the core, but her poker face never betrayed those concerns.

Before Dr. Freeman left he encouraged Kath to drink more fluids and suggested she take a hot shower, but he rebuffed her concerns about the risk of an incisional infection. "On the contrary," he said, "The shower will help keep it clean." But she had her doubts.

Later that morning, our neighbors Candy and Tom unexpectedly dropped in for a short visit. Initially, Kath felt a bit awkward as we reminisced about the wild Frisco Trail dinner parties and laughed our way through the famous raccoon sombrero story. As our guests prepared to leave, we all promised more good times once Kath recovered from this temporary medical detour. But as she waved goodbye, she realized that alcohol would no longer be a part of her life.

As we talked alone in the room, her concerns poured out as she spoke about all that had happened and all that might happen. She felt trapped within the dingy confines of the hospital as the medical community commandeered the last of her personal control and brazenly dictated her destiny. She laughed out loud when she recalled how ferociously she'd fought for some ridiculously hallowed minor personal principle back in her rebellious youth that in hindsight paled in comparison to what she now faced. But in that humorous moment she uncovered a part of her being that would never give up and felt a deep contempt toward death.

A knock at the door heralded our good friends Sandy and Tom from Sedona. As an intensive care nurse from the hospital where I worked, Sandy knew about healthcare and personally understood the lifestyle problems of a chronic disease. An attractively tall woman with a coiffure that complimented her apparel, Sandy understood that a woman felt better when she was cleaned and polished. When I suggested that she help Kath with a shower, Sandy wheeled Kath into the stall like a professional while Tom and I went for a walk.

The hot shower with a shampoo rinsed away all the accumulated negative energy, and after she dried Kath off, Sandy dressed the abdominal incision better than the nurse could. Sandy choreographed the hair brush with a curling iron and worked her magic in front of the mirror as if she had studied under Vidal Sassoon. She delicately applied the makeup in a way that accentuated Kath's blue eyes and highlighted the facial features of her wrinkle-free skin. She discarded that disgusting hospital gown and donned a new pair of coral colored pajamas with dark cranberry accents, which complimented the ensemble. Tom and I returned to the room and found a vibrant, transformed person, who felt prepared to tackle what life had placed before her.

While the four of us gabbed like we were back in our Sedona living room, Kath felt so oblivious to the hospital surroundings that she briefly forgot her troubles and for a moment felt like she did before cancer. But in the midst of laughter, there came that uncomfortable moment when the stillness settled in, as we simultaneously remembered the seriousness of the setting. Unsure of the politically correct thing to say, everyone suddenly shared an awkward look, when Kath suddenly broke the thunderous silence and shouted, "Fuck cancer!" We all howled in support of her defiant stand.

Kath slept well that night but awoke the next morning with a low-grade fever and a slightly reddened area along the abdominal incision. She felt concerned about these developments and asked the nurse to summon Dr. Freeman, who entered the room a short time later. He greeted Kath with his grandfatherly demeanor and asked her questions about her general well-being while he proceeded with an examination. He gently picked up her pajama top to better inspect her surgical site, but promptly lowered it and immediately discounted the obvious redness with an inconsequential huff. He then placed a stethoscope in his ears and positioned the working end on the right lower part of her ribcage. In less time than it took to listen to one shallow breath, he dangled the stethoscope from his neck and exclaimed, "Ah hah! I knew it. You have pneumonia".

We looked at each other in complete disbelief, as I immediately questioned the accuracy of his diagnosis. But he became very indignant and refused to discuss it. Kath knew she didn't have pneumonia because she'd had it before and her body felt different this time. But Dr. Freeman dismissed her input with a roll of his eyes. Clearly perturbed, he insisted that an infectious disease doctor be consulted to guide her care and ordered a chest x-ray. Then he left the room in a very unhappy state.

A patient's lung field is clinically assessed in a very specific manner. The stethoscope must be moved to six different locations along the upper back, then moved to four different parts of the upper chest, as the patient's deep breaths are carefully listened to. If any suspicious sounds are heard, percussion is performed around the suspected area (one hand with closed fingers is placed on the suspected area, while two fingers of the other hand thump the top of the resting fingers and the practitioner listens for different sounds). This entire process requires two or three minutes, but a non-healthcare person would never have noticed his embarrassingly careless assessment.

Dr. Stone, an infectious disease specialist, arrived shortly after the X-ray technician took the picture. He identified himself when he knocked at the door and announced the purpose of his visit but washed his hands at the sink before he entered the room. As he approached the bed, he asked very general questions about Kath's overall health while he visually assessed her physical state and concluded that what he saw correlated with what Kath said. She had no cough and did not feel short of breath but felt queasy with some abdominal tenderness. He carefully lifted her pajama top and meticulously studied her abdominal incision before he listened to her bowel sounds with his stethoscope. He then pressed on her abdomen and watched her facial expressions for any signs of pain and carefully listened to her lungs in a professional manner. When he completed his assessment, he announced his conclusions in a circuitous way that highlighted his concern about her abdomen but curiously never declared that she had pneumonia. When I asked to view the X-ray film or read the report, he referred me to Dr. Freeman but ordered some IV antibiotics before he left and promised to return the next day.

Kath's temperature increased overnight, and in the morning Dr. Freeman entered the room with a concerned look as he quickly proceeded with his examination. With an abridged version of his physical assessment of Kath completed, he said very little as he momentarily left the room and returned with a staple remover (a type of plier that removed the staples which held the incised skin closed after surgery). While Kath lay on her back, he lifted her pajama top and tugged down the bottoms, which exposed a slightly red abdomen as he carefully removed one of the staples.

Kath could not see the procedure, but she smelled the putrid yellow pus that immediately drained out of her now open incision and felt its warmth as it trickled down her side while the nurse sopped up the drainage with sterile gauge.

Kath's panicked eyes fixed on mine as everyone in the room realized she had a raging incisional infection. Dr. Freeman tried to minimize the situation and referred to the newly developed condition as a superficial dehiscence while he removed the rest of the staples. He then spoke quietly to the nurse, who left the room momentarily and returned with an arm full of supplies, which he used to cover the large open area.

Fortunately, Kath could not see the wound, which measured six inches wide by ten inches long, and exposed the muscles of her abdominal wall, which remained closed with large wired sutures that kept all of the intestines in their place. However, the opened area actually extended underneath the skin for an additional inch around the entire perimeter, which made for a huge wound. A yellow plasma-colored fluid mixed with pus quickly saturated the gauge and leaked everywhere, as Dr. Freeman reinforced a poorly secured dressing that did little to stem the flood. Kath felt completely overwhelmed as she lay silently on her back with her eyes locked on the ceiling tiles while the ramifications of this event rushed through her head. Dr. Freeman tried to allay her fears when he described the wound as a minor setback, but no one in the room believed him and, he left with the nurse after she finished the dressing.

I watched in disbelief, as Kath lay flat on her back in that dismal room afraid to move, with tears trickling down her cheek. She knew Dr. Freeman did not speak the truth about this misadventure, and if the wound healed at all it would take at least two to three months with the outdated "wet to dry" wound protocol that he had ordered, which had been the standard of care decades ago. He also failed to mention that less than two per cent of people with this type of surgery developed this complication and experience a thirty percent mortality rate, or that her blood may become contaminated from the wound with a potentially fatal infection called sepsis. He also failed to mention that chemotherapy would be delayed until the abdominal wound closed, and he clearly forgot to discuss the full ramifications of his earlier intimations about the aggressiveness of the cancer.

The full consequences of these truths became self-evident, and we felt that if she remained in this hospital she would die. I promised Kath I would get her back to the doctors I trusted in the small town of Sedona and asked the case manager to arrange that.

A hospital case manager coordinates the immense amount of information generated by the extraordinary number of specialists involved in a patient's care for an eventual discharge. Beth happened to be assigned to Kath.

Beth, a soft-spoken, middle-aged woman, who hadn't worked as a bedside nurse for years, introduced herself when she entered Kath's room. She had heard of our dissatisfaction with Kath's care and attempted to smooth it over with the usual political correctness of bureaucratic speak. I listened as Kath lay in the bed staring at the ceiling and the over-saturated dressing oozed down her side.

She explained why the hospital denied our request for a transfer to the local hospital where I worked even though a surgeon from there accepted her care and personally requested that she be transferred. Standard insurance rules allowed a transfer to another hospital only if the patient required a higher level of care that the current hospital could not offer. The services of the local Sedona hospital could not compete with that big trauma center in Phoenix, and insurance would not pay any of the hospital bills if they transferred her.

I pleaded and demanded that she be moved, but another day passed while the wound leaked around the dressing. Dr. Freeman refused to speak to me when he entered the room and only talked to Kath, while the nurses avoided the room as much as possible. Dr. Stone visited every morning but left quickly with little comment.

Phone calls to friends at the local Sedona hospital offered emotional support, but no one could find a way around this impasse, and a sense of desperation set in. Two more days had passed and nothing had changed when I caught Beth outside the door of Kath's room. She seemed surprised when I asked for the proper paperwork to file a complaint about Kath's care with the Arizona Department of Health Services. She tried to dissuade me from that path, but after I told her my list of complaints, I dared Beth to look Kath in the eye and tell her that she had received the best care anywhere. She hesitated for a moment and quickly excused herself.

She returned a short time later and announced that Kath could be discharged to home and followed by a home health agency. Apparently, Beth had persuaded the hospital cronies that this approach would be the least litigious way to proceed, but in reality, she arranged for nothing except a home health number for us to call once we returned to Sedona. She did manage to get us some sterile gauge with tape for the dressing change, but they offered no prescriptions for antibiotics or any medications for pain management. Their lack of responsible action remained unacceptable by any measure, but it didn't matter. We simply wanted to leave as soon as possible, and they wanted us gone even quicker.

When I wheeled her past the nurses' station, the staff offered no fond good-byes only a sense of good riddance. The wound continued to drain copious amounts of pus-like drainage, as we made the two-hour drive home and stopped twice along the way to repair the dressing. My anxiety level skyrocketed as we drove through an empty desert completely void of vegetation or medical services, and I couldn't tell if Kath had fallen asleep or passed out.

17 Home Again

Once home, I replaced the saturated dressing and promptly contacted Dr. Falino, who had been Kath's primary care physician for some time. She liked him for his sense of humor and his ability to make her laugh. Dr. Falino arrived at our front door within an hour of my call, and he wore his serious face when he knelt next to her as she lay on the couch. He performed a complete physical exam before he dismantled the dressing. He bent over Kath's abdomen and placed his nose next to the wound, sniffing like a bloodhound for any signs of infection. Then he sat down on the floor in a crossed leg yoga position and looked her in the eyes as he spoke of his findings.

He saw no sign of pneumonia and didn't believe the wound to be grossly infected but promised a prescription for an antibiotic. He explained that under normal circumstances the dehiscence would heal without much fanfare, but ovarian cancer complicated things because it became a big deal when the chemotherapy had to be delayed. The chemo for ovarian cancer proved most effective immediately after the surgical debulking, but its toxic effects severely impeded any surgical healing. This unfortunate medical mishap left Kath with no choice. The chemo had to be delayed until the wound healed, but as the clock advanced so did the cancer.

In Phoenix, Kath felt the medical deities determined her destiny and refused to have their preordained path of treatment questioned by anyone. They superficially placated her to think her input mattered, but she saw through their phoniness and in less than an hour a trusted local doctor had given Kath hope.

Wound closure became a priority, and Dr. Falino felt that debridement (the cutting away of dead tissue from the wound with a scalpel) would accelerate the process. He promptly called the physical therapist at a local care facility for an immediate appointment.

As Kath prepared to leave for the wound consultation, she secured her abdominal dressing with one hand and hugged the doctor with the other, conscious not to stain his suit with her drainage. She whispered, "Thank you," in his ear while her teary eyes shouted out the gratitude she felt. Within five minutes we arrived at the care center, and when we drove into the parking lot it felt like deja vu all over again.

In 1999, this same facility offered us the proof of employment documents we needed to buy the Sedona house, and we felt a sense of irony that we had returned with hat in hand. Ten years ago we were a healthy couple, excited about our Sedona adventure. It never occurred to us that we'd be back here at the dawn of a carcinogenic adventure we'd refused to believe would ever happen. For a decade, we had subconsciously buried the possibility of cancer deep in the land of denial and lived life as if those deadly seeds would never sprout again. But they had germinated into a full-blown health crisis that had careened out of control.

An uncertain future loomed large as we walked into the facility, but if Kath felt frightened she never showed it. It had been less than a week since her belly had been sliced opened and only hours since she had been lying in a hospital bed. Every step awakened her incisional pain, but she never complained as she moved forward with determination and grace. Kath always kept her emotions in check, which proved useful under the circumstances. She politely introduced herself to Jean, the physical therapist, who met us at the entrance.

As we walked to her work area, Kath discussed the details of the wound and the goal of debridement. The small room accommodated a large massage table covered with a clean sheet. A large, blue absorbent pad had been placed in the middle. The glass cupboards were filled with various wound care products while the drawers were neatly stocked with essential healthcare items and the uncluttered counters sparkled clean.

Kath clenched her teeth and lay frozen in place on the table without the benefit of analgesics, while Jean removed the dressing and inspected the area. The wound continued to produce a considerable amount of drainage and contained plenty of tissue that warranted debridement, but the dressing's tape had excoriated the skin around the entire perimeter of the wound, which complicated an already complex dressing change. As she laid on her back with her abdomen exposed, Kath wanted to see the wound she had never seen before, so Jean pulled out a mirror from a nearby drawer and gave it to her.

Kath struggled to properly position the looking glass. A subtle look of silent shock confirmed she had achieved the proper angle of reflection, and she remained motionless while she stared at the image that frightened her to the core. Fatalistic doubts fueled apocalyptic visions that nearly overwhelmed her. In a surreal moment, she frantically manipulated the mirror in the false hope the wound would somehow be smaller than the reflection suggested. With a defeated sigh, she dropped the mirror on the table and stared briefly at the ceiling before she stoically asked Jean to proceed with the debridement.

Kath squeezed my hand tightly as Jean cleaned the wound with a saline solution and trimmed the dead tissue with a scalpel. For twenty minutes we remained locked in a silent visual embrace as the excised tissue accumulated on the counter top. Finally, Jean declared a halt to the procedure and dressed the wound. Then she scheduled a follow-up appointment in three days. Jean made sure we left with enough supplies for two dressing changes, as Kath thanked her for the services and we returned home to an uncertain future.

Kath held on to the dressing and pulled herself out of the car, then slowly walked into the house. I followed with all of the supplies. When she passed the kitchen, she declined any offer to eat. "No thanks," she said, "I just want to go to bed." As she teetered down the hall, she cradled the wound with one hand and used the wall to steady herself with the other, while the cat did his best to run between her legs. She made it to the bed and sat down in an exhausted collapse, but she wouldn't lie down until she had placed a large towel on the mattress to absorb any drainage that might leak from the wound. When she finally laid down, her face telegraphed abdominal pain and the desperation she felt, but her exhausted state kept her from dwelling on her impossible situation. She quickly fell asleep lying on her back, too petrified to lie on her side.

The night provided little relief, as the wound required regular attention. As the night dragged on, Kath became disheartened. Rather than count sheep, she counted the nights until the wound would heal, but she concluded it might never heal, and that left her in near panic.

We were both awake when the sun peaked through the bedroom window and illuminated our dilemma. I repaired the dressing with the last of the supplies. As the daylight shined on the soiled dressings piled high in the trash can next to the bed, we conceded the obvious. We needed help. Kath asked me to call Dr. Wallace, a surgeon at the local hospital who had previously agreed to help her, but the Phoenix hospital denied his professional request. Fortunately, I had his cell phone number.

I was shocked when he answered the phone. While he detailed his plan to meet us at the hospital, Kath packed her over-night essentials and prepared to leave immediately. Dr. Wallace arranged for Kath to be a "direct admit," which meant she could bypass the line at the Emergency Room. After a quick stop at the admissions desk, we arrived at her preassigned room in short order. As the nurse helped her into bed, Kath splinted her abdomen and tried not to show the pain as her exhausted body melted into the mattress.

Before long Dr. Wallace arrived. After a brief discussion of recent events, he carefully examined the wound before he confidently assured her that it could be healed. When he asked how long it had been since Kath had eaten, he winced at her answer but replied, "I can schedule the debridement surgery today." A happy but exhausted smile replaced a nervous one.

Kath finally felt confident this abdominal disaster would be resolved. But its conclusion signaled the resumption of her personal fight with cancer, which presented its own plethora of hidden surprises. Although she had nearly drowned in the depths of despair, she finally pushed herself up with a reinvigorated sense of hope and found the courage to face the myriad of medical unknowns. This helped her to believe that with the proper help she could defeat any tumor.

Ann, the hospital's wound specialist, arrived at Kath's bedside shortly after she returned from surgery with the "wound vac" Dr. Wallace had specifically ordered. The device used a low level of vacuum suction that pulled the drainage out of the wound and collected the fluids in a plastic container. An absorbent material similar in texture to steel wool but with the thickness of a large kitchen sponge had been custom cut to fit the specific irregular dimensions of the wound. One end of a tube, about the diameter of a pencil, connected to a perforated plastic, flat-round "shower head," about the size of a silver dollar that laid on top of the absorbent sponge. A thin sheet of plastic, similar to Saran wrap with glue on one side, overlapped the entire area that stuck to the dressing as well as the skin and created an airtight seal. The free end of the tubing connected to a small vacuum machine, about the size of a large camera case. It provided the low level of suction that pulled the drainage from the wound through the tubing, and into the collection container. Historically, this device dramatically sped up healing time for wounds, and Dr. Wallace predicted it would be healed in less than two months. The pain-free process required approximately a half an hour to install, while the portable battery-operated machine offered her the freedom to walk around and not worry about a leaky dressing.

With the wound vac in place Kath moved off the bed. She no longer needed to secure the abdominal dressing with her hand and felt very confident walking with the "vac" in her hand as she moved toward the window. She looked like her old self as she leaned against the glass dressed in her monogramed pajamas and her blue, terry cloth robe while the sun warmed her back. She glanced around the room before she raised the "vac" up in the air with one hand and asked with a soft voice through slightly clenched teeth, "Why didn't Dr. Freeman think of this?" I assumed that was a rhetorical question.

Kath anxiously walked about the room while the case manager finalized the home health arrangements. Dr. Wallace arrived and announced that her wound had become infected with Methicillin Resistance Staphylococcus Aureus (MRSA). Kath's blue eyes opened nearly as wide as her mouth when she eked out, "You've got to be kidding me?" She slumped into a chair and stared in silence at no one in particular while the wound vac rhythmically drummed its mechanical beat.

He declined to say how she might have contracted the bacteria, but Kath was convinced it originated from that mildewed shower Dr. Freeman had suggested she use. Dr. Wallace calmly replied to her inevitable question of, "Now what," as he downplayed the severity of that notorious microbe for which he ordered a new antibiotic, Zyvox. He predicted the infection would not impede the healing process, but he failed to mention the two hundred dollar per day cost of the drug or the contagious nature of the saturated dressings that had leaked everywhere.

Kath felt concerned about the spread of this bug in our home as well the unexpected expense of the new drug. The case manager eased her mind when she informed Kath that our health insurance covered the full cost of this unusual medication, however, she offered no advice for the contaminated areas.

That night, while Kath stayed in the hospital, I went home and laundered all the bed linens and wiped every imaginable surface with a diluted bleach solution. When Kath returned home the next day, she walked into the house with a wound vac that dangled over her shoulder like a huge purse. She smiled when the cat ran between her feet, as she tried not to trip over the suction tube on her way to the bedroom.

After she plugged the suction device into the electrical outlet, she pulled back the blanket and let out an appreciative sigh, then floated down onto the bed. She tugged the covers up to her chin, which created an impenetrable cotton force field that protected her from further malfeasance, while her cat laid down next to her and acted as a lookout.

Kath viewed herself as an independent person who never accepted or solicited help from anyone. But this abdominal dehiscence, with all its complexities, boldly proclaimed to everyone that she had become dependent upon others, and that metamorphosis frightened her more than cancer. She reluctantly accepted the idea of a home health nurse and agreed to give it a chance, but she remained skeptical on the competency of the agency's representative.

The home health nurse arrived later that day to teach us the intricacies of the dressing changes and the complexities of the wound vac. I recognized Judy from her prior days as a nurse on the medical surgical floor at the hospital. Kath smiled when she entered the room and reached out to shake her hand as she approached the bed.

After Judy completed Kath's health history, Kath witnessed a subtle but concerned look on Judy's face as she inspected the dressing along with the wound vac. She abruptly admitted her lack of familiarity with the suction machine or the airtight abdominal seal. When she approached Kath for the dressing change, I altered Judy's course toward the sink and suggested that we wash our hands together. When we returned to Kath, I quietly insisted that she observe my wound vac technique, while I performed the entire dressing change.

With Kath's abdomen exposed, Judy peered closely into the wound and proceeded to document its measurements. I interrupted her appraisal when I asked to tie her hair back, as it dangled too close to the wound. After she cataloged the dimensions, I repacked the wound with an airtight seal and successfully initiated the suction without an audible alarm from the machine. That brought a misty-eyed smile from Kath.

With the business of the wound vac completed, Kath thanked Judy for her time, as I hurriedly escorted her out the front door. When I returned to the bedroom, Kath had pulled the blanket up to her neck. With an emphatic voice, Kath insisted that Judy never touch the dressing or manipulate the wound vac again. After a moment of awkward silence, we laughed uproariously at the incompetence we had just witnessed. But underneath that exaggerated levity lurked the stark realization that not all healthcare workers were created equal and discretion should be advised.

Intellectually, Kath resigned herself to the simple fact that cancer permeated her every conscious thought, and she was unable to escape its long dark shadow. But in the sleepy slumber of the morning twilight, she almost believed this debacle to be a dream. For a brief euphoric moment she doubted that she had cancer until she opened her eyes. Suddenly, when the plethora of visible reminders from this unwelcome intruder overwhelmed her senses, the irrefutable cerebral response shattered her wall of denial and revealed more than she cared to see.

Before cancer unceremoniously invaded Kath's world, the bedroom symbolized the center of her private life. It was an impenetrable fortress against an intrusive world where she enjoyed her meditative practices, read countless books, and reveled in her moments of passion. But overnight that sacred place had been turned into an infirmary.

A small end table recruited from the living room served as a bedside stand for the required wound supplies, while the bedroom closets stored the surplus medical stock. A large trash can that contained the contaminated dressings stood next to the bed.

The portable "vac" machine with the plastic umbilical cord didn't limit Kath's independence as much as the necessity of an airtight seal. The unfortunate anatomical location of the wound greatly affected its integrity. Any bend or twist of the abdomen stressed the airtight dressing, and the simple act of sitting in a chair or getting out of bed crimped her abdominal skin in such a way that the seal often failed. A compromised seal meant the vacuum had to be turned off until a new dressing could be applied. But a loss of suction for an extended period of time resulted in a build-up of secretions that slowed the healing process, increased the chances of reinfection, and further delayed the start date for chemotherapy.

The wound vac ruled Kath's world for two more months. She spent most of that time in bed, flat on her back, which minimized the leaks but amplified her social isolation. With a limited ability to leave her home or properly entertain the occasional visitor in the living room, the bedroom became the center for all social interactions. But the implied private nature of that room created a sense of personal intrusion, which further stoked her reclusive nature. With her last sanctuary breached, she had no place to be the solitary recluse she wanted to be. But as she laid flat on her back, she escaped the pressures of life with cancer through the world of books.

The first paperbacks from Amazon were biographies of the old Rock and Rollers of her youth. She always had a passion for the music makers of the 60s, not as a groupie but as an aficionado of minute details of their lives that few others ever knew, or wanted to know. In her younger days, she danced to the beat of Led Zeppelin, The Doors, and The Beatles. But when she read the personal stories of the individual musicians like Jimmy Page, Jim Morrison, or George Harrison, she drifted back to a time when diamond needles played vinyl records and death only happened to old people and junkies. Their personal triumphs and tragedies distracted her from the inescapable fears that roamed about in her head but also provided conversational topics about something other than cancer.

As a reluctant combatant in a relentless war waged by a ruthless enemy that infiltrated the very core of her being, these distractions dulled the roar from the cancerous cannonade that continuously exploded all around her. Her counterattack strategy remained very simple—divert the mind to win the daily skirmish and build a coalition of medical allies to defeat this implacable foe.

Every day, regardless of whether visitors were expected, she stood naked in front of the bathroom mirror and bathed herself in the sink. She watched as that reflected image stared back in disbelief at the plastic tube that dangled from a surgically scarred body, while the doppelganger's sad face regularly questioned whether she had the courage to run the cancerous labyrinth that lay before her. Each time she concluded with the same stern affirmation to never give up, and she found that her morning routine helped her cope with the unrelenting emotional stress.

She typically wore one of several monogrammed pajamas that she carefully buttoned around the vac tube before she leaned toward the mirror and applied her make up. But when she blow-dried her hair, she petitioned the chemo gods that she be spared from the alopecia that eventually accompanied the inevitable chemotherapy.

Dressed in pajamas and confined to the house, Kath felt increasingly isolated from the outside world. With social contact limited to healthcare workers, she needed more human interaction than her books or what the *Bold and the Beautiful* T.V. soap opera offered. She thought a dinner at a local high-end restaurant, the first such outing since her surgery in Phoenix, fit the bill.

After careful consideration, she picked out a dress that accommodated the wound vac tube and gazed into the mirror as she carefully applied her makeup. When the final dab of red rose lipstick had been applied, she pressed her lips together and checked for proper distribution before she turned to me for my approval.

Through misty eyes I saw a courageously beautiful woman and never noticed that she held the wound vac like a fashion accessory. She never appeared self-conscious about the tube that dangled from her abdomen when we entered the only decent restaurant in our small town. We enjoyed our extended dinner to the hum of the suction machine that we never heard and toasted its eventual departure before we returned home.

In the early days of the wound, Kath had convinced herself the nutritional supplements that she had learned about at Dr. Reynolds office would actually help heal the wound. She pushed herself out of bed three times a day no matter how bad she felt and made her way to the kitchen where she consumed high doses of glucosamine, Vitamins A, C, and E, plus a high-protein drink supplemented with aloe vera juice. Two months later, with the wound nearly closed, she no longer rolled out of bed like a telephone pole, but sat on the side of the bed with her feet on the floor and slowly stretched her sleepy muscles while she braced herself for the next challenge, finding a replacement for the now retired Dr. Freeman.

The Hunt for **18** Good Oncologist

Kath contacted the medical records department at the Phoenix hospital and, with surprisingly little effort, received multiple faxed pages that covered her entire hospital stay. When the avalanche of printed faxes finally stopped, she searched the pile of paper for the pathology reports and sat down to review them all. When she read the words *adenocarcinoma*, her jaw dropped as the papers fell to her lap. "This can't be right," she screamed. "Borderline tumors don't morph into adenocarcinoma." For the next several hours she searched the Internet for information that proved her point.

She found "Borderline Serous Tumors with Low Malignant Potential" referenced by many different names, each with its own little nuanced subtype that ranged from benign cysts to aggressive adenocarcinomas. But borderline serous tumors with low malignant potential accounted for only fifteen percent of all epithelial ovarian cancers while adenocarcinomas were less than five percent. Her spirits lifted when she read the five-year survival rate for an LMP tumor exceeded 98%, which supported Dr. Winter's prediction ten years ago. When she learned that a tumor with "invasive papillary implants" or "psammoma bodies" suggested a less than rosy outcome, a sudden chill ran down her spine. She recalled those names from both Dr. Winter's and Dr. Freeman's report.

Chemotherapy killed cells that rapidly divide, but the research suggested systemic intravenous chemotherapy produced less than optimal results with the slowly dividing borderline serous tumor cells.

Peritoneal chemotherapy that utilized Carboplatin with Taxol immediately after surgical debulking proved to be a therapy that most likely extended survivability, but Dr. Freeman never believed in that school of thought and the superficial dehiscence rendered it a moot point. Unfortunately, she found no other research that demonstrated any greater promise.

Kath felt the Phoenix hospital's report to be flawed and convinced their pathologist to re-examine the samples along with the biopsy slides he had from Dr. Winter's original surgery. She also insisted that upon completion all the pathology slides be forwarded to Dr. Jay Fleishman, the local Sedona hospital's pathologist, who promised Kath he'd personally review them.

In less than a week Kath received an addendum to the Phoenix hospital's report that substantiated her initial claim and surreptitiously stated that the hospital had mistakenly identified the original cell. She did not have adenocarcinoma and the tumor cells were identical in every way to the cells Dr. Winter first identified, while Dr. Fleishman reconfirmed these exact same findings.

When she searched the Internet, she found widely divergent theories on ovarian cancer. Some crazy, some not, but the most consistent piece of information suggested that an ovarian cancer patient who received care from a gynecological oncological surgeon had a better chance of survival than those who received care elsewhere.

Most cancer patients received their care from the oncologist their primary doctor recommended, but Kath's animosity toward Dr. Freeman made any of his Phoenix recommendations an unlikely choice. Sedona advertised three oncologists, but they were all hematologists that specialized in blood disorders and blood forming organs with little experience in the rare form of ovarian cancer that invaded her abdomen. With the wound nearly closed, Kath felt reluctant to travel out of town in search of chemotherapy and decided to visit one of those hematologists at the Sedona Cancer Clinic, a fifteen-minute drive from home.

She had never met Dr. Nafrun and knew little about him. The online data base of the Arizona State Medical Board revealed no complaints against him, but she discovered little else other than the usual promotional information on the cancer clinic web site. Frustrated with the lack of data that impeded an informed choice about the practitioner who may or may not be able to save her life, she sat in his waiting room and wondered if she knew more about this cancer than he did.

Dr. Nafrun's medical assistant escorted us to the office and sat us in front of an unoccupied desk to await his arrival. Other than a computer monitor, no medical folders cluttered his spotless desktop. Nondescript trophies lined the bookshelves and a few well-framed modern art prints adorned the walls, but prominently displayed on the wall behind his chair hung a large print of the *The Scream* by Edvard Munch.

The sounds of a busy office wafted through the open door when a tall slim figure suddenly burst into the room and rocketed past us. He zipped around the corner of the desk and landed in his chair with such force that he grabbed the edge of the desktop with one hand to stop his sideways momentum and reached across the desk with his other hand for an anticipated handshake. In a professional manner, he said, "Dr. Nafrun. How can I help?"

Kath eschewed the obligatory handshake but reached across the desk with a large manila envelope that contained her medical records and in an unflappable voice said, "Kathy Wilson." His face reflected a moment of uncertainty before he retrieved the packet and carefully stacked its contents in a neat pile. He methodically reviewed each page but carelessly scattered them about the desk as he finished each one. However, he sat very still when he read Dr. Freeman's surgical report before he fastidiously returned all of the papers to the envelope.

With the fingers of both hands interlocked behind his head and a distant look in his eye, he gazed at the ceiling as he contemplatively rocked in his chair. After several muted moments, he suddenly leaned forward with his eyes focused on the envelope that his hands aimlessly twirled on the desk and cleared his throat for an important announcement.

He readily confessed his limited experience with this particular form of cancer but referenced Dr. Freeman's note when he suggested a combination of taxol and carboplatin chemotherapy. Kath felt relieved that he admitted his limited exposure to the LMP tumors, but that lack of experience invalidated any advice he offered. When Kath pointed out the results of the "Onco Tech Scan" that Dr. Freeman had ordered, he readily dismissed the test as an unreliable tool.

The Onco Tech Scan measured the response of several chemo agents from the published results of multiple clinical trials against the known cellular characteristics of the LMP tumor, while an algorithmic equation defined the probable effectiveness of certain chemotherapies. That mathematical algorithm suggested both taxol and carboplatin would be ineffective in this particular instance. Dr. Nafrun conceded that he didn't know if the proposed cocktail would work, but he related his own experience with cancer.

He too had doubted the effectiveness of the prescribed therapy for his prostatic tumor but achieved remission shortly after he completed the chemo regime three years ago. And while the therapy left him weakened, he chose tap dancing for his physical rehab. He pointed to the trophies that lined the shelves of his office.

As a cancer survivor, he felt greater empathy for fellow cancer patients and believed that connection improved their outcome. But Kath wanted an experienced practitioner, preferably a gynecological oncological surgeon, who had successfully managed this rare form of cancer. While she genuinely liked Dr. Nafrun's quirkiness, she concluded the meeting with a smile and promised to think about his offer, but everyone knew she intended to look elsewhere.

There were no gynecological-oncological specialists in Sedona while Phoenix offered individual practitioners. But American Cancer Care offered an integrated medical approach that appealed to her alternative medicine beliefs, and the three thousand mile flight to Chicago to see Dr. Serena Beltane, a female gynecological oncological surgeon who had survived cancer, didn't seem as crazy as it sounded.

The ACC arranged all of the travel logistics but more importantly accepted our health insurance plan with limited out of pocket expenses. Two weeks later we checked into our room at the Illinois Beach Resort on the shores of Lake Michigan, ten miles south of the Wisconsin state line. There the travel weary woman from Sedona stared into the bathroom mirror and momentarily questioned the wisdom of her choice. But the next morning, as she prepared for a long day at the cancer clinic, those self-doubts evaporated along with the misty Lake Michigan fog.

The complimentary shuttle dropped us off at the front door of the cancer center where the concierge greeted us with a smile and reviewed Kath's information before he escorted us to the proper location. Their organizational skills shined as the myriad of admission papers and blood tests were completed with minimal fuss before they escorted her to a climate controlled exam room where she waited comfortably in a hospital gown. A gentle knock announced Dr. Beltane's arrival.

The doctor entered the room with a sense of professional purpose and introduced herself with a soft English accent. She extended one hand for a formal handshake and held the medical chart snuggly against her white coat with the other. The two finished the necessary small talk of personal introductions before they moved on to the true nature of the visit.

Dr. Beltane sat comfortably on a stool next to Kath and actively engaged in a true health care dialogue. She listened carefully to all of Kath's concerns and completed a thorough physical exam before she summarized her findings.

She believed the cancer to be of serous tumor origin, which consisted of hundreds of small fluid-filled sacs, much like giant-sized BB pellets, scattered throughout her abdomen and pelvic floor. The CA-125, the numerous PET-CT scans, and her physical exam supported those conclusions. But the pelvic floor tumors Dr. Freeman had left behind, which he failed to mention, posed significant future problems, which could not be solved with further surgery or radiation therapy. Dr. Beltane described the only two choices available to her—chemotherapy or do nothing. While the three of us sat together in a small, windowless room, Kath felt very alone.

For a moment her eyes grew distant and she appeared to be deep in thought, while the air conditioner hummed in the background. "What about Doxil?" Kath asked. "The Onco Tech Scan recommended it."

"Sure, it's an IV medicine given once a month, and it's ideal for your schedule." Dr. Beltane replied. "And if that doesn't work, we've got plenty of other drugs to try."

Kath didn't know exactly how Doxil, an anthracycline chemotherapy worked, but she knew the drug rarely caused alopecia. And since all intravenous chemotherapy drugs damaged the blood vessel through which they were delivered, Kath requested a "port."

The chemoport is a permanent large bore IV catheter surgically placed into a large vein through a small incision in the left upper chest wall but completely under the skin. It is ideal for IV chemotherapy and designed to negate the noxious effects of the toxic drugs on the smaller vein walls. Dr. Beltane scheduled the outpatient procedure for the next morning and chemotherapy in the afternoon.

Long frustrated with the delayed chemo treatments that the abdominal dehiscence empirically imposed and prevented any movement against this cancer insurgency, Kath felt the burden of inaction had finally been lifted from her shoulders. Kath had always been an impulsive, action-oriented person, but she felt stymied in her quest to battle this foe. For two unchecked months that alien had grown stronger, but now she found a competent person she trusted to lead the charge in her personal war on cancer. On the eve of the first battle she felt resolutely serene as we walked along the sandy beaches of Lake Michigan in the early evening.

The morning sun found Kath ready for the day. The painless port placement went smoothly, but as we stood at the entrance of the chemotherapy room she paused. The old world she once knew had changed forever, but if she wanted a life without cancer this new toxic adventure required a leap of faith.

She had read many scientific articles that clearly suggested serous tumors failed to respond to any chemotherapy. Many people with the same type of tumor had subjected themselves to this toxic potion and risked its detrimental side effects only to find the cancer had continued to grow unabated. That introduced a degree of un-certainty in a world with no guarantees. All of these doubts were racing through her mind as she stood at the entrance to the chemotherapy room surveying the site and a young nurse at a distant desk waved us in. Unsure as to the proper etiquette of a chemotherapy room, Kath tried not to stare at the occupied chairs as she followed the nurse to her assigned seat.

The recliner felt comfortable as the young nurse sat on a stool next to Kath and reviewed the necessary paperwork. After she completed a brief physical exam, they had a short discussion about the major side effects of Doxil. Then she left to obtain the chemo drug from the pharmacy while Kath waited nervously in her chair and looked around the room.

The chemo area held a couple dozen chairs mostly occupied by middle-aged to elderly females, many with headscarves and IV's that infused into their veins. They were attended to by daughters, granddaughters, or sisters, and all of them seemed happy but, curiously, very few men populated the room.

The background conversations included everything from mundane grocery lists to the current weather. Anything except the common thread that brought all of the occupants of the room together. But when someone finally spoke of cancer, they did so in hushed tones so as not to disturb the uninvited guest and only uttered that word when absolutely necessary.

For over an hour the Doxil infused without problems while a cadre of ancillary staff stopped by and offered support from their unique specialty. The naturopath brought a variety of suggestions in the realm of complementary medicine, which resonated with Kath. The pastoral minister espoused a strong Eastern philosophical lean and offered the chapel as a spiritual retreat. The mind-body medicine person offered therapies that Kath felt very comfortable with. The broad range of enthusiastic support stood in sharp contrast to the culture of indifference she had experienced at the Phoenix hospital, but more important, she no longer felt alone in her battle against cancer.

After the nurse disconnected the IV's and secured the newly placed port, we visited the scheduler who arranged all of our future travel needs and made appointments for next month's return visit.

Once a month for the next year and a half we traveled to Chicago for an overnight trip. Kath tolerated the drudgery of travel surprisingly well and never complained or felt reluctant to go, perhaps because Chicago held a special place in Kath's world before cancer had changed her life.

She recalled the train trip with her mother and sister from Ann Arbor to Chicago that left a permanent sentimental glow in a very non-sentimental girl. While the cancer clinics proximity to Ann Arbor afforded the occasional opportunity to see her family, Kath felt uncomfortable when Marianne visited during a chemotherapy session where she witnessed firsthand what her baby sister experienced. As the sisters traversed that chemo-day together, Kath felt self-consciously vulnerable and Marianne felt particularly helpless as the two struggled to reconcile their strong emotions, which eventually solidified the shaky rapport they'd historically had.

On occasion we extended the Chicago trip by a few days and visited her mom in Ann Arbor. The five-hour drive offered a time out from the relentless drumbeat of cancer as we headed back to the land she called home. But Kath knew her mother's angst at the possible loss of a second daughter to that deadly plague and vowed to allay her mom's concern about her imminent demise.

Carol listened as Kath explained the minimal effect chemotherapy had on her well-being and pulled on her hair, which emphasized the point. She gave a slight gasp when Kath displayed her abdominal scar but breathed easier when she understood her daughter had completely healed from that surgical debacle. She felt even better when they shared a meal and readily interpreted Kath's strong appetite as a sign of good health. The fear of cancer faded in the presence of their magical mother-daughter bond that transported them back to a simpler time when moms made everything better.

We took a short drive to Ann Arbor and walked the University of Michigan campus, which exerted a strong pull on her nostalgic strings. But when we sat on a bench in the middle of the diag, she sentimentally spoke of her three-speed Schwinn racer she had pedaled through this very spot on her way to class. Her voice slowly ebbed as her eyes squinted against the imaginary wind and she remembered how it felt when her long brown hair flowed in the breeze.

After a moment of solitude, she stood up and continued the tour toward the Del Rio bar where her stained-glass window that bore the pub's name still hung above the entrance. She stood in the doorway for a brief moment and stared at the work of art that she and Tom created back in the simpler times of the glass-work days. She smiled at the flood of happy memories and then moved on to the Blind Pig Tavern where the hip crowd still hung out after hours, just like she did when she was their age.

We returned to Sedona and continued the monthly Doxil therapy, but Kath soon doubted its efficacy. The CA-125 failed to respond to the chemo, which meant she had one of two choices, try a new drug or stop. She'd risk the toxic effects of a new chemo drug if it worked but feared she'd guess wrong again.

Plagued with indecision and nearly overwhelmed with situational depression, she sought counseling from the only local psychiatrist in the area who accepted our insurance. Kath felt the one-hour drive to Prescott for the fifteen-minute monthly therapy session proved beneficial and readily accepted her prescription for the antidepressant Zoloft, which Dr. Beltane supported.

After twelve months of Doxil therapy, the persistently elevated CA-125 showed no sign of improvement, and Dr. Beltane recommended that Doxil be replaced with Carboplatin. The Onco Tech Scan ranked that drug as possibly effective against serous tumors. That pleased Kath, but Dr. Beltane also suggested it be paired with Taxol. Dr. Freeman had originally recommended this cocktail, but with a low Onco Tech score for Taxol and a high risk for alopecia, Kath wanted to avoid that combo if at all possible. Dr. Beltane accommodated Kath's request and ordered the single therapy Carboplatin infusion, which she tolerated well. But she also included Zantac as a prophylactic medication for chemo-induced gastrointestinal ulcers.

After two months of Zoloft and private therapy Kath felt emotionally better, but she also complemented that success with the various alternative therapies that ACC offered.

With four months of Carboplatin completed, one September morning began like any other. But when Kath brushed her hair she noticed the brush had accumulated more hair than usual. She stared at the tangled collection for a moment before she leaned toward the mirror and breathed out a silent sigh that confirmed her hair had indeed thinned. "Great," she said to herself. "I'll be bald by Christmas." She turned her back on the mirror and leaned against the counter top as she mindlessly cleaned the brush and pondered how unprepared she felt for yet another battle in this endless war on cancer.

Back in Chicago, we all felt disappointed that the CA-125 exceeded three hundred and the PET Scan confirmed that the Carboplatin had failed to stem the rising tide of cancer. Kath somberly listened while Dr. Beltane reviewed a number of other chemotherapies that might work, and Kath pulled on her hair when she mentioned alopecia as one of the possible side-effects. All of the chemotherapies proposed by Dr. Beltane carried risks, which, among others, included a decreased ability to fight infections. Being immunosuppressed on a crowded airplane concerned us, but with no other suitable alternatives we mentioned Tarceva as a potential choice.

For many years we had studied borderline serous tumor with low malignant potential and probably learned more than we should have. This tumor proved to be estrogen dependent, and we long suspected the hormonal supplements Dr. Reynolds recommended years ago had poured gasoline on its dormant embers. Conventional chemotherapy usually proved ineffective against this tumor and often created near fatal conditions that significantly compromised the patient's longevity well before the disease would have caused their demise. We understood this tumor on a molecular level, but the complexities of its inner signaling exceeded our knowledge base. We were not molecular biologists but our studies suggested Tarceva, an oral chemo drug for non-small-cell lung cancer tumors, might be effective against the serous tumor. We were surprised when Dr. Beltane sat back in her chair and pondered our suggestion, but we were even more shocked when she agreed with our conclusion.

For the next three months the CA-125 steadily decreased and the PET Scans confirmed a reduction in the tumors. Kath continued the monthly therapy sessions with the psychiatrist in Prescott and faithfully took her Zoloft along with Zantac, which continued to be part of her morning medication ritual. Her life seemed to be back on track in time for the holidays, but then she developed a urinary tract infection, which she considered a minor nuisance. Her primary care physician successfully treated it with the antibiotic, Ciprofloxacin.

In early December Kath developed an occasional dry cough that initially went unnoticed but quickly progressed to a frequent non-productive harsh hack. She suspected Tarceva to be the culprit, but with the documented tumor reduction she hesitated to stop it. To better understand this condition, we studied the metabolism of this drug and what we found surprised us. We believed Kath had fallen victim to a perfect storm.

The Tarceva proved very effective against this tumor, but even with a correctly prescribed dose, Kath demonstrated signs of drug toxicity, which the chronic dry cough hinted at. The drug failed to be efficiently metabolized in the liver and slowly built up to a toxic level, yet her liver functioned properly. However, further investigation revealed a web of drug interactions that created this perfect storm.

Tarceva is metabolized in the liver by an enzyme called CYP3A. As long as this enzyme is available the drug is successfully metabolized.However, Zoloft, Zantac, and Ciprofloxacin are known to decrease the availability of the CYP3A enzyme in the liver. The decreased enzymatic levels meant Tarceva could not be fully metabolized, which increased plasma levels of the drug and produced signs of toxicity.

Dr. Beltane listened to our concerns and performed a complete physical exam before she consulted a pulmonologist who ordered a chest x-ray. After our trip to radiology we returned to the clinic and were greeted by the pulmonologist.

Dr. Chin, a slim, young Chinese man, who spoke with a heavy accent, escorted us to the exam room and proceeded with a chest examination as careless as Dr. Freeman's had been. He barely listened to her lungs, did no percussion, and failed to look at her throat before he reviewed the chest X-ray. "Your lungs are fine," he said. "You have post nasal drip." We were stunned. After a moment of uncomfortable silence, we explained our toxicity theory, but he really didn't listen nor did he care. He stood up and, with a thick Chinese accent, said "You RN's read too much on Internet. This is postnasal drip. That's all," then quickly left the room. We felt infuriated and speechless.

A few moments later Dr. Beltane entered the room and discussed the X-ray results but ultimately supported the lung specialist's opinion. Postnasal drip would be the final diagnosis, and she handed us a refill prescription for Tarceva. Dr. Beltane's eyes suggested that she didn't believe the pulmonologist's theory, but we knew she wouldn't contradict the hierarchy of medicine.

As healthcare nurses, we had done our medication homework. But in an arrogant fashion Dr. Chin could not be bothered with the facts. He refused to discuss the metabolic pathways of the medications he knew nothing about and unapologetically scoffed at our concerns.

Dr. Beltane seemed sad as we said goodbye before we arranged for our flight home. Later that evening, the shuttle-limousine picked us up, and we toured the local neighborhood with its many Christmas lights before we returned to O'Hare. We were completely disenchanted with the ACC.

As Good As It Gets

With the Tarceva prescription in hand, we arrived in Sedona and immediately saw Dr. Arnold, a pulmonologist at the local hospital. He listened to our theory and excused himself while he researched this dilemma in the privacy of his office. After some delay he returned with a concerned look and sat down before he discussed his findings.

He confirmed our suspicions that Tarceva toxicity had occurred and strongly advised Kath to stop the drug immediately. The law required he formally file his findings with the FDA. Kath's harsh cough signaled early pulmonary involvement, which if left unchecked would have developed into pulmonary fibrosis, a fatal condition. The healthcare community never recognized the interactions between the four drugs and never recommended the cessation of nonessential medications, which may have allowed the continued use of the only drug that worked against the cancer.

For eighteen months, Dr. Beltane had proved to be an ardent ally who always put Kath's well-being first. But now Kath felt abandoned and adrift in a sea of unknowns, just in time for the Holidays.

We put up the tree, decorated the house, and completed our Christmas cards, but the joys of the season were tempered by the concerns of cancer. Before Tarceva, Kath had no magic bullet against this borderline serous tumor. But now she felt confident the tumor could be destroyed and enlisted Dr. Donacheck, a gynecological oncological surgeon in Scottsdale, Arizona, for help.

After a two-hour drive, we waited in Dr. Donacheck's comfortable, well-decorated, modern deco office as the efficient staff processed the necessary insurance papers then punctually escorted us to the exam room, where we awaited the doctor's arrival. A soft knock announced his entrance. After formal introductions, Dr. Donacheck sat down and listened to Kath's story, before he completed a thorough physical exam.

We followed him back to his office and sat in front of a large computer screen that displayed Kath's most recent PET-CT Scan. When he compared the older scan to the newer one, he pointed out many areas that had improved. When correlated along with the two-hundred-point drop in the CA-125, the story painted a happier picture. He agreed that Tarceva might have influenced the tumor's regression. That assessment complicated his thesis that serous tumors failed to respond to chemotherapy, but given Tarceva's toxicity, he recommended the drug not be renewed. "This is as good as it's going get," he said. After eighteen months of bad news, we smiled in stunned silence.

Celebratory disbelief punctuated with hysterical laughter filled the car on the return trip to Sedona. Kath wanted to believe the cancer had become a manageable, chronic condition that no longer threatened her life, so she tried to stifle the incessant inner voice that for years had screamed, "Cancer kills."

She lived as if she had a future and returned to the activities that made her happy before cancer had stolen her joy. Spirituality found its way back into her daily life, as did yoga and regular meditation. These practices brought her closer to the Zen of life, but in a characteristically impulsive whim, she committed to a two-year plan to straighten her teeth with Invisalign braces.

This impetuous decision attempted to resolve her long perceived self-conscious flaw of an inconspicuous overbite. The dentist convinced her this minor malocclusion could be easily corrected in two very short years, and her appearance would be greatly improved for a mere five thousand dollars. That two-year horizon helped her believe she had some longevity in this world, but all she really wanted was a normal, cancer-free life.

Marital intimacy had been difficult under the gloom of cancer, but as that shadow faded Kath cautiously reached out and hoped to be that partner again. She recalled the Valentine weekend years ago in San Juan Capistrano when she had planned an amorous getaway that rivaled any romantic movie. It had been a long time since she felt the comfort of an intimate night, but the overnight Valentine package she arranged in Sedona proved just as memorable. Physically, emotionally, and spiritually blessed, Kath finally felt whole again. However, a follow-up appointment with Dr. Donacheck changed all that.

The CA-125 had been stable in the months that led up to her May appointment, but a slight increase in the April cancer number prompted Kath to schedule a consultation with Dr. Donacheck. The preparatory workup had become very routine. First obtain another PET-CT Scan and CA-125 and then schedule an appointment to get the results.

It had been six months since Kath's last visit, but as she entered the office on a beautiful spring day in Phoenix, she felt the life she hoped for probably would not be the life she'd get. She didn't fear the bad news as much as she wanted the cancer to stop its relentless subconscious chant. Her body imperceptibly jumped when the office nurse called her name and her palms got sweaty as she walked the final distance to his office.

We sat in front of the computer screen that displayed the PET Scan, as Dr. Donacheck greeted us from behind his desk. Kath held my hand while he reported the bad news. The scan revealed increased tumor activity, and the elevated CA-125 corroborated it. Kath stopped listening as he delved deeper into the details. When he had finished, Dr. Donacheck sat back in his chair and, with a solemn face, waited for her reply.

With hands folded on her lap, Kath carefully processed what she had hoped to never hear again. With resolute eyes, she glanced at me before she leaned forward and said, "What about Topotecan? The onco tech scan suggested it might work."

"Yes," he replied. "That medication has some history with ovarian cancer. But I have to be honest, I don't think this tumor will respond to any chemotherapy." The tick of the clock became the only noise in the room as we despondently looked around for another answer. Kath said, "I can't just sit here, waiting for this thing to kill me. I have to try something." She leaned forward with her arms folded over on his desk. He leaned ever so slightly toward her, and they sized each other up in a locked stare.

After a few seconds he sat back in his chair and outlined the side effects for Topotecan, which included bone marrow depression. If she wanted to risk the possibility of an infection or significant anemia for an unlikely chance at success, then she could start the medication that day.

The nurse escorted us to the chemo room, where a dozen female patients sat in various stages of alopecia with different colored IV bags dangling over their heads. A subtle but distinctive metallic odor lingered in the air, as Kath walked toward the only available recliner in the room. After the nurse completed the preliminary procedures, the Topotecan infused through her port. For sixty minutes Kath exchanged cancer stories with her chemo neighbors. And when the Topotecan finished, she walked past her new-found friends with a strong sense of camaraderie. Once a week she repeated this scenario and chatted with those she recognized. But as time passed, unfamiliar faces with familiar stories occupied many of the same chairs and she tried not to think about those who were no longer there.

For five weeks she continued this routine, but a few days before her next infusion date she felt feverish and detoured to see Dr. Kevin Wilson, her new local primary care physician.

Many years Kath's junior, a well-dressed Dr. Wilson looked younger than his stated age. His compassion and excellent bedside manner mixed with his self-effacing humor made her feel comfortable with his care. As we waited in the exam room, she felt much better than earlier in the day and thought she may have over reacted to symptoms that could easily be attributed to the side effects of chemotherapy. Lost in the midst of her self-doubt, the door suddenly flew open and Dr. Wilson entered the room much like Cosmo Kramer of Seinfeld fame.

He greeted her warmly and engaged in perfunctory small talk as he washed his hands, being fully aware of her immunocompromised state. He sat directly in front of her and listened as Kath relayed her symptoms, while he indiscreetly looked for any physical signs that suggested a problem. He reviewed her current medications before he checked her vital signs and carefully examined her, paying particularly close attention to her lungs. Then he returned to his chair and announced she most likely had contracted a community-acquired pneumonia. He recommended four days of IV antibiotic therapy in the hospital followed by a ten-day course of oral antibiotics at home and a temporary cessation of chemotherapy.

She received the IV antibiotics shortly after admission to the local hospital. Her most recent blood work confirmed that Topotecan had lowered her white blood cell count and compromised her ability to fight an infection. The neutropenia explained why she had developed pneumonia, but the hospital had not implemented reverse isolation which protected an immunocompromised patient from an accidental infection from healthcare workers. Worse, the nurse assigned to Kath was also caring for a patient with clostridium difficile colitis (C-Diff), and another patient with Methicillin-Resistant Staphylococcus Aureus (MRSA).

We found it unimaginable that a nurse caring for patients with the most contagious diseases found in any hospital was also caring for a patient prone to infection. When asked for the assignment's rationale, the supervisor shrugged it off and said, "All of our nurses practice excellent universal precautions."

Kath quickly replied, "If I become contaminated with C-Diff or MRSA, my lawyer practices excellent lawsuits." The nurse's assignment changed shortly after that conversation, and four days later Kath went home.

It took a month before she returned to Dr. Donacheck and found the CA-125 had climbed higher, unaffected by the Topotecan. But the suspected tumor growth had no deleterious effects. She had no pain and her appetite remained strong with a GI tract that worked just fine. If it weren't for the PET Scans or the CA-125, Kath wouldn't have known she had cancer and that made future decisions about therapies that much harder. She always remembered that many cancer patients died from well-intentioned medical interventions long before the disease would have killed them.

Dr. Donacheck knew Kath never intended to stop chemotherapy and didn't flinch when she suggested Etoposide, the number one chemo drug on the onco-tech report. Confident that Kath had fully recovered from pneumonia, he dutifully reminded her this potent drug had a long list of potentially bad side effects, and he doubted it would be effective against serous tumors. But without an alternative medication, he wrote the prescription for Etoposide, one pill a day.

Nothing happened for the first week, but Kath's anxiety level increased after the second week. She managed her uneasiness with

Clonopin, an anti-anxiety medication. In the third week Clonopin no longer controlled her higher anxiety levels, and after many days of restless insomnia, she finally stopped the Etoposide. Two days later the symptoms subsided, and two weeks later she returned in his office for another round of tests.

We stared at the computer screen in disbelief as Dr. Donacheck pointed out the areas of increased tumor growth from the most recent PET scan. But the eight-fold increase in the CA-125 removed all doubt the multiple chemotherapies over the last two years had proven useless against this very resilient cancer. In a self-realized moment Kath understood that Dr. Donacheck may have been right about the ineffectiveness of standard chemotherapy. She felt hopeless as he discussed the only option that remained.

Clincal Trials

Clinical trials are the "Hail Mary" passes for cancer patients who have failed at least one chemotherapy regimen, and Dr. Donacheck recommended a phase three clinical trial that utilized two VEGF (vascular endothelial growth factor) inhibitors. Vascular endothelial growth factors are proteins that are produced by both healthy cells and cancerous ones. They start a chain of physiological events that ultimately built new blood vessels in the desired areas to those specific cells.

For tumors, the new vessels provide an additional blood supply that enables the cancer to grow. The VEGF inhibitor stops the cancer's initial signal to build new blood vessels and ultimately starves the tumors of the needed blood supply, so eventually the cancer will die. Dr. Michael Graham, from Doughton Oncology in Scottsdale, Arizona, readily pointed out the experimental nature of the trial and never promised a cure, but he offered hope.

Kath slowly navigated the bureaucratic maze of clinical trial documents, but she never read the countless papers she signed. She readily accepted the unknown liabilities of an experimental drug and willfully signed away any culpability. But the convoluted costs of this medical adventure needed to be fully understood before she swallowed the first pill.

The medications were free, but most of the tests were not. A preauthorized agreement from the insurance company was required and that further delayed the start date. That hiatus fueled Kath's doubts that she had once again waited in vain for another failed chemotherapy drug that would deliver only side effects and allowed the tumor to progress unchecked.

After all the obligatory conditions had finally been met, we counted down the days to an extended stay in Scottsdale. But my admission to the local hospital's ICU for a bleeding ulcer that required two blood transfusions on the day the chemo trial had been scheduled to start yet again postponed her search for a cure. Kath sobbed quietly in the corner of my hospital room as I apologized for another delay and predicted that the trial could be started in a few days. But I misinterpreted her distraught reaction. She didn't care about the delayed start date. Instead, she blamed herself for my predicament. She felt so self-absorbed with her cancer drama that as a wife and a nurse she had failed to recognize her husband's ghost-like pallor that clearly foretold my compromised health. Overwhelmed, she buried her face in her hands, as the tears seeped through her fingers. And when I peered over the bed rail, I saw a magnificently magnanimous woman hit an emotional rock bottom.

It took a few days, but Kath felt like her old self when we finally arrived in Scottsdale for the clinical trial. We waited patiently in a well-worn waiting room in a strip mall type building that could have used a facelift. A fresh coat of paint would have improved the aesthetics of the clinic area, but at least the place looked clean. Clinical trials received funding from government grants, pharmaceutical companies, and foundations. But in the upscale neighborhood of Scottsdale, this business did not appear to be an affluent enterprise.

The nurse introduced herself before escorting us to a small exam room. We all squeezed in and listened to Dr. Graham as he reviewed the test results, which suggested the tumor had progressed unabated. His physical exam found Kath to be in good health, if he excluded cancer, which boosted his confidence that she could tolerate the VEGF therapy. Although Kath had become accustomed to bad news, she felt anxious but eager to start the trial.

We left the cramped exam room and entered a large open chemotherapy area with two-dozen recliner chairs. Individual IV pumps lined the walls, and the overhead fluorescent lighting cast a slight greenish-yellow glow on patients who already looked ill. The family area within that large room had a well-worn couch and a large table covered with an ever-present thousand-piece jigsaw puzzle next to a coffee machine and styrofoam cups.

The nurse led Kath to another semi-open area within that large room separated by lightweight aluminum privacy screens for an EKG. Finally, after all the preliminary work-up had been completed, the nurse handed her a cup containing the two experimental pills and a glass of Phoenix chlorinated tap water. Without hesitation, Kath swallowed the pills.

For the next six months, we took a day trip back to Doughton Oncology every two weeks for a follow up evaluation and eventually became acquainted with those involved at the clinic. Many of Dr. Graham's patients appeared sicker than those she had met at other clinics. Kath never disturbed those ashen-gray people with sunken faces and dark circles around their closed eyes as they slept in their recliners while the chemotherapy infused. She felt empathetically overwhelmed by despondent family members as they struggled to maintain upbeat facades. Most would tear-up at the slightest provocation.

As a self-confessed loner with limited social interaction for the last three years, Kath missed the occasional friendly conversation about something other than cancer. She savored the opportunity to speak with the younger healthcare workers on things she cared about like music, books, or spirituality.

At home Kath resumed the biographical pursuit of her favorite musicians and devoured George Harrison: *Living in the*

Material World by Olivia Harrison which brought a welcomed escape. But the metaphysical Beatle's story also rang her spiritual bell. She resumed her astrological studies and rekindled an appreciation for the mystical magic of the cabalistic arts. But when she re-read the *Mists of Avalon*, she charted a new spiritual course.

Kath tried to reconcile the enchanted history of English lore, Eastern philosophy, and Celtic Christian tradition with the duotheistic mythology of Wicca for a single unified theory of spirituality. She joined an online Wicca school based in Glastonbury, England, that offered an avenue for advancement in Wiccan degrees and rites of passage. She fancied herself a solitary Wiccan practitioner and shopped online for the necessary tools of the trade, which included *The Book of Shadows*.

She created a sacred space with an alter in a secluded area of the bedroom for her ritualistic practices, which the cat regularly disrupted. Dressed in her robe with an athame (sacred knife), wand, and chalice, all ceremoniously placed on her small altar, Kath regularly cast spells from *The Book of Shadows* intended to bring about inner peace and healing. She never shared this part of her life with others, but these mythological rituals felt true to her and offered a sense of personal power at a time when she felt powerless.

Kath responded to life with cancer in an intellectually compartmentalized way. She tried to live a normal life but could never escape cancer's omnipresence. It dominated her conscious mind and crept into the unconsciousness of sleep, but she never let it block her view of life. She did her best to ignore the world that crashed around her and tried to focus on the beauty she saw in front of her.

Kath never understood the molecular biochemistry of cancer and left the nitty-gritty of mutated cells to the medical community. But during the first six-months of the clinical trial, the experimental medications failed to reverse the upward trend of the CA-125. Without any physical symptoms from the relentless tumor, Kath seemed begrudgingly content with the status quo. Dr. Graham encouraged her to stay the course, but the current medical regime seemed destined for failure, and with no alternatives on the horizon I offered to look for one.

An Internet search provided a multitude of cancer cures, ranging from the sublime to the ridiculous. All them had the professed legitimacy of supported science, but most of those purveyors preyed on the desperate hopes of sick people. Kath knew the VEGF pills didn't work and became skeptical of the medical community whenever they dangled the fruit of success from their "tree of hope." But she feigned a half-hearted interest with the legitimate clinical trials I found across the country. Unfortunately, many of those ovarian cancer trials required extended stays and were not financially practical. But one program at a Cancer Center in Houston, Texas, offered a medication that seemed perfect for Kath's predicament.

A group of gynecological oncologists at the Houston Center completed various clinical studies that proved estrogen dependent borderline serous tumors might be controlled with drugs that blocked estrogen's stimulative effect on the tumors. While Kath's prior hysterectomy had removed the major source of estrogen, a small amount continued to be produced by the adrenal glands, which may have fueled the tumor's growth. Kath felt that a trip to Houston might be worthwhile, so two weeks later we arrived for our appointment at the Center's gynecological oncological department.

Everything in Texas seemed big as we navigated the congested freeways through the country's fourth largest city. We arrived at our hotel room in time for an early bird dinner before we surrendered to the king-size bed on the eve of another cancer safari. The wake-up call rousted us to the suitcase routine of cancer travel. Kath primped herself in front of the bathroom mirror and sipped the coffee I had retrieved from the buffet bar before we joined the other hotel guests for a light breakfast.

We arrived at the towering Cancer Center and gawked like tourists as we wandered through the huge atrium. Eventually, we found a concierge, who directed us to the gynecological oncological area. The receptionist confirmed Kath's appointment and processed all the insurance information.

We rested comfortably in a crowded waiting room. Muted conversations were interrupted every ten minutes by a nurse who stood in the doorway and unceremoniously bellowed out the next patient's name, much like the caller of a bingo game. But the winner never looked excited to claim the prize. The nurse escorted the patients down a long hall and eventually disappeared into an exam room. Meanwhile, a young female doctor in a white lab coat with shoes that clomped along the tiled floor darted from room to room.

When Kath's morning appointment time had long since passed, the receptionist repeatedly assured us she would be called back at any moment. But when the crowded waiting room emptied, the clinic activity suddenly stopped and the staff announced their intention to go to lunch. We sat alone in a deserted waiting room.

Frustrated and hungry, we questioned the wisdom of the trip over a hurried lunch in a crowded cafeteria. We felt hostage to an impersonal system that dangled the allure of a cure but remained unabashedly unaccountable for our wasted time.

We returned to a fully repopulated waiting room, as the nurse once again shouted out the patient names and we heard the clomp of the doctor's shoes as she traveled from room to room. The crowded waiting room had once again dwindled to near empty when the nurse finally announced Kath's name six hours after her appointed time. Like so many others before us, we finally walked down that long corridor and, with mixed emotions, sat in the exam room as the clomp of the doctor's shoes grew louder until they stopped in front of the closed door. After a brief silence, the doorknob slowly turned, and the mysterious doctor finally entered the room.

Her knee-length skirt exposed a pair of not-so-thin legs, while the white lab coat with a stethoscope stuffed in the right lower pocket barely disguised a somewhat protuberant belly. A small coffee stain had strategically landed in the busty crevasse of the full-figured doctor, but the stain barely stood out against her pastel dress. Slightly frizzled, jet-black shoulder-length hair outlined her round, chubby face, and bright-blue eye shadow contrasted a pair of dark brown eyes. Her glossy red lips barely moved when she confidently stretched out a hand and said, "Dr. Harmond."

Seated next to Kath, Dr. Harmond silently rustled through Kath's medical information completely oblivious to our lengthy delay. Periodically, she peered over the chart with a question that clarified some nebulous historical point she deemed relevant. After all the necessary background information had been obtained, she proceeded with a brief physical exam eerily reminiscent of Dr. Freeman's.

With the chart on her lap, the doctor confirmed the serous tumor had remained estrogen dependent and most likely would respond to oral dosing of Femara. Then she espoused the exceptional response obtained in her published serous carcinoma studies. Kath felt relieved that IV chemo therapy had not been discussed and readily agreed to start a well-documented therapy that held the potential for an easy fix. Kath smiled while the doctor wrote the new prescription for Femara. She felt elated about the minimal side effects associated with this drug but cringed when Dr. Harmond requested a follow-up appointment in one month. Satisfied with the outcome, Dr. Harmond gave Kath a warm smile followed by a big hug before she clomped down the hall and disappeared into another room.

For the next month Kath nearly convinced herself the malignancy had finally retreated. She tried to step out from its tumorous shadow, but the cruel realities of the last few years suggested a stalemate might be the best outcome she could hope for.

Free from any Femara side effects, she nearly dismissed the asymptomatic cancerous calamity that besieged her and enthusiastically embraced her esoteric pursuits. They provided a pleasant distraction from the emotional turmoil she rarely discussed. Stymied on the physical plane, Kath sought fulfillment in the spiritual one and returned to her cabalistic nature in time for the observance of Beltane, a Wiccan celebration of life on the first day of May.

She busied herself in the kitchen and made Beltane bannocks in accordance with Gaelic tradition, which were really nothing more than oatmeal cookies that were offered to friendly spirits in attempts to gain their favor. Dressed in her Wiccan ceremonial garb, Kath used the gas fireplace as a substitute for the Beltane bonfire as she cast her spells from *The Book of Shadows*. When the ceremony had ended, she set the cookies out in the backyard as a symbolic gesture for the javelinas to enjoy.

Astrological charts once again littered the bedroom floor along with various books that fed her diverse passions. But one book, *The Mists of Avalon*, sparked an intense interest in Celtic England, Glastonbury, and the myth of Avalon. Kath became a self-taught expert on the long lineage of the British monarchy and how the early Germanic invasion influenced world history. Her deep knowledge of Christian worship led to an in-depth study of the great cathedrals of England. This rekindled her interest in the Freemasons with their secret society and outsized influence on world affairs. She loved everything British, and as the stereo played George Harrison's *All Things Must Pass*, she abruptly announced a desire to visit Great Britain.

Many viewed this idea as a welcomed distraction from all Kath had been through, but Kath saw through the illusion of a so-called cancer holiday. She knew the fallacy of such a thing, as the carcinogenic companions of fear and doubt traveled with her on every path in life, like an uninvited guest who couldn't be ignored. She questioned if she had the stamina for this "Bucket List" trip and secretly worried about some unforeseen cancerous complication that might leave her stranded far from home. But once again she jumped into the deep end of the pool and hoped for the best.

Kath returned to Houston for a follow-up visit and experienced deja vu all over again as she listened to the muted murmur of the crowded waiting room punctuated by the familiar sound of Dr. Harmond's shoes as they clomped down the hall before they faded into an exam room. We felt increasingly frustrated as the hours ticked by as the waiting area slowly emptied of patients who arrived long after we did. But when the nurse unceremoniously announced "Barbara Wilson" four hours after Kath's scheduled appointment, we breathed an exasperated sigh of relief. Kath acknowledged her presence with a raised hand and sarcastically complimented the nurse on the improved wait time, as they walked down the long corridor toward the exam room.

The nurse chatted politely as she recorded Kath's vital signs and apologized for the delay before she left us alone in the room. We passed the time in uncomfortable chairs and made light of our mutual irritation with the inefficiency of the clinic. But we laughed uncontrollably when we heard the familiar clomp of Dr. Harmond's shoes as they crescendoed to a stop in front of the closed door. Caught by the sudden silence, we desperately tried to stifle our giggles as we listened to the rustle of crinkled paper from the medical chart and sheepishly watched as the door slowly opened. Dr. Harmond smiled like an old friend when she entered the room and exchanged small-talk pleasantries before she proceeded with a poorly executed physical exam that proved unremarkable. She complimented Kath on her progress and said she believed Femara had stabilized the CA-125. Delighted with the overall result, Dr. Harmond suggested the next visit could be done by phone to avoid the long-distance travel.

When Kath asked about her planned overseas travel, Dr. Harmond encouraged it. She briefly pontificated about her own need for a vacation and jokingly asked if Kath needed a doctor to go along with her. Ironically, Kath would have loved a doctor to accompany us to England, but not her. The visit ended with a six-month refill prescription for Femara and a big bear hug from the doctor, before she clomped down the hall and entered another room.

Since her last visit to Houston, Kath's energy had returned to pre-cancer levels. She volunteered at the Sedona Library, attended regular yoga classes, and swam laps at the Hilton Spa. Her voracious appetite for books now included anything with tourist spots in Great Britain. She grew more excited by the day as she planned for the September 4th trip to England in honor of our twenty-sixth wedding anniversary.

In the midst of this personal renaissance, Kath received the first phone-visit from Dr. Harmond. Kath reported all of her good news and felt very upbeat, especially with a stable CA-125. But Dr. Harmond had a different point of view. She suggested that Kath should return to the clinic as soon as possible because she no longer felt Femara would be the most effective drug against ovarian adenocarcinoma.

After a long silence, Kath said "I don't have adenocarcinoma. I have borderline serous tumor with low malignant potential."

"No," the doctor replied. "You have adenocarcinoma and need to change the chemotherapy."

Kath literally looked at the phone in disbelief before she said, "Where did you get the idea that I have adenocarcinoma?"

"From the pathology report in your medical record," the doctor replied.

"But there is no such report in my medical record," Kath responded.

Kath took a moment to gather her wits before she said, "Do you have my chart in front of you right now?"

With no immediate reply, Kath said, "You don't have my chart in front of you, do you?"

The doctor confessed, "No, I don't."

Kath immediately became furious, and with an angry voice said, "You're going from memory, aren't you? You want me to stop the only medication that may be working and recommend a chemotherapy with potentially fatal side effects to kill a cancer that I don't even have based on information you erroneously remembered from another person's chart. Wow! That takes the cake. I'm sorry," Kath said. "I have completely lost what little confidence I had in you. I'm going to hang up now and don't you dare bill me for this phone visit." With that Kath slammed the phone down.

It took a while for Kath to shake off the self-doubt Dr. Harmond had created. But after she reviewed all of her pathology reports, Kath realized she had almost become a victim of negligence. In a rare display of anger, she slammed the stack of medical reports onto the desk. She jumped up and punched the air several times with her fists as she screamed obscenities at the absent Dr. Harmond.

As her lungs struggled for air, Kath stopped her punch in mid-swing and silently stared at the scattered pathology reports. She fell back into the chair, and in a final emotional outburst, pounded her fist on the desktop and whispered, "Now what?"

Completely distraught, she sat for a few minutes before she felt the slow eruption of a huge smile bellowing up from deep inside.

"Oncologist? she muttered in a guttural tone. "I don't need no stinkin' oncologist." Then she laughed so hard it bought tears to her eyes.

For years Kath's life had been hijacked by major medical events that dictated the terms of her existence. But with a six-month Femara prescription and a stable CA-125, she waved goodbye to the medical community and boarded a British Airways flight to England for a three-week vacation to celebrate our wedding anniversary.

Mind the Gap

After a few days in London, we arrived very early at Henry VIII's castle at Hampton Court, well before the usual hordes of tourists. As we roamed the castle rooms and walked the spacious grounds, we found ourselves at the entrance of England's oldest Hedge Maze, originally planted in 1690.

As we read the plaque that dared the reader to find the heart of the maze, Kath pushed by me and disappeared into the living puzzle. My head immediately filled with thoughts of failed rescue attempts, as I hustled to keep up with her. I watched as she moved deeper into the evergreen maze, one turn after another. In less than ten minutes she stood in front of a plaque that welcomed the reader to the heart of the maze.

When I asked how she had arrived in the center without one wrong turn, she said, "I don't know, but it's as if I've walked this path many times before."

"Well," I said. "Can you get us out of here before lunch?"

Kath stared at me for a moment before she accepted the challenge and disappeared into the labyrinth. I ran to keep up and in less than ten minutes she stood at the exit without one wrong turn. I raised my hands in befuddled disbelief when she said, "I don't know how I did it. I just followed a voice in my head that told me which way to go." Completely unfazed by her remarkable feat, she simply said, "I need to find a bathroom," and set off to find one.

A plaque outside the restroom described a ghost, affectionately known as the Grey Lady of Hampton Court, that had been frequently sighted around the estate since 1592. As I leaned against the plaque, Kath returned from the privy, and in typical understated fashion said, "I just saw a ghost in the bathroom."

I stared at her in a moment of disbelief before she went on to say, "I sat down to do my business in an empty, dimly-lit bathroom when someone walked by the closed stall door. I found that odd, since I never heard the entrance door squeak open, nor did I hear the sound of footsteps as she walked by. When I stepped out of the stall I saw a ghostly figure walk around the room and stop in front of a mirror that didn't reflect an image. We looked at each other for a moment and exchanged smiles before she disappeared through a wall." Kath went on to say the apparition lasted less than a minute, and when I pointed to a picture of the ghost on the plaque, she moved in for a closer look. "Yep," she said. "That's her."

"That's it?" I said. "You see a ghost and that's all you have to say?"

"Yeah. Kinda weird huh?" She never spoke of the apparition again.

After we finished all the touristy things, we boarded the train for the return trip to London and prepared for our road trip through the English countryside.

Kath's well-planned itinerary took us on a driving tour around the entire southern half of England, but she declined the opportunity to drive a car built for the English motorist. Instead, she navigated us along the byways to the many cathedrals and ancient ruins she had previously studied but had never seen. If the historical site offered guided tours, she energetically engaged the docent with such innocent enthusiasm that the two of them often continued a willing conversation long after the tour had finished. One of those historic sites included Glastonbury.

Originally settled in the Stone Age with a history steeped in Gaelic tradition, Glastonbury lived at the very center of Avalon lore, where the legend of King Arthur came alive and the town's Chalice Hill gardens remained center stage for the modern Wiccan practice. Kath breathed it all in as she strolled along its pathways and drank from the Lions Head Well, long known for its curative powers, before she meditated next to the ancient Chalice Well steeped in early Christian history.

After a short walk through town, we picnicked in the ruins of the Glastonbury Abbey as Kath told the story of how Oliver Cromwell and Henry VIII destroyed the very grounds we sat upon. At the end of the day, we found ourselves at the base of the Thor, the epicenter of all things Avalon. But she declined to walk the easy five hundred foot climb up the well-groomed path to the tower perched on top of the hill that offered a magnificent view of the enchanted kingdom of Avalon. Lost in thought as she stared at the obelisk, Kath had the look of a disappointed person who knew her life energy had begun to fade and sadly asked that we return to the hotel.

Kath enjoyed the scenic views of the English countryside as we motored through the southern coastal towns of her self-described genealogical homeland of Cornwall. When we arrived at the secluded outpost of Tintagel, the mythical birthplace of King Arthur and the land where Merlin the Magician roamed, she declined the easy half-mile hike to the castle ruins. Instead, she sipped coffee and wandered through the tourist shops.

Imperceptible to the casual observer, Kath's overall stamina slowly diminished as the trip progressed. But she never seemed sick and always kept up her appearance. She enjoyed short walks, particularly in the Cotswold countryside around the River Eye in the tiny village of The Upper Slaughter a few miles from Bourton-on-the-Water. In a picturesque town with country homes that bordered a small winding stream, we stood in the shade of giant oak trees that guarded its banks and listened to the brook as it babbled past this heavenly spot. "I want to be buried here," Kath whispered, as she looked into the distance and held my hand in silence. The tranquility of the moment revealed its natural beauty in the autumn-colored leaves that floated by and slowly disappeared around the bend.

Kath had reluctantly resigned herself to an inevitable future that she suspected would prematurely end her branch of the family tree. But she gained strength from the legacy of her heritage as she traveled through her ancestral homeland. Her thoughts gravitated to all who had passed before her and pondered their fate in the Samsara (cycle) of life. But as she stood next to the entrance gate of Friars Park, the home of her adolescent icon, the late George Harrison, the music and words of *My Sweet Lord* filled her head.

She stared through the huge, wrought iron gate at the spectacular gardens he had personally tended and sensed that he had learned to live his song *Beware of Darkness* even while the illusions of Maya completely surrounded him. Her eyes grew distant as she stood in front of the gate and prayed to find her elusive God in the land of illusion with the time that remained in her shortened life.

Weary from weeks of travel, Kath boarded the return flight to Phoenix with great ambivalence. Our trek through the enchanted land had rejuvenated her psychic energy but not her physical stamina. That simple concession meant she was losing the skirmish with her personal war on cancer.

No Direction Home 22

The abrupt transition from carefree tourist to cancer warrior robbed Kath of the post vacation glow. And the continued rise of the CA-125 presented an unwelcome reality check and urgent need to find a new gynecological oncological surgeon. Dr. Barden's credentials with borderline serous tumor with low malignant potential seemed to fit Kath's requirements, so in two weeks we made the drive to Phoenix to meet the new doctor.

As we walked with an armful of medical records toward the high-rise office building, Kath hoped the ominous upward trend of the CA-125 could be reversed. But the thought of more chemo with miserable side-effects completely distracted her when she tripped over the curb. The stack of documents went flying in the air, and she landed on the hard, concrete street. Papers floated down around her as she broke the fall with her hands, and her knees skidded to a stop on the pavement. Visibly shaken, she struggled to stand as blood trickled down her leg through the torn nylons. With scraped hands, she desperately tried to keep the blood from staining her colorful dress. I helped her up and quickly collected the papers, but she seemed unsteady on her feet as we made our way through the concrete courtyard and into the building.

Kath felt self-conscious as we rode the crowded elevator to the tenth floor, and the occupants stared at her obvious injuries. When we arrived in Dr. Barden's office her bloodied, disheveled look immediately caught the attention of one of the office staff, who came out from behind the Plexiglass sneeze-guard and attended to Kath in one of the treatment rooms.

When Kath returned, her injured knee was covered with a large Band-Aid that pushed through her torn hose. She had brushed her hair with the palms of her hand that burned from abrasions, and her eye make-up remained slightly streaked. The staff spoke in hushed tones with fleeting glances through the Plexiglass window as we silently sat in the crowded waiting room while Muzak played in the background.

Before long the nurse who had bandaged Kath's knee escorted us to Dr. Barden's dimly lit, but spacious office. When she announced our arrival, the Doctor never looked up or acknowledged our presence. Instead, he remained seated with his combed-over baldhead tilted down as he read a medical report through thick, horned rimmed glasses. A young man in a white lab coat leaned over his shoulder to get a better view of the document as we sat quietly in oversized leather chairs on the business side of his desk. After he put the paper down, he folded his hands and looked at Kath through thick glasses that eerily magnified his hazel eyes. "Hello," he said. "I'm Dr. Barden, and this is Dr. Belzman, a third-year medical resident."

Kath acknowledged him with a half-smile. He ignored her attempt to introduce herself and spoke directly to the resident doctor about her medical status as he described the indolent long-term nature of borderline serous tumor with low malignant potential with such detachment that she felt like a rat in a lab experiment.

Kath tried to interrupt this one-man lecture by offering him the original CAT Scan films she held in her lap, but he never looked at her. He abruptly brushed her off with a wave of his hand and continued his monologue to his obedient resident.

Incredulous at his abhorrent behavior, Kath offered a false smile, as she calmly sat back in the chair and waited for him to say something of value. He confidently claimed all borderline serous tumor cells divided slowly, which rendered them completely chemo resistant, and deemed any further surgery as unwarranted, since she would grow old before the tumor growth adversely impacted her life. He summarily dismissed the elevated CA-125 as an unreliable test for this type of cancer. He believed those results inaccurately predicted mortality and confidently forecast a long life for Kath with the caveat that she should spend that time wisely. She promptly dismissed his claims except for the last one.

Dr. Barden never performed a physical examination or checked her vital signs. He derived all of his conclusions from information Kath had sent him. He ignored the CT films she knew confirmed the explosive tumor growth. Her life would have been much easier if she had believed him and simply returned to her Sedona lifestyle. But she had one major problem with Dr. Barden, she didn't like him.

When the consultation concluded, neither party offered a parting handshake. Kath politely acknowledged him for his service before she walked toward the front office and personally thanked the nurse who had helped her. Alone in the elevator, she smiled and waved good-bye to the staff. When the doors closed she sarcastically whispered, "What an asshole!"

Back in Sedona, Kath busied herself with all the distractions of the Holiday Season, but she couldn't escape the Ghost of Cancer Past. The serous tumor remained impervious to every recommended intervention, and its continued proliferation predicted an unhappy future. Concerned with her diffuse abdominal discomfort, she worried that her lack of physical stamina signaled the start of an inevitable slide. But without any oncological guidance, she found herself in a downward spiral of desolation that darkened her very soul.

Troubled by the thought of her last Christmas on Earth, Kath felt deserted by the divine powers of the unseen universe she had once believed in and abandoned by a medical community that only offered empty promises. Spiritually lost and emotionally exhausted, she sought solace in her mother's words. She reached out through the phone for the comfort of her mom's verbal embrace, which soothed Kath's fears more than any ten-minute psychiatric counseling session ever could.

The power of the mother-daughter bond rejuvenated her inner soul and galvanized her will to fight, but she needed the chemical weapons of an oncologist if she hoped to defeat the enemy within. Unfortunately, most of Kath's relationships with the previous eight cancer doctors had been inimically dissolved, so her options in the Phoenix area were limited. And starting a new doctor-patient relationship necessitates the transfer of an enormous amount of information between various medical offices. Consequently, it seemed that any new consultation would be delayed until well past the Holidays.

Kath's urgent need for oncological intervention necessitated reconciliation with an established oncologist, and she felt Dr. Beltane at the American Cancer Care in Illinois would be the best choice. Kath regretted the Tarceva fiasco that had forced her to prematurely abandon the deep rapport she'd established with Dr. Beltane and the ACC staff, and she soon found herself back in the familiar exam room of the Chicago area cancer clinic.

When she entered the room, Dr. Beltane embraced Kath like an old friend and exchanged the warm pleasantries of personal updates, but she awkwardly avoided any discussion of the past Tarceva mess. After she had completed a through physical exam, the doctor reported small but palpable lower abdominal masses that matched the CAT Scan reports and gave credibility to the CA-125. Dr. Beltane reviewed a few chemotherapies that might be effective and recommended Hexalen, an alkylating antineoplastic pill taken three times a day. Kath agreed to the oral therapy, thankful to have avoided IV chemo. She hoped to escape Hexalen's many side effects with a number of supplements recommended by the clinic naturopath. Armed with a bag full of complementary medicines, we returned to Sedona hopeful for success. But the harsh memories of past failures tempered the festivities of the Holidays.

Kath always felt a depressive cheer in December and struggled to feel the Spirit of the Season. Her Christmas youth held the allure of promised toys, but as the years went by the meaning of the season matured, particularly when she converted from Lutheranism to Catholicism.

During her adolescent years, Kath had learned that early Christians used the festival of Saturnalia as a recruitment tool when they incorporated that pagan holiday into the celebration of the birth of Christ. For Kath, that cast a dark cloud of suspicious intent on the very origins of the Church. But as her Wiccan views grew, she tended to meld all of those existential beliefs into her own unique theory of existence. Her endless battle with cancer gave her a greater appreciation for the spiritual birth of all sentient beings. She celebrated the Christmas season in her own unique way, but she understood that with every birth there had to be a death. The cycle of life for her mother seemed to be approaching a full circle.

Kath became concerned about her mother's well-being when she noticed that Carol occasionally lost her train of thought during their regular phone calls. But she felt buoyed by the sharpness of their recent conversations, especially on Christmas Day, Carol's ninety-sixth birthday, and again on December 28th, Kath's fifty-seventh birthday.

They chatted for over an hour as Carol shared stories of Kath's early years and Holidays past. Her mother offered insights from a life well lived with few regrets and encouraged Kath to find the joy in life. They also spoke of death with the conviction of those who had faced the abyss.

Kath shared her weariness from the incessant medical procedures and broken promises that hinted at an upbeat future. But she felt particularly frustrated that she had not yet achieved her main goal in life, to see the inner light of God. Carol fully understood her daughter's Eastern view of reincarnation and left her with a quote from John 3:2: *"Unless you are born again you cannot see the kingdom of God."* Kath drew incredible strength from her mother and made plans to visit her in Ann Arbor on her next visit to the Chicago clinic. But shortly after that conversation, on December 30th, her mother died in her sleep.

Her mom's funeral in Michigan left her somber and withdrawn. Kath smiled politely to those who gathered at the mortuary to pay their final respects, but she spoke very little with them. With the family gathered on a snowy winter's day at the family plot in Royal Oak, she stared intensely into the frozen excavated grave while thoughts of final goodbyes tumbled through her mind. In a hushed voice, she whispered, "I wonder when I'll be laid next to you and dad?"

A few days after we returned to Sedona, Kath developed intolerable neurologic side effects from the Hexalen, and the supplements meant to control those symptoms were ineffective. She felt highly anxious and wanted to crawl out of her skin as she paced around the house. But three days after she discontinued the medication, the symptoms slowly subsided. Disheartened, she scheduled an appointment with Dr. Beltane and visited the psychiatrist in Prescott who responded with more antidepressants.

Back in Chicago, Kath fully expected what Dr. Beltane's physical exam, the PET-CT scan, and the increased CA-125 suggested—that the abdominal-pelvic mass continued to grow unchecked. Frustrated with yet another failed chemotherapy, Kath asked if the breast cancer drug, Tamoxifen, an estrogen receptor inhibitor, would be effective against the estrogen dependent tumor. After a lengthy discussion, Dr. Beltane wrote a prescription for the pill.

Relieved to be back in Sedona, Kath felt fortunate to have avoided IV chemotherapy again. But after years of failed cancer treatments, she hoped Tamoxifen would be that elusive magic bullet. Kath didn't care to understand the complexities of serous tumor growth or estrogen receptor inhibitors. She just wanted to feel better. But as the tumor relentlessly pressed against her gastrointestinal tract, she felt bloated and constipated. And that made the monthly trip to Chicago very uncomfortable.

American Cancer Care had recently opened a center in the Phoenix area. For two months Kath tried to receive care there, but they continually declined the identical insurance that the Chicago center accepted. But one day in early March, everything changed when they called to announce the ACC had altered their policy.

ACC invited Kath to receive care at the Phoenix branch where she met Dr. Rexlon for the first time. He entered the exam room with a gentrified stride and greeted her with a warm smile before he introduced himself with a soft Carolinian accent and a firm handshake. A tall, slim grandfatherly man, who sported a full head of neatly trimmed grey hair, Dr. Rexlon sat with us while he reviewed Kath's medical history and politely asked questions. As an oncological hematologist, he did not have the lengthy resume of Dr. Beltane, but Kath liked him anyway and accepted his care.

He recommended a long list of outpatient tests that took the rest of the day to complete and necessitated an overnight stay in an ACC guest room that resembled a very nice hotel suite. The next day we enjoyed a full breakfast in the clinic's cafeteria before Dr. Rexlon reviewed the results.

The CA-125 had skyrocketed to frighteningly high levels, and the PET-CT scan confirmed his suspicions that the tumor activity had dramatically increased. But curiously, the results differed significantly from the historical average. The tumor had always grown at a slow, steady pace in tandem with the CA-125, regardless of the previous chemotherapies. But this sudden nefarious escalation worried Dr. Rexlon. Something had clearly changed.

He suspected Tamoxifen had caused the CA-125 spike and recommended the medication be stopped. But he never speculated on how the estrogen receptor inhibitor may have impacted the tumor. The explosive cancerous growth lent an air of urgency to his discussion. Kath listened apprehensively about the necessity of immediate IV chemotherapy with Gemzar, a nucleoside metabolic inhibitor that had a twenty-one-day dosing cycle. After his argument, Kath felt she had no choice. She anxiously walked through the corridors of the new ACC hospital toward the chemo IV infusion center.

We peered through a open door into a large, dimly lit room, unsure if we had arrived at the proper place. In the far corner, bathed in the glow of fluorescent lights, a nurse stood in the midst of occupied chairs and waved us over. We passed a dozen empty chairs on our way to the only illuminated section of the room, where Amy introduced herself as one of the chemo infusion nurses, and then offered Kath a recliner.

Kath sat among a half dozen others in the midst of their chemical infusions. All had a family member nearby. Some of those patients appeared to be very ill as their support person hovered nervously around them, unsure of how to help.

After the initial introduction and signing of consents, Amy prepared Kath's double lumen chemo-port for the Gemzar infusion. Meanwhile, Kath calmly adjusted the TV as she sat in the recliner to await the start of her favorite soap opera, *The Bold and Beautiful.*

The nurse administered a variety of IV medications designed to minimize the chemotherapy's side effects, and Kath tolerated the Gemzar infusion without any problems. Back home in Sedona, she psychologically prepared herself for the thrice-monthly drive to the ACC in the open desert west of Phoenix for the remainder of the scheduled doses of Gemzar.

ACC's short-stay guest rooms provided a comfortable respite. We always arrived the night before the scheduled infusion and returned to Sedona immediately afterward. Kath felt safe at the ACC and befriended a plethora of people at the center. She regularly talked with Sandy, the volunteer in the gift shop, as they shared a common cancer story. She also became acquainted with many of the servers in the cafeteria. Kath trusted Dr. Rexlon and bonded with many of the nurses who regularly cared for her.

Sadly, after a month of chemo, the CA-125 continued to rise. To Kath, it felt like deja vu all over again, with yet another ineffective poison that did nothing more than weaken her already damaged immune system and hastened her demise.

In the quiet of the ACC guest room, Kath experienced an unusually severe bout of insomnia. But rather than pace about the room in the wee hours of the morning, she walked to the portico entrance of the cancer center to breathe in the cool desert air, stare at the stars, and ponder her fate.

A tall young, muscular security guard, dressed in a well-pressed uniform approached and checked on her welfare. Kath rarely espoused her troubles to anyone, let alone complete strangers, but she quickly bonded with this young man. His dark skin and warm smile accentuated his straight white teeth, while the sincerity of his brown eyes matched the benevolence of his voice. They sat under the stars as she briefly explained the dilemma of her health. The young man listened more than he talked, and when

Kath had finished her story she shifted the conversation to the starry constellations in the clear desert sky.

She ascertained the birthdate of her new acquaintance and pointed out his zodiac sign of Pisces among the heavenly host of stars. She described the Sign of the Fish as the most humanistic of all the astrological signs and said those born under it possessed great compassion. Their discussion on life continued for some time. Before he returned to his security rounds, they shared a prayer under the starlit desert sky. Kath believed that encounter did more for her mental health than any antidepressants or professional counseling ever had.

Kath felt drained from the years of incessant combat against a relentless foe with body armor that deflected every chemical arrow ever launched at it. She despaired at her imagined demise, but she received an unexpected victory at the next chemo visit when she learned that the tumor marker had significantly declined.

"The Gemzar worked," howled Dr. Rexlon. A slap of high-fives followed, but Kath tempered her response with the thought of past failures burned deep in her memory. She wanted to believe the tide had turned against the tumor.

As the CA-125 declined in the months that followed, Kath dared to believe the cancerous beast could be beaten. With Gemzar's continued success, she cautiously lowered her guard and warily considered herself a cancer survivor.

With cancer firmly in the rear-view mirror, the thrice-monthly overnight chemotherapy sessions turned into mini vacations and included upbeat dinner conversations at various local restaurants where she cautiously dared to outline future travel plans to the United Kingdom. Confident in her newfound longevity, she saw the chemo infusions as a minor inconvenience in a life that had finally turned for the better. She gave little credence to the subtle abdominal uneasiness that she dismissed as gas.

She expanded her wardrobe with online purchases of flowing printed dresses and comfortable tops she supplemented with an occasional outfit from Chico's in Sedona for our planned trip to England in September.

With a newfound interest in physical exercise, she regularly swam laps for twenty minutes at the Sedona Resort and consumed large amounts of antioxidants along with mega doses of vitamin C, convinced it absorbed the free radicals created from the chemotherapy. She resumed her yoga practice, rekindled her interest in Wicca, and kept those books along with astrological charts stacked up beside her bed.

An Uninvited Guest

For three months, Kath barely thought about cancer. Then in August, she felt a golf-ball-sized-lump just under the skin of her lower right abdomen. Her mind raced for a plausible explanation before she reluctantly concluded this protuberance to be the previously unseen foe that had chosen to brazenly show itself.

A cloud descended over Kath's psyche when she realized this cancerous lump laughed in the face of Gemzar. After the initial shock had faded, she arranged for an immediate appointment with Dr. Wallace at the local hospital for an urgent surgical consultation to extricate that exposed alien.

Kath entered the surgeon's Cottonwood medical office with the nervous calm of a warrior on the eve of a major battle. She patiently sat in a crowded waiting area before a nurse escorted her to the exam room followed by Dr. Wallace, a stocky young man who could have been a rugby player.

Dr. Wallace greeted Kath with a warm smile as we walked into a small room that looked like all the other exam rooms we had visited. Kath sat on the exam table while the medical assistant checked her vital signs. The doctor understood the main reason for her visit but listened while Kath reiterated a condensed version of her long medical history. She lay back on the table and with one hand pulled her yoga pants down. Then she lifted her blouse with the other and exposed the obvious lump.

She stared at the ceiling while he manipulated the painless extrusion. After he explored the depth of the mass with a portable ultra sound machine that displayed the ghostly images of her inner abdomen onto a video screen, he concluded the lump to be a serous tumor that could be easily excised on an outpatient basis.

Kath knew that sole metastatic scout represented the first of many tumors that would soon infiltrate other areas of her body. Its presence contradicted all of the previous pontifications made by numerous oncologists and left her with a sudden sense of doom. Dr. Wallace could not allay her concerns as he too feared the cancer had metastasized. But he guaranteed the surgery would not affect our overseas travel plans.

Determined not to display her doubts, Kath sat on the edge of the exam table and with a wry smile scheduled the procedure. On the way home, she stared through the car window into the distant desert and spoke to no one in particular when she declared that this trip to England would likely be her last.

She had the lumpectomy the next day, and two weeks later we were in London.

24
Cherrio

The fully reclined British Airways seats offered a comfortable sleep on the overnight flight. The next morning we arrived at Heathrow fully rested to begin our four-week vacation. With Kath's surgical site completely healed, we toured the northern part of the island Kingdom in our rented Passat, but after few days she rediscovered her limited stamina. We arrived at Hexham and found that Kath lacked the energy to walk the gentle rolling hills of the Roman archeological site of Hadrian's Wall.

Shortly after that, her legs nearly gave out as she navigated the steep cobblestone streets at Edinburgh Castle and took an extended rest in the citadel of St. Margaret's chapel. She fared no better when we walked the downhill slope of The Royal Mile and barely made it to the halfway point at St. Giles Cathedral. As she sat in the pews of the medieval church, Kath noticed many masonic symbols prominently displayed throughout the stained-glass building, and she stumbled upon the Cathedral docent.

Excited about the Freemason imagery, she spent a great deal of time with the Scottish guide as he pointed out the plethora of symbols embedded throughout the enormous structure. Invigorated by the tour, she returned to the city's oldest street and meandered through the small shops before she purchased a Wilson Clan tartan skirt to honor her family's heritage.

With perfectly applied makeup, Kath looked healthy in her snappy travel outfits, but she tired easily and rarely ventured far from the car or the hotel room. As the trip navigator, she remained vigilant for points of interest with short walks that included Celtic or Roman historical sites, medieval Cathedrals, or the plentiful ancient standing stone monuments scattered around Scotland. We drove the scenic byway of the Malt Whiskey Trail in the Speyside region of Scotland and stopped at the Glenfiddich Distillery on the banks of the River Fiddich. We declined the walking tour but found a seat at a lone table in the small tasting room, where we sipped an array of vintage malts. We retreated to the beautiful outdoor gardens to sample the mini-bottles of whiskey we had purchased along with a pack of cigarettes.

Although we hadn't smoked for decades, we sipped and puffed the afternoon away in the midst of a gorgeous green glen that overlooked the river, as songbirds added to the serenity of the moment. Dressed in her recently purchased skirt with a bright red cashmere turtle neck sweater and a waist-length black leather jacket to ward of the coolness of the shade, Kath sat with me sat at a picnic table where we exchanged our views on the essence of life. We were like newlyweds excited to be in each other's presence.

Kath spoke of her successes and laughed at her failed attempts to find inner peace with the various theological creeds she practiced. But she grew serious when she talked about the life she wanted to live as the scotch spoke about her uncertain future. Her laughter rang out as she reminisced about the Ann Arbor days of old and the unlimited potential of her young life. She regretted the missed opportunities of the free postgraduate education her father had offered. She stared into the distance with melancholy eyes as the white smoke from the cigarette danced in the air. She coddled an eighteen-year old scotch with her free hand and thought of all the people she knew who had passed on before her.

A calm enveloped her as she experienced the beauty of an ephemeral moment that transported her back to a happier time. She tenaciously clung to that feeling as we drove off in our Passat,

217

both of us clearly over the legal alcohol limit, through a tunneled archway of large oak trees with autumn-colored leaves that lined the narrow two-lane road. In the distance, the sunset turned the horizon into a brilliant red-orange hue. We toured the English countryside for three more weeks before a nonstop British Airways flight returned us to the serenity of Sedona's Red Rocks.

Our regular routine at home restored Kath's inner balance and diminished the somatic issues that had plagued her holiday. When Kath returned to the ACC in the Phoenix desert, she learned the CA-125 had not changed after the hiatus. That valuable piece of information convinced her that she had a chronic condition that required maintenance chemotherapy.

The Indignant Words of
Corporate Speak

The Gemzar therapy continued through November, but an unexpected and persistently elevated CA-125 left Kath terribly frustrated. After a spirited discussion with Dr. Rexlon, she eloquently announced her weariness with all things cancer. She desired to return to a world she once knew, so against his advice she stopped the chemotherapy.

To an outsider, Kath's decision appeared rash. But for the past five years she had rigorously adhered to the regimen of non-stop cancer care that consumed every moment of her existence. Meanwhile, she had imperceptibly morphed from a strong-willed woman who lived life on her own terms into a cancer patient who passively accepted the medical community's treatments that were no more effective than her Wiccan spells. In Dr. Rexlon's office, Kath realized she had become the acquiescent patient she abhorred. She impulsively decided she wanted her life back, if only for a little while, and chose this moment for her last hurrah.

Back in Sedona she attended regular yoga classes at the local gym. Every morning she navigated through a pile of metaphysical books stacked haphazardly next to the bed on her way to the cramped meditation area she reluctantly shared with Ziggy the cat, who preferred to sit in her cross-legged-lap while he meowed his mantra.

Each morning after meditation, Kath carefully applied her makeup in front of a mirror that reflected back a nearly full head of hair she masterfully styled, grateful the chemotherapy had left it intact.

She routinely flossed her teeth and maintained regular check-ups with the local dentist who periodically adjusted her Invisalign braces. When she renewed her contact lens prescription, the ophthalmologist discovered she had advanced cataracts that required surgery. While the clinician expressed muted surprise, she didn't dispute Kath's thesis as to the circumstances that had accelerated the aberrant process which resulted in this premature condition.

Kath felt a diffuse anger at the numerous faceless culprits who'd exposed her to years of accumulated radiation from more than forty PET-CT scans. The medical community completely ignored a lifetime of exposure to these deadly rays, as they thoughtlessly ordered more scans that collectively contributed to the opacity of her lens.

If a single PET-CT Scan delivered the radiation equivalent of five hundred chest X-rays, then she had been exposed to the equivalent of twenty-thousand chest X-rays in her lifetime. She felt particularly incredulous about the lack of culpability from anyone in the medical world, along with its collective unspoken implied response of "caveat emptor."

A local eye surgeon completed the procedure in less than two months, and with new prescription glasses she saw things much clearer, particularly when an unexpected medical bill arrived in the mail from the ACC for over $100,000.

Healthcare bills are notoriously complicated and their accuracy endlessly questioned, but Kath knew the ACC had erred. They just needed to be persuaded. Nervous that such an obvious misunderstanding threatened her financial future, she briefly forgot about the cancer.

Kath's mind pondered the innumerable scenarios of fiscal disaster as she sat in an oversized cushioned chair in front of the chief financial counselor for the ACC. A conservatively dressed young woman, Mindy spoke the uncomfortable truth about the money owed as she outlined an easy payment plan she believed minimized any financial hardship. When she had finished, Kath launched into a well-documented rebuttal against the erroneous information the ACC had presented as fact. The discussion quickly escalated into a controlled banter, but Kath refused to be denied as Mindy spoke less and listened more. Kath finished her argument with a deep sigh and slowly eased back into her chair. The sullen counselor politely excused herself to seek advice from her superiors while we pondered our financial fate.

The five-minute absence seemed like an eternity before Mindy returned with a pleasant smile and announced the hospital had rescinded the entire bill. She followed with a sincere request that the ACC continue to be Kath's treatment center of choice. Dumfounded but grateful, we were impressed by the actions of nameless administrators who did the right thing. Kath agreed to have her monthly lab work reviewed by Dr. Rexlon but abstained from any further chemotherapy.

For the next few months Kath's overall health remained stable. But on the next trip to the ACC she arranged to meet with Dr. Adebahoe, a pain medication specialist, to re-evaluate the effectiveness of the Clonazepam, Oxycontin, and oral Morphine she had taken for years.

In a small windowless room with neatly framed prints that hung on white clinic walls, we waited in comfortable chairs around a walnut coffee table. When the pain specialist entered, we all politely shook hands before he sat down next to Kath.

A tall thin man dressed in surgical scrubs, Dr. Adebahoe spoke with a thick Nigerian accent and asked how he could help. While Kath described her multi-year history with pain medications, the doctor struggled to stay awake. He helplessly nodded backwards and bumped his head against the wall that abruptly shook him awake. Staring momentarily bewildered through blood shot eyes, he apologized, saying he'd just worked a twenty-four-hour shift. He scribbled notes in the chart and offered her a prescription for the same drugs but at a higher dose. Kath knew the abdominal pain she felt represented a larger issue that would not be resolved by these drugs. Unconvinced the new prescriptions would do anything different, she accepted them without pretense.

The CA 125 remained unchanged while Kath continued her hiatus from chemotherapy, but the monthly cancer test still needed to be completed. When we arrived at the small ACC clinic room for the blood sample, the nurse discovered that the chemo port regularly used for blood draws had become plugged. A routine "clot buster" medication had to be injected directly into the catheter to salvage the surgically implanted port. After the nurse carefully prepared the catheter site for injection, she instilled the drug directly into the catheter. A few seconds later Kath unexpectedly cried out from the recliner chair, "I'm having a reaction to the drug. The room is spinning, and I'm going to pass out."

With the empty syringe still in her hand, the nurse's eyes grew wide in panic as Kath repeated the same phrase but in a weaker voice. The nurse fumbled with the syringes that were still attached to the catheter. Clinic staffers congregated outside the exam room door after they heard Kath's muffled plea for help but offered no assistance.

"Push some Benadryl," I yelled. The nurse opened the "emergency medicine drawer," and with tremulous hands delivered a single dose of IV diphenhydramine through the partially patent chemo port. The Kath responded quickly to the medication and slowly returned to normal.

That allergic episode discouraged any frivolous future use of Kath's chemo port and that presented a problem at the next lab draw. Her notoriously poor arm veins challenged even the best of phlebotomists. Multiple Band-aids marked their many failed attempts on her bruised arms. When a frustrated technician stepped away for a moment to recruit another phlebotomist, I pilfered the necessary blood draw equipment from their unattended supply cart and planned to draw the blood myself. When they returned, Kath requested a short break from the procedure to rest her arm, and we returned to our ACC overnight guest room with the pilfered supplies.

Within the privacy of our rented room, I successfully filled the necessary blood tubes from her battered arm and returned to the lab area with the specimens properly labeled. But the same technician we had left just moments before refused to accept the sample because "it couldn't be verified for accuracy."

Kath displayed her battered arms and pleaded with the technician to accept the sample, but her argument fell upon deaf ears. Dejected, we left with the blood-filled tubes. Soon, a well-dressed ACC employee noticed our frustration and asked if we needed help. After Kath explained the immediate conundrum, the employee identified herself as the Director of the Laboratory and said she saw no problem with the lab tubes. Armed with our contact information, she offered to resolve the matter after her morning corporate meeting.

Relieved that common sense had finally prevailed, we returned to our guest room and awaited her call. But in less than an hour she informed us the lab sample could not be accepted, as it could not be verified. Stunned, we reiterated our desperate plea. She quietly listened but once again referred to the company policy before she politely hung up.

We immediately found our way to the corporate offices with the lab tubes still in our hands and after a short wait spoke to the vice president for clinical services. He politely explained that the blood sample would not be accepted, as it could not be verified. And he went on to say that we were engaged in an ego contest with the hospital. Shocked at the corporate politics we found ourselves muddled in, we thanked him for his time, as we stared at him in utter disbelief. He leaned back smugly in his chair, before we politely excused ourselves. We returned to Sedona and never again associated with the ACC.

Kath requested all of her medical records from the ACC, and they arrived one month later. She planned to transfer her care to Dr. DeMarco at the Sedona Cancer Center, but when she read Dr. Adebahoe's report, her jaw clenched in righteous indignation. She angrily read multiple inaccuracies documented in the summation of his ten-minute consultation that physically described another patient and included an erroneous narrative of Kath's alcohol dependency. When she discovered he billed $1,997.00 to the health insurance company for the consultation he slept through, she felt outraged. Kath filed a formal grievance with the insurance company as well as with the ACC, but her calls to his office went unheeded.

Kath felt victimized by a system that offered no recourse. She quickly discovered that once an electronic patient medical record is created, it is rarely deleted. Dr. Adebahoe never corrected this error, but he accepted the $235.00 reimbursement offered by the insurance company as payment in full. And somewhere in cyberspace an encrypted note detailing the sordid alcohol-fueled forays of Kath's doppelgänger stubbornly remained.

Second Verse Same as the First

Kath washed her hands of big city healthcare providers and felt relieved to return to the Sedona Cancer Center where things seemed far more manageable, as she waited in a nondescript exam room in the small but busy office of Dr. DeMarco.

The soft-spoken petite doctor brushed aside her silver-white hair as she peered over her glasses and read aloud the most recent labs reports that suggested the cancer had continued to grow, and Gemzar with Carboplatin might be helpful. The oncologist's words echoed in her head as she relived the troubled world of past chemotherapies. She knew she could tolerate the side effects of those combined drugs, but the thought of losing her hair again upset her.

The Sedona Cancer Center's chemotherapy area resembled all the other chemo rooms Kath had visited in the past. Mature women occupied most of the recliner chairs and predominately female family members assisted them. IV poles stood like sentinels next to each chair as the automated drip systems infused the toxic potions. Many of those patients received the caustic chemicals through a temporary IV placed in the smaller vessels of their arms, which increased their risk of phlebitis or vessel wall damage. Fortunately, Kath's surgically implanted a dual lumen chemo port limited blood vessel damage from the toxic drugs.

For three weeks the chemo drugs minimally disrupted Kath's lifestyle of ethereal pursuits, until one morning after she shampooed in the shower, the water unexpectedly pooled over her feet as the hot water continued to cascade over her. With her toes, she pushed aside the brown hair that had mysteriously obstructed the drain and stared through a cloud of steam at a ball of wet hair haphazardly gathered on the side of the shower.

In a flash she suddenly realized what had just happened and her knees grew momentarily weak. The stream of water washed away her tears as she slowly tilted her head back and yelled a silent scream of exasperation. Unsure of what to do, she leaned against the wall until the hot water ran cold and forced her to exit.

Wrapped only in a towel, she gazed into the mirror and gently tugged on a strand of hair that partially detached in her hand. She stared in disbelief at her closed fist as the lifeless strands dangled between her fingers. She frantically shook them free and watched in utter astonishment as they floated toward the floor. She hesitated for a moment before she turned on the styler to blow dry her hair, but the brush completely filled with emancipated hair after only one stroke.

Completely shocked, she absentmindedly placed the still running hair dryer on the vanity. As she pulled detached locks from the brush, the blow drier blew the tufts of hair from her hand, and she watched in horror as they floated across the room before they landed in lifeless clumps on the floor. Kath quickly leaned toward the mirror and inspected the barren patches that exposed her naked scalp. After a few moments she reluctantly retrieved the dryer and gently dried her hair without the brush as the loose strands scattered in the air behind her.

In the days that followed Kath retreated into the solitude of books. She felt embarrassed by the glabrous state that had stolen her femininity. And the asexual denuded prepubescent androgynous girl she saw in the privacy of her daily bath didn't help. When her knees unexpectedly buckled one morning in the loneliness of the shower, she slowly slid down the wall until she sat on floor. The hot water mingled with her tears, and her muffled sobs echoed around the enclosed room as despair nearly overwhelmed her.

The next day Kath spoke very little as we drove to Prescott through the secluded Mingus Mountain Pass for her monthly counseling session with the same psychiatrist she had seen for years. That ten-minute session offered no help for her despondent state, nor did the new prescription for an increased dose of the same ineffective antidepressant.

She left the office frustrated and angrily silent as we drove through town in search of the Wigwam, a beauty salon that specialized in wigs. Parked in front of the small nondescript store, she paused to fully comprehend the journey that ultimately led to a wig store. With a heavy sigh, she pulled down the sun visor and stared at the disconsolate face reflected in the courtesy mirror. She adjusted her headscarf unconvinced this strip mall salon in the small town of Prescott offered any solutions.

A middle-aged woman with a curled flip at the end of her bouffant-styled shoulder length, dyed brown hair graciously greeted Kath when she entered the salon without an appointment. Mary Jo had grown up in a family of professional Hollywood make-up artists, and the autographed pictures of "Tinsel Town" celebrities that decorated the salon walls testified to her personal connections in the glamor business. Although the salon's core business catered to those who actually had hair, Mary Jo preferred to work with those who had chemo-induced alopecia.

As the two shared personal cancer stories, Kath realized her first impression had been wrong and she developed a strong respect for her new stylist. Together they inspected the numerous wigs resting on top of lifeless plastic heads that lined the shelves. Mary Jo elaborated on the specific attributes of a quality wig as she pointed out the different styles that complemented Kath's facial structure and selectively removed a couple of samples before they returned to the salon area.

Kath stared back at her reflected image in the full-length mirror as she stood in front of the oversized parlor chair. She slowly removed her headscarf, sat down, and quietly sighed in vanquished disbelief at the unvarnished image that hauntingly gazed back at her. Unlike the mythological character Narcissus, she saw no beauty in her reflection.

Mary Jo fluffed up a wig before she stepped in front of Kath and fitted the hairpiece into place while her anxious customer fidgeted about the chair in a fruitless attempt to find an unobstructed view of the mirror. After Mary Jo's pic comb finalized the look, she stepped aside and watched in delight as Kath's astonished expression signaled her approval.

The blonde highlighted piece that MaryJo had chosen resembled Kath's pre-alopecic look, and the uncanny parallel momentarily froze Kath in place. She jumped out of the chair for a closer look and slowly twirled around in front of the mirror capturing different views. Satisfied at the reflected image, she turned back to Mary Jo and delivered a huge hug before she leapt into the chair and asked to sample more wigs.

Mary Jo retrieved a seemingly endless supply of wigs, and Kath created a new personality with each one. Sometimes she pretended to be Jennifer Aniston or Madonna, and one time she mischievously danced around the salon like an exotic Egyptian dancer much to the delight of the other customers. Completely lost in the moment of frivolity, Kath forgot her cancerous past and became the belle of the salon while everyone applauded her antics. Eventually, she settled on the very first wig and bought a second one she named "Cher." The Wig-Wam did more for her emotional state than all the antidepressants in the world, and that good cheer reverberated for some time.

The simple solution of a high-class wig instantly restored Kath's lost femininity and changed how she viewed the hopelessness of cancer. New hair and the magic of Merle Norman revived a look the chemo had stolen. She felt reinvigorated to live life with cancer as a simple sideshow.

Buoyed by a recent retreat of the CA 125, Kath once again dared to believe cancer no longer presented an immediate threat to her life, so she passionately pursued the activities consistent with her introverted personality.

She studied online for a Masters certification in astrology from Kepler College. She created charts that were regularly critiqued by instructors and discovered forums and chat rooms. The socially reclusive Kath, who disdained small talk, found the concise discussions of online forums a perfect opportunity to be socially active. The anonymity of the Internet maintained the boundaries of her personal space but allowed her to engage in conversations with those who shared a common interest in astrological charts, ethereal topics, or cancer. She felt particularly qualified to answer any questions about chemotherapy or life with cancer, and that's how she met Lori Michaels.

A New Friend

Recently diagnosed with Primary Peritoneal Cancer, Lori posted her concerns on a popular cancer forum, and when Kath read her story, she felt compelled to answer. PPC and borderline serous tumor with low malignant potential unfortunately shared similar attributes, so the difficulties Lori experienced with that new diagnosis were well-known to Kath. Their conversations initially focused on treatment options and side effects but slowly shifted to personal stories of hope and loss.

In her early forties, Lori had married late in life and felt guilty about the unintended burden she had inadvertently placed upon her new husband as she struggled with questions that had no answers. Kath understood how cancer impacted those around her and tried to use her own life as an example of how she had moved past that.

Kath had always prided herself as an independent woman, but she eventually realized that cancer could not be fought alone. She reluctantly accepted help from those who loved her, which opened up a surprisingly synergistic energy with them. As Kath tried to express that revelation in an online chat, Lori unexpectedly asked if their conversation could be continued on the phone.

Kath picked up on the first ring, and Lori introduced herself with a soft, high-pitched voice that imperceptibly quivered. This caught Kath by surprise. Her on-line friend sounded different from what she had imagined.

The impersonal nature of the Internet gave way to real intimacy when Kath heard a somber but determined voice talk about the frustrations of failed treatments and the helpless feeling that engulfed her as the life she loved slowly disappeared into the abyss of cancer. Kath recognized herself in her new friend's words.

Levity followed that dismal discussion as they shared their awkward moments of well-intentioned visitors who had never experienced cancer but boldly spoke of a chin-up approach. Most days Lori preferred to stay in bed with the covers pulled snuggly over her head, but she often played the unwilling nauseated hostess who entertained the unannounced caller. Lori knew the cancer had spread to her liver and beyond. She fully understood its ominous implication and had grown tired of wearing the face she kept in a jar by the door. Then, after a brief moment of silence, Lori said she had decided to stop all chemotherapy. Kath nearly dropped the phone when she suddenly realized that no one else knew of her decision.

At first she wanted to scream, "Are you crazy?" But she remembered how she too had halted all chemotherapy and had contemplated assisted suicide as a possible alternative if life became too unbearable. Kath felt the tragic despair of her sister and niece as they had capitulated to cancer, so she understood Lori's position.

Kath shuddered as she envisioned Lori's motionless body on the bed under the blankets with her head peacefully resting on a pillow. Her eyes gently closed, and her husband's face flooded with tears, as he tightly squeezed her limp hand.

Kath's stalemated cancer differed greatly from the terminal nature of Lori's condition. She refused to be Lori's cheerleader for further futile treatments. Kath fidgeted in her chair as she wiped away a tear and said in a heartfelt voice, "Sometimes you just have to say good-bye."

Lori broke the silence that followed with a deep sigh, and said, "Yeah, I know." The strangers who shared the battle fatigue of cancer bonded like two soldiers in the midst of combat. They shared a mutual respect few would understand, as they solemnly parted ways and bid each other farewell.

In the days that followed, Kath secretly hoped her solicited advice hadn't influenced Lori to give up the fight. Through a sense of guilt, she avoided the cancer forum. Kath grew introspectively quiet as she sat in the Sedona Cancer Center's chemo chair and contemplated the fate of her friend, as well as her own fate, while the toxins that infused through her port waged war in her body.

Once back home, Kath placed her wig on the mannequin's head. The vanity mirror reflected her disgusted look as she briefly inspected her alopecic scalp, then wrapped her baldhead in a colorful scarf and ignored the queasiness in her stomach. The cat joined her when she climbed into bed and curled up with one of her many astrological books for an afternoon read. But soon the gastrointestinal upset proved so great that even Zofran couldn't relieve.

As the intractable nausea increased, she desperately fought the urge to vomit. But when a single, sharp abdominal pain abruptly sent her into a fetal position, the startled cat jumped off the bed. Curled up under the covers, Kath felt a second wave of intense pain and gave an audible gasp. But when a sudden spike in body temperature bathed her in sweat, she kicked the covers off in a vain attempt to cool down. The nausea and abdominal pain abated long enough for her to sit on the side of the bed as the sweat dripped from her forehead. But the intense diaphoretic state concerned us both. We sat together on the side of the bed while I contacted Dr. Wilson, who instructed her to go immediately to the ER.

While we waited in the emergency room, the hospital staff rewarded Kath's repeated requests to be segregated from the sneezing, coughing, contagious crowd by giving her a paper-thin mask. We hid in a corner far away from the huddled masses while Kath tried not to vomit.

We eventually worked our way through the hospital's bureaucratic labyrinth before she arrived at her room hours later and sighed in great relief when she slid under the covers of her hospital bed. Only her colorful headscarf remained visible after she pulled the blankets snuggly around her nose and for a few hours fell into an exhausted sleep.

Sometime later, Dr. Wilson entered the room with the grace of Cosmo Kramer. In the remote distance of Kath's deep sleep, she heard the doctor's familiar voice beckoning her to wake up. But as her slumber slowly retreated she abruptly sat up and found herself in a strange bed. Half awake, she struggled to orient herself to the unfamiliar surroundings. When she saw Dr. Wilson's face, her head flopped down on the pillow and the reality of cancer crashed down around her.

Dr. Wilson sat on the edge of the bed and asked what had happened at home. With her head nestled deep in the pillow, Kath looked at him and explained in detail all that had transpired, but she concluded the symptoms were simply side effects of the chemotherapy.

He listened without interruption. When she had finished he completed his physical exam with the efficient speed of an experienced practitioner before he returned to the edge of the bed to discuss what he had found. Left vulnerable to infection from the chemotherapy, Kath had developed a bad case of pneumonia that could be easily resolved with a five-day course of intravenous antibiotics. But a partial bowel obstruction had developed that caused her nausea and abdominal pain which presented a greater dilemma.

For the price of another dose of accumulated lifetime exposure to radiation, the CT Scan accurately confirmed what Dr. Wilson had suspected, a bowel obstruction from abdominal adhesions. These adhesions stretched across the abdomen like a spider web and often wrapped themselves around the intestines like a tight rubber band which eventually blocked the flow of food as it passed through. If the adhesions also cut off the blood supply to the obstructed bowel, it could prove fatal.

Medications proved ineffective against abdominal adhesions, which greatly narrowed the scope of potential treatment options, and surgical intervention would only be considered if the strangulated bowel lost blood flow. Within these constraints, Dr. Wilson decided on a conservative medical course of treatment and rested Kath's bowel. That meant she couldn't eat or drink anything for a few days, but Kath didn't mind. She ate very little anyway. However, the absence of morning coffee presented a real problem.

Kath stared at the ceiling as Dr. Wilson discussed his treatment plan. But she never heard a word of his proposal because her thoughts drifted to another time before cancer, when she had some control in her life.

Before cancer, Kath would busily plan her day after the warm morning sun peaked through her bedroom curtains and gently nudged her awake. But mornings were no longer a pleasant experience, as the nausea, abdominal distention, and health emergencies that usually happened to other people with cancer were now happening to her. The unpredictable nature of cancer held hostage any activity she might have planned because that metastatic monster had hijacked every aspect of her life. Cancer had made her a prisoner, subject to its metastatic whims. And she felt particularly enraged when it suddenly occurred to her that she had been captured.

When ovarian cancer first appeared in Kath's life, everything had screeched to a halt, and she believed death stalked her at every corner. But after the diagnostic horror had faded, the innate need for survival soon distorted the reality of her physical condition. She convinced herself she felt fine, even after years of continuous chemotherapy or when some cancer related health crisis landed her in the hospital. Her body had been battered for so long that she mistakenly took that pummeled feeling for normal. All of those thoughts ran through her mind as she looked around the hospital room in a befuddled gaze and tried to understand exactly how she had arrived at this catastrophic juncture.

Before Dr. Wilson left the room, he told Kath to get out of bed with such a stern voice that it abruptly interrupted her dazed preponderance. The covers suddenly slid to her side and she momentarily sat on the edge of the bed before she slipped her feet into her sheepskin, fleece-lined slippers. She retrieved her blue, terry cloth robe from the closet and slipped it over her mono-gramed sienna peach pajamas before she snuggly wrapped the colorful headscarf around her bald head.

As she strolled the corridors of the nursing unit, Kath initially failed to notice two orange isolation signs that decorated the neighboring doors on each side of her room. But on her second lap she stopped to read the posted note that declared a strict isolation procedure for all who entered those rooms. This prevented inadvertent dispersion of the occupant's infectious disease.

Kath backed away from the door as she struggled to control her immediate sense of panic and silently questioned why the hospital, once again, had assigned her a room next to obvious contagions. But as she walked another lap, she concluded that if she never entered the contaminated rooms and avoided contact with those who did, she wouldn't be at risk. Her sense of panic faded until she stopped at the busy nurses station and read the staff assignment board. She discovered her nurse had also been assigned to both of those isolation rooms! Kath became incensed. How could the faceless hospital bureaucracy willfully ignore her immunosup-pressed state and carelessly jeopardize her life?

Kath vociferously demanded to speak with her nurse, and the conversational hum from the huddled healthcare workers at the nurses' station suddenly fell silent. All eyes discretely watched Kath's nurse as she approached. But before she could say a word, Kath pointed to the assignment board and vehemently stated her views on that irresponsible assignment. The station's occupants busied themselves with imaginary work and abandoned the nurse to fend for herself. The nurse initially defended the assignment with scripted corporate replies of strict adherence to universal precautions. But Kath refused to abandon her fight and insisted that she be moved or the nurse assignment be changed. The exasperated nurse deferred to the charge nurse who then referred the matter to the director of the nursing unit. Meanwhile, Kath impatiently leaned against the counter and stubbornly remained until she arrived.

The matronly middle-aged director approached from the end of a long corridor with the struggled swagger of a heavyset person with bad knees. Her unbuttoned white waist-length lab coat partially covered a full length, brightly colored flowered dress that swayed with each step. When she arrived at the station, the director extended her hand and greeted Kath with a firm handshake from well-manicured, pudgy fingers. She breathed a bit heavy and small beads of sweat appeared on her brow. A warm smile from her chubby, round face revealed one crooked tooth, and the oversized clipboard that she held shielded the small openings between the severely stressed buttons from her undersized dress. She formally introduced herself and politely listened to Kath's concerns but reiterated the scripted response about universal precautions.

Kath knew the hospital standards specifically segregated the care of infectious patients from the postoperative joint replacement patients. She indignantly asked why her immune suppressed state failed to qualify her for the same treatment. She also questioned why the nurse failed to implement a rudimentary form of reverse isolation, which would protect her from a potentially fatal cross contamination. With her steely erect posture, Kath defiantly stood inches from the director's face as the two maintained strained eye contact and sized each other up. After an awkward moment of silence, the director leaned slightly toward Kath and promised all of her concerns would be accommodated.

Kath suppressed a jubilant smile and struggled not to thrust her fists into the air for a celebratory win. Instead, she politely shook the director's hand as she watched the charge nurse change the assignment board. The occupants of the crowded nurses' station silently smiled their approval. Kath returned to her bed satisfied with a minor triumph in a war that saw few victories.

Kath's pain gradually retreated over the next few days, just as Dr. Wilson had predicted. And one morning, as the sun brightened the confines of her hospital room, Kath awoke to a new type of pain that she immediately recognized as hunger. Astonished that she felt the pleasant discomfort of a ravenous appetite, Kath climbed out of bed dressed in her pajamas, with her headscarf slightly askew and braced for the return of a deep abdominal pain that never arrived. Doubtful this unlikely moment would last, she went about her morning routine. After she had applied her makeup and the pain still hadn't returned, she felt a hint of skeptical satisfaction as she replaced her headscarf with the wig. Kath stared in disbelief at the pain-free person the mirror reflected. She smiled a mischievous, congratulatory wink and then walked the corridors with a guarded exuberance few would understand.

Giddy with a sense of forgotten normal, she returned to the room and found that a stack of freshly made French toast awaited her. Smothered in maple syrup, each bite of toast produced a gustatory delight followed by an audible "hmmm." When Kath had consumed the entire stack, she gently pressed on her belly but felt only a full stomach. She pushed the tray aside and sat back in the chair with a smile.

Back home, with a newfound energy and an enormous appetite, Kath focused on healthy meals and exercise. Kath abhorred aerobics. Instead, she practiced yoga, convinced it would reduce the chance of future adhesions. With far less time in bed, she filled her days with online Wiccan studies and astrology classes. She became enchanted with old English lore and read all of Joseph Campbell's lengthy dissertations on ancient myths. Kath felt happy to finally have some sense of normalcy in her life and a real chance at longevity.

One evening well past sunset, I returned home from work and found a mysteriously darkened house. A slight aroma of cigarette smoke had permeated the air. Perplexed, I followed the scent but stopped when an orange-red glow suddenly appeared through a window that overlooked the deck. I watched as the glow moved about in a rhythmic manner in the darkness of a new moon.

I joined Kath outside as the smoke danced in an upward spiral from a recently lit cigarette that dangled loosely between her fingers. She sat alone in a chair and stared off into the abyss unfazed by my arrival. An uneasy silence filled the air before she looked at me with eyes that watered from a recent cry. A single teardrop trickled down her left cheek, and our eyes unexpectedly locked in an extended embrace. The cigarette glowed eerily brighter when she abruptly took a very deep drag. As her lungs exhaled a cloud of white smoke into the night air, she said, "Lori Michaels died." The dark news had cast a shadow of gloom over her soul. Kath silently finished her cigarette and pondered the role she may have played in Lori's unfortunate demise.

Earlier that day Kath had searched the cancer forum for Lori's updates but instead had found an emotional eulogy posted by her husband. He described in detail, how Lori had controlled her own destiny and refused to be persuaded by the healthcare dictums that predictably promoted just one more chemotherapy trial. He went on to say how she had courageously faced the tragic facts of her predicament and exited this life with tremendous dignity.

Kath understood better than most why Lori had stopped all treatments. Kath angrily recalled how the medical community had offered the same false hopes to her late sister, Joan, and niece, Patty, long after their time had run out. She also wondered if that animosity may have disproportionately influenced her advice to Lori. Kath filled the ashtray with cigarette butts as she spoke of how a cancer patient's mind tricked itself into thinking death could be delayed with the next magical chemo bullet.

Kath finally went to bed long after the sun had set and awoke in the morning uncharacteristically disheveled. Her breath smelled like stale cigarettes and her post-pneumonia cough sounded like a barking dog. A whiff of hot coffee from a cup held tightly between her hands temporarily distracted her from the depressive thoughts of the previous night. But when she looked through the dining room window at the overfilled ashtray that littered the deck with cigarette butts, she wondered if she would have Lori's courage when her time finally came to say goodbye.

A Reflective Repose

The persistently elevated CA-125 highlighted the futility of Kath's chemotherapies, and the radiographic images confirmed that this uncommon form of ovarian cancer continued its relentless advance. Meanwhile, the cancer doctors downplayed this information and regularly proclaimed their upbeat prognostications for longevity. For over fifteen years, the medical community had optimistically stated that an early diagnosis of borderline serous tumor with low malignant potential rarely implied a premature death if the surgeon properly removed the abdominal tumor. But years earlier, Dr. Winter had failed to live up to that standard and thus set into motion a health crisis that Kath believed should never have happened.

Dr. DeMarco, the Sedona oncologist, never mentioned the omentum quandary when she declared Kath cancer free eight years after Dr. Winter's initial surgery. And she never discouraged Kath when she requested bio-identical hormone replacement therapy from Dr. Reynolds. Both doctors failed to recognize the documented facts in the medical literature—cancer cells of a borderline serous tumor with low malignant potential tend to be hormone dependent. Everyone in the medical community, except Kath, seemed perplexed when the tumors mysteriously exploded one year after the replacement therapy had started.

When Dr. Freeman described the tumor-ridden omentum he had surgically removed from Kath's abdomen ten years after Dr. Winter's first surgery, she knew that Dr. Winter had done her a great disservice. She felt incredibly angry at his intentional omission.

With Dr. Winter's blunder, the cancer festered unchecked for years, while the very stewards who could have prevented it denied that it even existed. As these unfortunate events coalesced into a perfect neoplastic storm, those same stewards expressed outrage that this metastatic disease refused to be reined in by their toxic potions.

The dozen different medicinal poisons Kath received over the years had left her with a badly beaten body and persistent tumors that seemed to have morphed into a potentially deadlier strain of cancer. The restrained anger she felt toward the multitude of culprits who directly contributed to her predicament eventually faded away as she simply tried to survive.

Kath never felt the fatalism that Lori did before she stopped all of her cancer treatments, but she never truly reconciled her hope for the future with the despair of death. The medical community consistently encouraged a false sense of optimism that gave Kath the intellectual cover to deny the obvious. She preferred to ignore what a dozen failed chemotherapies unambiguously implied, and she simply refused to acknowledge that borderline serous tumor would shorten her life.

Frustrated with Western medicine's lack of progress, Kath augmented the ineffective chemotherapy with multiple alternative health options like acupuncture and Reiki, while she consumed large quantities of supplements recommended by the local practitioners of complementary medicine, all readily found in Sedona.

Preoccupied with Wiccan spells that restored health, Kath searched the Internet for potions that promoted her cause and gathered the necessary supplies from local New Age stores. Dressed in her Celtic robe, she created her magical elixirs and recited her incantations with talismanic sincerity in the secrecy of her bedroom, as she conjured the guardian spirits to rally to her cause. She studied Deepak Chopra's mind-body medicine program and practiced his version of restorative chakra energy. This dovetailed nicely with her regular meditative practice that unfortunately continued to be disrupted by Ziggy the cat.

Each night as she lay in bed, Kath retrieved the quartz crystals from the bedside stand and strategically placed the healing stones across her abdomen, focusing the beams of restorative energy toward her cancerous tumors.

Determined to know her future, Kath breathed new life into the large collection of cabalistic metaphysical methods she had known in the past. In the solitude of her bed, she regularly scrutinized the Celtic Spread from the Rider Waite Tarot cards for any hint of her fate, as she searched for clues in the Rune Stones that she threw in her secluded meditation area. She spread her Vedic astrological birth chart across the desk, along with graphs, rulers, and reference books, as she searched for information that might be chronicled in the stars. But the muddled messages she conjured from the cosmic beyond gave no clear path forward and led Kath to believe whatever her future would be came down to pure luck.

Not Again

Kath no longer expected her hair to grow while the therapeutic chemo toxins continued to poison her body. The alopecia would have been an acceptable trade-off if the CA-125 had at least responded and the cancer had remained unchanged.

Her comfortable routine blew up one morning just before her shower. The metaphysical mumbo-jumbo had not predicted nor prevented the golf-ball-sized lump that appeared overnight at her beltline near the umbilicus.

The newly discovered lump filled Kath with such dread that it seriously threatened to destroy her carefully crafted cancer survival story and nearly cracked the wall of denial that she had carefully constructed over the years.

Emotionally shaken, Kath flung her monogrammed pajamas into a disheveled heap before she feverishly inspected every inch of her naked, abused body for any additional tumors. After an extended search in front of the vanity mirror, she breathed a heavy sigh of relief when no others were found. Kath leaned in toward the mirror and her imperceptible smile slowly faded. She studied her sad face without the benefit of makeup and no longer recognized the gaunt, baldheaded stranger who stared back at her.

On the rare days when Kath felt physically strong enough to do what used to be considered a normal routine, her "out of sight, out of mind" cancer adage sufficiently distracted her. But when the hidden metastatic monster protruded through her skin and her fingers felt its ominous presence, she nearly vomited. Her knees buckled and her hands instinctively clung to the vanity top for support.

When she regained her balance, Kath slowly shook her head and questioned the efficacy of a chemotherapy that allowed the spread of this serous tumor. Completely disgusted, she stared at the reflected image for what seemed like an eternity before she gave a deep sig, and then quietly dressed herself in her retrieved pajamas as she pondered her response.

Kath recalled that one year ago, just prior to our month-long trip to England, Dr. Wallace had removed an identical lump without complications. She convinced herself this time would be no different. Determined to have the tumor excised as quickly as possible, she arranged to be evaluated by Dr. Wallace the very next day.

Kath slept very little that night as the sickly image of the baldheaded stranger that she saw in the mirror haunted her dreams. But she rolled out of bed early the next morning determined not to look like a cancer patient and started her journey with a carefully selected outfit that accentuated her curves.

Determined to be happy with what she saw in the mirror, Kath gathered her cosmetics from the various drawers and with deliberate strokes applied her makeup with Van Gough-like precision. Then she meticulously primped her hair until it no longer looked like a wig. After she finished this arduous task, she scrutinized her appearance for several minutes before she half smiled at the person in the mirror, confident her restorative efforts had succeeded.

She arrived at Dr. Wallace's office well before her scheduled appointment and nervously fidgeted in the waiting room chair as she passed the time with nameless magazines that were neatly stacked around the room. She discussed the benign nature of the tumor with anyone who would listen, but underneath her facade of nervous calm lurked an unspoken fear. The clock had meandered well past her scheduled appointment time, but when the nurse finally called Kath's name, she energetically bounced out of her chair and walked with a determined stride into the examination room, completely confident of the outcome.

Kath sat on the exam table as the nurse asked the obligatory questions. She documented Kath's vital signs and updated her medical history before Dr. Wallace entered the room. He greeted Kath with the warm smile of a well-acquainted friend and expressed his regret that another tumor had emerged. She lowered her pants before she laid back on the table and raised her blouse. The doctor carefully manipulated the golf-ball-sized protuberance then concluded the new growth was identical to the one he had previously removed. He recommended the same procedure with the same minimal risks, but expressed concern about the efficacy of the current chemo regime, as it had failed to check the spread of these serous tumors that were likely scattered within her abdomen, well beyond his reach. That unsettling piece of information quickly retreated to the back of Kath's mind and she chose not to think about the likely implications. Instead, she focused on the immediate problem and scheduled the outpatient surgery for the next day.

The procedure went as Dr. Wallace had predicted. Kath returned home later that afternoon with a small gauze patch that covered a two-inch steri-stripped incision. Although the surgical site remained tender, she felt confident the worst had passed and insisted that I fly out the next day for a long-planned visit to San Jose, California, for my mother's 85th birthday. Against my better judgement, I left her alone at home for the three-day trip.

For two of those days Kath brushed off the diffuse abdominal symptoms as nothing more than post-operative pain. But when a high fever accompanied the abrupt onset of abdominal pain, she recognized her physical condition had deteriorated and prayed my return flight from San Jose would not be delayed.

Home alone with no one to call for help, Kath tried not to panic. But she lacked the energy to do anything other than lay in bed under a thick pile of blankets while beads of sweat dampened her bright headscarf. She almost called 911 but changed her mind when she calculated that I'd be home in a few hours. She anxiously watched the digital clock next to her bed as the red numbers silently counted down the minutes until help arrived.

The house seemed eerily quiet as I found my way to the bedroom where the cat stared at me from the foot of the bed with complete indifference. Kath acknowledged my presence with a warm smile from under a mountain of blankets as her blue eyes peered over the top of a thick down comforter.

When I sat next to her on the bed, she downplayed the events of the last few days. But the sweat-soaked headscarf betrayed her calm tone and suggested a serious medical issue lurked beneath the blankets. The surgical site appeared clean, but the pain radiated in spasmodic waves from the incision site across her entire abdomen. She agreed to be evaluated by Dr. Wilson in the emergency department.

The ER nurse who triaged Kath expedited her passage from the waiting area into an exam room. I never knew if my employment status at the hospital accelerated her placement or if Kath appeared so ill that she automatically moved to the front of the triage line.

Her vital signs reflected an active infectious process that included an elevated temperature accompanied by profuse sweating, low blood pressure, and a rapid pulse. Aware that Kath remained dangerously immunocompromised from the chemotherapy she had received ten days prior, Dr. Wilson admitted her to the hospital for possible sepsis (an overwhelming blood infection). He immediately started her on IV antibiotics delivered through a newly placed intravenous PICC (peripherally inserted central catheter) line in her left upper arm. That offered additional long-term IV access for up to six months in addition to the chemo port that had been surgically implanted in her shoulder years ago. She arrived in her hospital room later that evening and felt much better by morning.

Convinced Dr. Wilson's antibiotics had staved off a potential disaster, Kath felt upbeat and joked with the nurses who remembered her from the many previous admissions. She gleefully chatted over a French toast breakfast, which she said tasted almost as good as her mother's, and speculated on when she could go home.

The jovial conversation continued when Dr. Drake, a thin, younger man with a full head of well-groomed silver hair, entered the room with a three-person entourage and introduced himself as the surgeon on-call for Dr. Wallace. Together they reviewed the events of the last few days. He also felt encouraged that her condition had improved over night, and that boosted her hopes for an early discharge.

Their upbeat dialogue continued as he lowered the head of the bed which gave him a better view of the recent surgical incision. Kath nervously chatted to no one in particular as she stared at the ceiling unable to see the exposed wound. All the other occupants of the room leaned forward for a better look as Dr. Drake carefully removed the dressing and revealed a drainage that looked mysteriously like partially digested French toast. Everyone except Kath immediately understood that her bowel had perforated and formed a gastrointestinal fistula.

Anxious to sit up, Kath pressed the button that raised her head high enough to see the solemn faces that surrounded her. Dr. Drake sat on the side of the bed and explained what his examination had discovered.

The mesh Dr. Wallace used for abdominal muscle support in the recent surgery had inadvertently punctured a hole in her intestines and leaked partially digested contents into her abdominal cavity. The drainage from the perforated intestine formed a small river through the abdomen that exited through the surgical incision site very near the umbilicus.

The perforated bowel had flooded the abdominal cavity with bacterial laden content and had caused a type of infection that often proved fatal. Dr. Drake asked Kath to immediately stop eating, since any food she swallowed would drain directly into the abdomen and exit out of the newly formed fistula. He feared the worst and requested a surgical intervention first thing in the morning, if Kath agreed.

A sense of silent urgency filled the room as everyone coldly stared at Kath for what they perceived to be an easy decision, but her thoughts were far more complicated than they ever magined. As a nurse she understood the gravity of her predicament with all the unforeseen consequences. But as a cancer survivor she wondered if this catastrophic episode would be the final crisis that led to her "Lori Michaels moment."

Kath sat upright in bed with perfect posture and as much poise as possible for a person whose French toast had just oozed out of her abdomen. She studied the somber faces of those who surrounded her, as the quiet in the room crescendoed to an uncomfortable loud roar. She paused for a moment before she answered in a subdued but resigned voice and agreed to the surgery. After the healthcare team filed out of the room, we spoke about her decision. Kath simply recited a verse from *Tangled Up in Blue,* one of her favorite Bob Dylan songs. "The only thing I know how to do is to keep on keeping on." With that I cleaned up the French toast that had collected in her bellybutton.

After surgery Kath returned to her room somewhat groggy but otherwise in good spirits. Instead of repairing Kath's perforated bowel, Dr. Drake simply removed the surgical mesh that Dr. Wallace had previously inserted. This left a deep, silver-dollar-sized hole in Kath's abdomen that overflowed with gastric contents from the fistula and trickled its caustic juicy contents down her skin.

Dr. Drake had purposefully avoided the extremely complicated and potentially fatal surgery required to repair the perforated bowel because he hoped the fistula would close on its own. In reality, this happened only twenty-five per cent of the time.

The fistula originated in a part of the small intestine called the jejunum, several feet down-stream from the stomach. The abundant drainage consisted of digestive juices that quickly saturated the makeshift dressing in less than an hour. Those same gastric enzymes excoriated the exposed skin around the edge of the wound. Initially the nurses changed the dressing whenever Kath reported it was saturated, but this method soon proved to be unsustainable.

Dr. Drake offered no plausible solution to this dilemma, but the nurses soon concocted an unorthodox Rube Goldberg plan that collected the biliary juices with an ostomy bag. That worked well until Kath bent at the waist. That movement broke the seal between the skin and the gummed adhesive designed to protect the skin from the digestive enzymes.

Weary from a day filled with surrealistic events that she had vaguely experienced through an anesthetic fog, Kath slept through the night in an exhausted sleep. In the confused twilight of her morning slumber, she prayed the hazed memories from the previous day would be nothing more than a bad dream. But when her eyes snapped open from the ambient noise of the hospital, she awoke to the realities of her inescapable nightmare.

With shell-shocked eyes, Kath silently watched as the nurse removed the empty intravenous TPN bag that infused her only source of nutrition and replaced it with multiple antibiotic solutions. Kath's temperature had returned to normal, which suggested the sepsis now appeared to be well controlled. Unable to eat or drink, Kath had an extremely dry mouth and when she tried to voice a celebratory cheer, she garbled her words. Deeply frustrated, Kath flopped her hands down against the mattress. But when they landed in a wet mess of saturated sheets, Kath realized she had slept in a puddle of gastric ooze that had seeped from the ruptured seal of the colostomy bag and soiled the bedsheets as well as her pajamas.

For the next three weeks, Kath remained hospitalized, unable to eat or drink, while all of life's vital nutrients were supplied through the TPN. The fistula remained unchanged and drained into a colostomy bag that leaked its gastric contents at least twice a day. That further excoriated her skin and required the replacement of the entire makeshift collection system.

As the days pressed on, hope that the fistula would close on its own slowly faded. Out of options, the doctors suggested a wound vac to control the drainage and possibly close the fistula. But as soon as the suction had started, Kath screamed out in pain. "This fuckin' thing is sucking my guts out!" It was the only time in all of her ill-fated endeavors that Kath ever complained about severe pain.

The doctors offered no surgical solution for this fistula and washed their hands of any responsibility for either its cause or its resolution. But the fistula's continued presence suspended all chemotherapy, which allowed the tumors to grow unchecked. Although the fistula hadn't closed, the septicemia had been success-fully treated, so on Halloween, the doctors declared victory and dis-charged her from the hospital with an enormous home care burden.

The hospital finalized the logistics of home delivered intravenous TPN and arranged for frequent visits by a home health nurse, but they refused to order any colostomy supplies for home use. The discharge coordinator handed Kath a medical supply catalog the size of a phonebook and suggested she use it to order the necessary fistula supplies that would be delivered to our home.

With no hospital guidance, we flipped through countless pages of irrelevant medical equipment until we found the supplies that closely matched what the hospital used. We ordered them by phone, but they couldn't be delivered for two days. The nurses gathered some supplies for us to take home, but not enough to bridge the gap. Kath could have stayed in the hospital until the complete shipment arrived, but she wanted to go home and no one argued against it.

The  Bile River

The fistula collection system survived the ride home, and Kath tried not to trip over Ziggy when she entered the house. Through misty eyes, Kath watched as Ziggy continually rubbed against her legs while his meow begged her for attention. But she feared a fractured seal on the collection bag if she bent down to pet her faithful friend.

She stood in the middle of a kitchen that she could not use and, out of habit, briefly looked inside the refrigerator. The shelves may as well have been empty since all of her meals were now intravenous. She closed the fridge door, wiped away her moist eyes, and carefully stepped over Ziggy on her way to the bedroom.

After weeks of poor sleep on a hospital mattress, the Tempurpedic bed looked incredibly inviting. She pulled back the sheets and carefully logrolled into a supine position on the bed. Her body relaxed and she smiled as she sunk comfortably into the mattress. For the next several months, she would have to sleep on her back.

Relieved to be in her own bed, Kath pulled the covers snugly under her chin and smiled when Ziggy joined her for a heartfelt emotional reunion. He purred like a diesel motor as she gently caressed his silky black fur. For a brief moment, she forgot about the ordeal and drifted off into an exhausted sleep while the cat snuggled next to her. A few hours later the doorbell announced the arrival of the home health nurse and abruptly interrupted her catnap.

Renee stood at the front door dressed in blue hospital scrubs. Her short, highlighted brown hair flowed neatly over the collar of her a waist-length white lab coat that partially concealed a slightly overweight belly. After introducing herself with a limp handshake, Renee maneuvered the hand truck loaded with supplies into the kitchen and placed the TPN in the refrigerator. She then proceeded towards the bedroom and introduced herself to Kath while she stacked the remainder of the supplies in a nearby closet.

Kath watched as Renee fumbled through her health history and conducted a not so thorough physical exam. But when she attempted to check the fistula, Kath only allowed a visual inspection, as she feared the unnecessary manipulation would create a leak.

Renee struggled to assemble the CADD (continuous ambulatory drug delivery) IV pump for the TPN and nearly contaminated the sterile IV tubing. When she prepared to improperly access the PICC line, Kath calmly touched Renee's hand and suggested that I complete the procedure. Although Kath never trusted Renee's nursing skills, they found a shared interest in quartz crystals and alternative medicine, which they discussed on her weekly visits.

On her first night at home, Kath laid on her back and stared at the ceiling while the mechanical beat of the infusion pump provided a constant reminder that her fate rested on the hope that the fistula would miraculously close on its own. But until then, three hundred cc's of gastric juices would flow through the fistula unimpeded every day.

The four liters of TPN fluid that infused into the PICC line every night provided all the necessary nutrition but compressed a full day of hydration needs into twelve hours which caused a frequent need to urinate. Two hours after the infusion started, Kath cautiously logrolled out of bed and carried the light weight portable CADD pump to the bathroom, mindful not to get tangled up in the IV tubing.

When she sat on the commode, the adhesive seal separated from her skin and bile leaked onto her pajama top. She quickly pulled the soiled garment above the fistula and placed a towel over the defective bag. She waddled to the sink with the CADD pump in one hand, a bile-stained towel held snuggly against the fistula with the other, and her pajama bottoms around her ankles. After she placed the I.V. pump on the countertop, she leaned forward over the vanity, stared into the mirror, and questioned her ability to continue the fight. Just when she felt she couldn't go on, a sparkle from her diamond wedding ring caught her eye and a determined resolve rumbled up from deep inside her. She leaned closer to the mirror and studied the subtle smile that reflected back. She returned to the bedroom, placed the pump on the nightstand, and arranged the absorbent blue pad on top of the sheets. She pressed the towel against the fistula bag and logrolled back into bed.

I removed the bile-filled bag and placed an unsecured four-by-four-inch gauze into the open fistula, but it soon became obvious the gauze supply wouldn't last until the colostomy stocks arrived. So, on Halloween night, I traveled to the neighborhood grocery store and pushed my empty cart past rows of candy before I found myself in the feminine hygiene aisle. I planned to replace the wicked hospital gauze with a tampon that would fit snuggly into Kath's fistula hole and absorb the bile.

I was dumbfounded by the various sizes and brands of tampons. I had no idea which one absorbed best or what size would fit the hole. I stood in the aisle next to my cart and studied box after box as fellow shoppers passed by with silent, quizzical looks. I finally gave up and emptied the shelves of all the sizes that I thought would meet the requirements. As I stood in the checkout line, the fellow shoppers silently pondered what kind of Halloween costume required so many tampons, as the cashier politely rang up over a dozen boxes.

When I returned home, Kath was lying on her back. A wicked gauze protruded from the hole and a pile of used ones filled the garbage can next to the bed. She laughed when I showed her the dozen boxes of tampons, but after I explained my plan she realized it just might work. Kath's knowledge of the product helped us choose the most appropriate brand, which I unwrapped and inserted into the hole. We laughed hysterically when it slipped into the cavity and self-expanded to a snug fit.

Throughout our married life Halloween had always been a special night. As we periodically changed the soiled tampons, we reminisced about the Halloweens that stood out over the past twenty-nine years.

When we lived in Salt Lake City, we attended a private Halloween costume party. Kath went as the Queen of Hearts from *Alice in Wonderland,* and I dressed as the White Rabbit. She looked absolutely stunning in her costume. We were quite the young couple.

As the night progressed, our spirits soared proportional to the wine we consumed, and we found ourselves next to a hot tub full of naked revelers. We gave each other approvingly subtle glances before we discarded our costumes and jumped into the huge jacuzzi with the other au naturel revelers. The rest of that night remained a blur, and for the next few days we suffered a hangover with a tincture of Catholic guilt. We shook our heads at the foolishness of youth, while I changed out another tampon.

We recalled another Halloween in San Diego when we handed out candy to almost two hundred Trick or Treaters while we listened to Garrison Keillor's *Prairie Home Companion* on the radio. For a woman who had been unceremoniously denied the opportunity of childbirth, Kath reveled in the innocence of the children, as they paraded to our front door while we gorged on all the extra candy. Once in Sedona, we dressed up as vampires and won first place in a costume contest at a popular nightclub. The next day our picture made the local paper.

We smiled at the memories, as we lay in bed with a tampon inserted into Kath's fistula and watched *Interview with a Vampire,* which made this All Hallows Eve the most memorable of them all.

The large shipment of medical supplies arrived the next day. Multiple boxes of IV tubing, syringes, needles, glucometer supplies and intravenous saline solutions filled the closet, while many single dose IV medication vials were squeezed into a very full medicine cabinet. Numerous boxes of colostomy provisions replaced the depleted stock of tampons, and I stacked a week's supply of TPN bags next to the food in the refrigerator.

While Kath was in the hospital, the nurses had connected the intravenous TPN bag to the PICC line every day at 5 P.M. for a twelve-hour overnight infusion, which provided all of the vitamins, minerals, glucose, and water she needed to survive. A separate bag of intravenous lipids infused three times a week and ran in tandem with the TPN solution. Kath never experienced a problem with the TPN or the independent lipid bag, but once she returned home the pharmacy combined those two separate solutions into a single bag. She experienced a near disaster when the first combined bag infused into her body.

Kath attached the new mixture to the PICC line, and over the course of thirty minutes the mechanical CADD pump gradually increased the speed of the infusion rate until it reached maximum speed. But an hour later she felt short of breath with mild itching over her entire body. Her concern mounted, as the symptoms seemed eerily similar to the near anaphylactic reaction she had to a medication called Alteplase that required intervention with I.V. Benadryl and averted a near disaster.

In a near panic state she sat up and immediately decreased the infusion rate of the CADD pump to near zero. Her eyes telegraphed a sense of urgency as the reaction escalated. Kath suddenly fell back onto the bed and struggled for air as her chest tightened. Her eyes quickly lost focus, and her consciousness started to fade.

I immediately stopped the TPN-Lipid infusion and disconnected the IV lines. I retrieved a bottle of IV diphenhydramine from the stash of emergency medications stored in the nearby medicine cabinet and rapidly pushed the drug through her PICC line.

Kath's symptoms quickly faded, but her eyes struggled to focus. She sat up in bed and looked around the room in a bewildered state before she turned to me for reassurance. When our eyes met, she struggled to verbalize her gratitude, but a dry mouth exacerbated by the IV Benadryl made it very difficult for her to enunciate the words. She shook her head in disbelief and stared at me for a few moments with watery eyes before she silently mouthed a heartfelt, "Thank you."

She leaned her head back against the pillows with the covers pulled snuggly around her neck and pondered the potentially fatal consequences of this near disastrous reaction. The root cause of this unusual episode forever remained a mystery. But Kath refused to infuse any TPN from the newly arrived batch which meant that she received no nutritional support or fluid replacement until the pharmacist delivered a new TPN bag the next day.

The aura of serenity that descended upon her from the intravenous Benadryl suddenly gave way to an inner sense of doom as she moved her legs nervously beneath the blanket and small beads of sweat formed on her brow. Her restlessness crescendoed before she declared herself hot and flung the covers off the bed, catapulting Ziggy through the air.

Kath sat up in a wide-eyed panic and scooted to the side of the bed. A sudden attack of vertigo nearly knocked her to the floor, but she managed to remain seated as she steadied herself with both hands placed firmly on the mattress. With her head bowed low, Kath failed to understand the diaphoretic state that made her sick to her stomach. She watched in hypnotic horror as drops of sweat tumbled from her forehead and splashed onto the carpet below.

We did not realize that Kath was experiencing insulin shock. When a new TPN bag is started, the speed of the intravenous infusion is gradually increased over the course of thirty minutes before the maximum flow rate is achieved. This allows the pancreas time to upwardly adjust its native insulin secretion to efficiently manage the increased glucose load. Conversely, when the bag is nearly finished, the infusion rate is slowly decreased to zero over the course of an hour. This gives the pancreas time to lower its insulin production and insure an orderly decline in the patient's blood glucose levels. But the allergic reaction necessitated the abrupt cessation of the TPN infusion and resulted in insulin shock.

I immediately retrieved the glucometer from the supply closet and tested her blood sugar. It read 65, while 80 - 120 represented a normal result, and a second check recorded a glucose reading of 55.

A symptomatic hypoglycemic person would simply eat a candy bar or drink a sugary soda. But Kath couldn't eat or drink anything, and the emergency medicine cabinet filled with supplies from the hospital lacked any IV dextrose to treat a hypoglycemic medical emergency. I ran to the kitchen and created a thick paste of sugar and water that I rubbed on her gums. But when her glucose dropped to 35, I called 911.

Although it seemed like hours, the EMS arrived in less than five minutes. And much to Kath's disoriented hypoglycemic delight, the bedroom instantly filled with several buff young firemen. I explained the circumstances of the emergency to the unit commander. He altered the normal protocol and only infused one half of an ampule of the IV dextrose, which instantly raised her blood glucose to 180. As her symptoms quickly subsided, the paramedics discussed the absurdity of how a patient in Kath's condition would be sent home from the hospital without an emergency ampule of IV Dextrose. With a sheepishly reoriented grin, Kath thanked all of the young men for their service before they left the room. Out of caution, I placed the unused portion of the dextrose ampule in the emergency medicine cabinet.

The next day Kath sought answers from Dr. Wilson. He offered no explanation for the mysterious episode but agreed that the intravenous lipids and the TPN could be infused simultaneously but from their individual bags. This prevented any further reactions. However, the medical community remained hesitant to surgically repair the fistula and self-closure seemed very unlikely, which would leave her tied to the TPN forever.

The precarious nature of the bile collection bag limited her mobility, as the gastric enzymes regularly leaked under the wafer and excoriated her tender skin. The elusive search for a well-sealed fistula bag remained a perpetual work in progress.

Kath felt sullied by the bile that frequently dribbled down her side and between her legs. The days of a relaxed bubble bath surrounded by scented candles as New Age music played in the background had long since passed, while the fistula precluded any immersion in water. The collection bag tolerated a shower, but the PICC line needed to be securely taped with a plastic Saran-Wrap-like cover. She showered once a week and settled for a morning sponge bath the rest of the time.

The bulky collection system forced a change in Kath's social attire. Before the fistula she had dressed in fashionably tight jeans.

Now she wore loose fitting sundresses whenever she left the house. She spent most of the time in bed dressed in her pajamas and quickly morphed into a recluse.

Kath filled those long, lonely days under the cotton sheets reading novels by Thomas Hardy or Jane Austen and listening to audio books of mystic religious leaders, like Paramahansa Yogananda or the Dali Lama. She used her laptop computer to resume her online astrological studies. From the comfort of her bed, Kath developed an Internet-based social life that successfully substituted for the one she lacked in the real world. Her online friends never knew the emotional turmoil that lurked just below her stoic surface.

Outwardly everything seemed normal. But the relentless cascade of Kath's physical troubles tested her emotional resolve and she resorted to an array of pharmaceuticals to manage that incredible stress. For years, a 72-hour Fentanyl patch, Oxycodone, Lorazepam, and Xanax had filled her medicine cabinet. But the fistula rendered all oral medications useless. The new drugs included IV Lorazepam for anxiety and IV morphine for breakthrough pain that she never experienced but conveniently cited to get the medications refilled. Kath always had a penchant for drugs, whether illicit or prescribed and readily accepted Dr. Wilson's prescriptions, but she never viewed herself as a drug abuser. Kath self-administered those drugs through the intravenous PICC line, but always within the prescribed limits, even when the emotional rigors of her infirmity nearly overwhelmed her.

In her life before cancer, Kath often surrounded herself with house guests who shared a laugh over an impeccably set dinner table with a menu that she'd fretted over for days. But those halcyon times had faded into a distant memory, overshadowed by an endless cascade of cancerous related catastrophes that left her emotionally strained and socially awkward.

Kath longed to relive those heady times, but in her physically ravaged state she found it difficult to be the perfect host. She hesitated to invite the occasional guest who called ahead for an audience. As a self-proclaimed recluse who felt comfortable in her solitude, she never refused a visitor, but she frequently muttered to herself the Greta Garbo line, "I vant to be alone."

But guests did come. They found Kath semi-recumbent in bed under the covers, dressed in her monogramed pajamas with her makeup meticulously applied and a wig primped to perfection in a room that resembled a hospital suite. She tried to make the guests feel comfortable, as she had before cancer, but with no table to set or food to be served. Being constrained by a flawed collection system she feared would leak at any moment, she politely listened as the conversation cautiously danced around the elephant in the room and inevitably led to nervous small talk she absolutely abhorred.

Guests came with good intentions, but the awkwardness of ill health made everyone feel a bit uncomfortable. They didn't know what to say, while Kath tried to convince them things weren't as bad as they seemed. When the visitors said their goodbyes, they enthusiastically offered their rosy outlook for a condition they knew little about. And when her solitude finally returned, Kath felt emotionally exhausted.

Kath never felt drained when Mika, the housekeeper, or Renee, the home health nurse visited, as neither required a hostess. Renee understood and empathized with Kath's predicament slightly better than most visitors, while Mika didn't really care.

Renee arranged her biweekly visits to coincide with my twelve-hour workdays which provided an opportunity for a wellness check on Kath while I was away. Although Renee lacked basic clinical nursing skills, she practiced a New Age theory that corresponded closely to Kath's beliefs. Their discussions provided a momentary distraction from the woes of Kath's world, as they chatted about the latest dogmas of alternative medicine.

Once a week Mika provided an additional wellness check when she cleaned the house on a day that I worked but opposite of Renee's schedule. The thin, young Eastern European spoke excellent English with a noticeable accent that displayed a certain charm, but she always remained distantly cordial whenever she engaged Kath in brief conversations.

Kath never established a rapport with her like she did with Renee, and Kath felt no particular allegiance to Mika as the two shared little in common. Mika represented the apathy of quasi-well-intentioned healthy individuals whose busy lives had no time for genuine empathetic personal rapport. She offered half-hearted condolences with little insight into Kath's personal trials. Motivated by money, Mika cleaned the house quickly. But any disruption that slowed the process, like extended personal conversations, extended her time spent on the job and reduced her productivity.

When I returned late one evening to a freshly cleaned home, Kath greeted me from the bed with a voice that seemed slightly distraught. Outwardly, everything seemed normal. But the unusual quiet in the room, broken only by the rhythm of the CADD pump as it delivered the TPN solution, hinted at a different story.

I routinely changed the collection system when I returned home from work. As I started the process, Kath mentioned that Mika had accidentally broken her red ceramic dragon that doubled as an incense burner. The creature had emerald green eyes with coal black oblong pupils and vented the smoke through its nostrils. Kath's voice crescendoed as she explained how Mika never apologized for the accidental breakage or offered to pay for the damages.

The dragon represented more than just an incense burner that Kath had carefully carried back from England. She had struggled with her health on that particular trip, but she felt unusually well the day we drove through the small Welsh town of Corris and stopped at a roadside attraction that recreated the land of Camelot deep within an abandoned mine that had long since flooded.

An electric boat filled with tourists navigated the dark underground waterway, while the damp aroma of a subterranean river filled our senses. The helmsman's voice mesmerized her as he chronicled the legend of King Arthur while we floated past life-size displays tucked into well-lit caverns that illustrated his story as the *Mists of Avalon* came to life before Kath's eyes.

After the tour, we strolled through a colorful outdoor garden. Dozens of ceramic incense burners molded into the various Avalon characters stood guard like sentinels under live plants and wafted their distinctive scent throughout the large flowered area. Out of all the mythical figurines of Camelot that dotted the floral landscape, the red dragon caught her attention.

As a pragmatic woman, Kath rarely attached emotional sentiment to inanimate objects. But when an aloof Mika stood next to her bed with a dustpan filled with the shards of the shattered dragon, an anger welled up inside of Kath that extended beyond the smashed symbol of that Avalon moment.

She wasn't angry at the apathy of people like Mika. She wasn't upset that her life would end much like the aromatic smoke that once flowed from the dragon's nostrils and lingered for a while in the land of the living before it too dissipated into nothingness. Kath was angry because she felt cheated in life. She recalled the togetherness we shared in the flooded mine of Camelot and realized that we would never grow old together. She felt the despair of Morgaine when she said goodbye to the love of her life and buried Arthur in Avalon. A torrent of multifarious emotions flowed through her mind as she stared at the lifeless shards gathered in the dustpan.

She resigned herself to the inevitable end and simply pulled the covers up to her neck and withdrew into her books

Thanksgiving holiday arrived with an empty table in a house absent the aroma of the traditional meal. It had been over a month since Kath had tasted any food or drink, and the scent of a feast with all the trimmings would have been tortuous. She passed the day in bed with her books just liked the previous day, and at 5 P.M. set up her own holiday meal of TPN followed by some IV morphine for dessert. Then she fell asleep with her headphones on as she listened to Deepak Chopra's audiobook *Life After Death*.

When Christmas week arrived, a faux holiday spirit filled the house, while Kath tried to guess the presents stacked under the fully trimmed tree. The stereo played the usual carols, but the silent cryptic message eerily heard between the stanzas of the seasonal hymns hinted this Yuletide season might be her last.

In classic Wiccan fashion, Kath celebrated the winter solstice in front of the Yule altar she had arranged in her meditation area. A large bronze sun with radiating sunbeams and facial features hung on the wall overlooking an altar with colorful candles encircled by fresh evergreen boughs and scattered pine cones. Frankincense filled the room and golden flames flickered from the candles, as Kath sat on a chair dressed in her long red robe. She methodically chanted her incantations as Ziggy slept peacefully next to her on the floor. She bid farewell to the darkness and celebrated the rebirth of the sun on its return journey from its nadir. She praised the lengthening light of spring that would rejuvenate all that seemed dead or asleep in the world.

Two days later, Kath celebrated Christmas wearing a floor-length burgundy velvet dress that successfully hid the collection bag. She wore a golden, Celtic cross that dangled from a gold braided necklace. The tight sleeves revealed the slight bulge of the capped off PICC line. Her diamond wedding ring glimmered on her left hand. Her meticulously curled hair looked nothing like a wig, and her make up covered the ashen look of a cancer patient.

Kath abandoned the hospital-like bedroom for the festively decorated living room where we opened gifts and reminisced about past Christmases with particular attention to Kath's propensity to preside over elaborately prepared meals.

Kath longed for the pageantry of midnight mass and the dignified solemnity of Holy Communion, but she laughed when we took bets on how long it would take before the white wafer exited the fistula and landed in the bag. She tried to strike a happy pose for the obligatory Holiday pictures but she had a subtle sadness in her eyes that reflected a reluctance to leave this world and meet the Holiday's guest of honor.

Kath's reclusiveness accelerated in the days before her 59th birthday, as she lay in bed buried under astrological charts. She searched the cosmic constellations and planetary alignments for some insight into her future but doubted the upbeat conclusion that her studies suggested.

She contacted a well-known East Indian astrologer and arranged for a long distance telephone consultation of her personal star chart. For thirty minutes, they spoke with doctoral thesis precision in cosmological verbiage as they dissected the planetary alignments and debated their meaning. His upbeat synopsis predicted a period of troubled health followed by a return to normalcy, which curiously coincided with her own studies. But he stipulated his prognostications were limited to the next twelve months and refused to speculate on events beyond a year's time horizon.

When the consultation concluded, Kath sat back in the chair and grinned a hopeful smile. But her smile quickly faded when the collection bag suddenly leaked its biliary juices on her pajama top.

Her emotions instantly changed from newfound hope to familiar despair. She left the office and went to the bedroom, where she tossed her bile-stained clothes into the corner.

After she cleaned herself up, she pondered the strange disconnect between the upbeat astrological predictions and the persistent reality she found herself in. Alone with her thoughts, Kath struggled to keep her mind focused on an eventual positive conclusion to this fistula disaster. The upbeat astrological news bordered on magical thinking and may have been born out of desperation or from the profound effect that Peter McBeltane's book, *You Can't Afford the Luxury of a Negative Thought,* had upon her psyche.

Kath had fought depression for many years, but now she simply tried to maintain her sanity until the fistula finally closed. Freud postulated in *Mourning and Melancholia* that depression is simply anger turned inward. This seemed to be true with Kath as she had plenty to be angry about.

My ill-fated attempt to lift her from those dark clouds of doom with a surprise 59th birthday party inadvertently released all that pent-up anger. Kath disliked surprise parties and still carried a grudge from the last one I'd had for her fifteen years earlier. But when I told her of the event just a few hours before the guests arrived, I realized the error of my ways. Her face turned beet red as she angrily screamed her objection to the clandestine gathering of friends. Thick sprays of spit flew out of her mouth in a frustrated rage and showered my shocked face. Her rant detailed a preference for a secluded life with no extra energy to be the life of the party. She went on to say that she never understood how to be the center of attention.

She screamed out the story of the party her mother had planned for her sixth birthday when she lived on Audubon Street in Grosse Pointe Park. They worked out the guest list days ahead of time, but as the big day approached Kath's anxiety increased. When the party date finally arrived, she constantly peered out the front window for the friends she never believed would come. But when the first group arrived, she hid in her bedroom, too afraid to come out.

Kath stared at me with a look meant to kill. She threw herself in front of the mirror and applied her make up as quickly as possible. She pulled the wig over her straggled thin locks and primped it as best she could. She chose a loose sundress and completed the transformation just as the doorbell announced their arrival. She looked at me and said, "This bag had better not leak!" And went to answer the door. She sat with the guests in the living room and pretended to be a gracious hostess, but she refused to look at me the entire time.

Kath's wrath eventually dissipated after the New Year. She returned to her meditative seclusion in the shelter of her bedroom surrounded by books, but beneath the stoical facade of a cancer survivor she slowly spiraled down into a depressive funk. She struggled to find the bright side of a bad situation but awoke each day to the grim reality of a bag full of bile and soon questioned the futility of the effort. As these doubts permeated her very soul, Kath recognized the need for professional counseling and arranged for an appointment with Dr. Wild, her long-time psychiatrist, in Prescott.

On the morning of her consultation, Kath spent an inordinate amount of time in front of the mirror applying her makeup and trying on clothes. She refused to look like a cancer patient who hadn't eaten in months.

Kath had long since mastered the art of entering the front seat of the car without bending at the waist. While her "stiff-as-a-board" movement may have looked humorous to the casual observer, it preserved the integrity of the collection bag's seal. She laid back fully reclined in the car's front seat. Her black-rimmed wrap-around sunglasses obscured any hint of her emotional state as she stared at the ceiling for the one-hour ride to Prescott.

Kath occasionally emerged from her distant inner place and engaged in brief conversations with me, but for most of the trip she remained lost in thought. As we approached the clinic her anxiety noticeably increased. When we parked, she retrieved Lorazepam from the emergency bag of supplies and injected the intravenous medication through the PICC line.

The receptionist greeted Kath by name, and they exchanged pleasantries while Kath signed in. She sat down in the empty waiting room and silently chuckled at the *Muzak* elevator music that quietly played in the background. "You need some *Led Zeppelin* in here," she half shouted to the receptionist, who remained sealed up in her office behind the glass window and acknowledged her comment with a slight smile.

Kath fidgeted in an uncomfortable chair and nervously paged through an outdated large print *Reader's Digest*. She occasionally peered over the top of the periodical to monitor the doctor's closed office door at the end of the hall for any sign that the current client had completed the session.

The door unceremoniously opened as a well-dressed, middle-aged woman wearing oversized, square sunglasses exited the office and aristocratically walked down the dimly lit hall followed by the psychiatrist. They exchanged a pretentious hug at the entrance to the glass enclosed office before the well-healed lady said in a sultry voice, "Au Revoir, Darling" and sauntered out of the clinic.

The doctor stepped into the glass enclosure and casually skimmed through a patient's chart she retrieved from the secretary's desk. Kath quickly put the magazine down and nervously watched while the doctor flipped through the pages of an unknown medical record. Suddenly, a profound sense of apprehension welled up inside of her.

Kath anxiously waited as the doctor engaged in a business-like discussion with the secretary in the privacy of the enclosed office. Dr. Wild closed the chart and smiled through the thick glass partition at the only patient in the waiting room. Kath quickly acknowledged the doctor's inferred summons with a broad smile and rose from her chair with a Cheshire Cat grin. "The doctor is in and she charges more than five cents," she whispered in a perfect ventriloquist-style voice and followed Dr. Wild to her office.

Dr. Wild closed the door and skimmed through Kath's chart as Kath shifted in the overstuffed armchair trying to get comfortable. The thought of a ruptured seal oozing putrid green bile onto her dress overrode her strong sense of social decorum. She slowly slid down in the chair and unbent her waist, then extended her legs and tucked both feet unceremoniously under the doctor's metal desk.

Dr. Wild walked to her desk but abruptly slowed her pace as she quizzically peered at Kath over the top of her black-rimmed reading glasses. After placing the opened chart on her uncluttered desk, she sat down in a faux leather swivel chair that looked like something from Walmart. The doctor rested her hands upon her chest in a prayer-like fashion and slowly rocked in the chair. She seemed deep in thought as she stared past Kath but eventually broke the silence with summarized minutes from their last encounter, several months ago.

When she had finished, Dr. Wild sat back in the chair and asked Kath for an update. She listened closely as Kath factually described the relentless nature of the ovarian cancer and leaned slightly forward as Kath's voice crescendoed in anger when she described the debacle that created the fistula.

"You seem to be angry about that," Dr. Wild said.

"That mistake changed my life and may ultimately kill me," Kath replied.

"They didn't intend for that to happen," the doctor said.

"Oh, that's supposed to make me feel better?" Kath asked. "I have been the recipient of multiple medical mistakes and no one has ever apologized to me, not once. For a long time I blamed myself and fell into a deep despair as I pondered what I could have done differently. How sick is that?"

"None of this is your fault, but it's understandable that you feel despondent. What helped with your previous bouts of depression?" the doctor asked.

"The antidepressants you once prescribed seemed to have worked, but they are useless to me now" Kath said, as she pointed to the collection bag under her dress. "Since this fistula occurred, I lie in bed all day imagining my life before cancer. And those thoughts become darker as the days drag on. At times I've felt that assisted suicide seemed like the only answer, and I actually researched what the Oregon law required."

"Do you want to commit suicide?" Dr. Wild asked.

"No," Kath emphatically replied. "I just want my life back. I'm emotionally exhausted, and I really don't know how much more of this I can take. I need a miracle but I'm losing faith."

The doctor remained silent for a few moments before she said, "I have no magic solution for you. People struggle with health issues all the time. Yes, yours is uniquely troubling, but when the hard reality of a life-threatening illness becomes totally undeniable, an inevitable emotional panic sets in, which causes people to react in different ways. Denial is the most powerful drug on earth, and some people act as if nothing is wrong. They try to live their life as they always have until they can't, and then they suddenly give up. Some create a bucket list and pursue unrealistic dreams that temporarily divert their attention from the crisis at hand, while others fall prey to con artists and charlatans who, for a price, promise unsubstantiated cures. Others use prescribed or illicit drugs to withdraw into themselves and deny the troubled waters they find themselves in. Many fervently plea to their religious deities in the belief that death can somehow be miraculously avoided. While none of these methods adequately address the fear that death brings to each life, they all share a common thread with Dr. Kubler-Ross's well-known thesis on death and dying."

"I've faced death a few times. It didn't frighten me then, and it doesn't frighten me now," Kath said. "But the physical pain I will experience before I finally break on through to the other side is what causes most of my angst. It's not about death or dying. It's whether I possess the inner strength to emotionally survive this impossible situation I have been thrown into. The only way this emotional struggle can end is when the fistula is repaired and the cancer is obliterated. But neither you nor anyone else seems to be able to do that. I came to you for help, but that may have been a waste of my time. You have no magical potions to offer me, and there is nothing you can do or say to change my life."

"Well, your cancer is a problem," Dr. Wild retorted.

"What did you say? Don't call this MY cancer," Kath angrily said, stressing the word "my." "This is not MY cancer. I didn't ask for this, and I don't claim it as my own. I've been held hostage by a parasitic invader who will take its sweet time eating me from the inside out. I haven't had a meal in over three months, and this fistula may never be resolved. But I will survive it. I appreciate your sincere offer to help, but unless you're an abdominal surgeon there is nothing you can do. I will probably die from all of this, and if that comes to pass I can only hope to emulate the unbelievable grace I've seen in the many courageous patients I've met along the way.

I'm no fool. I know there will be more bad days ahead, but I refuse to be a sniveling whiner constantly wishing for a better day. This cancer may destroy me, but it can never destroy the love I have found along the way."

With that, Kath slowly pulled her feet out from under the desk and stood tall in front of the doctor who remained seated. Kath politely expressed her gratitude and offered an outstretched hand that the doctor stared at but never shook. They shared a short visual embrace before Kath quickly exited the office. Dr. Wild spun around in her chair and tried to catch up to her. Kath waved goodbye to the secretary as she whisked passed the entrance to the glass enclosed office. But Dr. Wild stopped her pursuit at the secretary's desk, and they both watched Kath walk out the clinic door.

Kath put her sunglasses on and sat back in the front seat of the car. Staring at the ceiling, she never uttered a word for the one-hour ride back to Sedona.

Days turned to weeks, but Kath's routine remained the same. She rarely ventured off the bed, but she continued to read her books and interact with her social connections on the Internet. The home health nurse maintained her biweekly vigilance, and the various doctor appointments remained a large part of her real-world social interaction. Over the course of many months the size of the fistula gradually became smaller and the amount of excreted bile decreased to a mere trickle, which improved the longevity of the bag.

When the fistula hole had diminished to the size of a sewing needle, Kath dared to believe that she might be in the 25% category of intestinal fistulas that closed by themselves. But the painful memories of overhyped promises pitched by various doctors for previous chemotherapies, or cancer surgeries that inevitably failed to meet their inflated expectations, tempered her cautious optimism. She warily clung to the favorable forecast previously predicted by the astrological reading completed some time ago, and cautiously embraced a new found hope that slowly displaced the endless despair that had inundated her over the past several months.

For three consecutive days, no bile oozed out of the invisible fistula. This emboldened her newfound optimism, but she feared any oral intake would ruin this unexpected progress. Her self-imposed social isolationism slowly diminished, and her dry sense of humor tepidly re-emerged, as she cautiously processed the potential promise implied with the fistula's recent changes.

In the midst of this guarded euphoria, Kath's sister, Marianne, called from Ann Arbor, Michigan, and announced her planned visit to a local Sedona golf resort with her husband over the fast approaching Easter weekend. In a family replete with collegial diplomas, Marianne never earned a four-year degree, but she had studied hard under the tutelage of Grandpa Ernie and Aunt Betty and had received an advanced degree in high society. She had the discernment of an elite Cartier jeweler and easily understood the value of a true antique from a garage sale knock off. She could spot a Sennah knotted live wool Persian rug from across the room, and she excelled in the art of fine country club etiquette. Kath secretly admired all of those traits but never fully reconciled them with her own 1969 anti-capitalist hippie heritage that formed the foundation of her ethos.

The momentary silence that screamed through the phone underscored the sisters long tempestuous relationship. It extended beyond simple sibling rivalry and hinted at something far more perfidious that lurked just below the surface. After an awkward moment of uncomfortable quiet, Kath heard herself say, "Sure, that would be great."

That troubled pause had its roots in a drunken night they shared together more than thirty years ago. In a swanky Ann Arbor bar, Kath proudly boasted to Marianne that she had ended her

273

extended affair with Dr. Banks. But when Kath continued to brag about how she unabashedly twisted the spiteful knife into her adulterous co-conspirator's back, and revealed the seedy details to his aggrieved wife in a vindictive late-night phone call. Marianne was appalled.

Kath's affair with Dr. Banks didn't upset Marianne nearly as much as the unfortunate event that transpired at the annual office Christmas party that Marianne attended shortly after Kath's drunken boast. It was there that Marianne expressed her sincere apologies to Dr. Bank's wife for her sister's inexcusable actions. Marianne never forgot the stunned look on the aggrieved wife's face, nor the moment when Marianne realized the dishonored wife had no idea that her husband had been unfaithful. Marianne's embarrassed anger nearly exploded when it became abundantly clear that Kath had blatantly lied to her and had never revealed the illicit details to Dr. Bank's wife.

Marianne had long since forgiven Kath, but she had never forgotten Kath's fabricated story that unexpectedly humiliated her in front of her husband's medical office crowd. Kath never spoke about that alcohol-fueled lie and wished it had never been told. She struggled to suppress the tremendous guilt that percolated up whenever she saw her sister.

Kath braced herself for the inner turmoil that frequently surfaced whenever her sister visited and the unintended disruption that out of town guests brought to her secluded domicile. But the recent good news about the fistula buoyed her spirits and helped her prepare for visitors that she'd rather not entertain.

Dressed in her best pajamas, Kath warmly embraced Marianne and Chuck at the front door when they arrived in the late afternoon after a round of golf at the local country club. After a few moments of entryway awkwardness, she graciously accepted an attractive white box handsomely wrapped in a very wide, gold colored ribbon with a single large bow in the center. The guests followed her back to the bedroom as she read the card that said, *"Hope you feel better. Love Mari & Chuck."*

Kath wore a wiry smile under her carefully styled wig and meticulously applied makeup that easily deceived the casual observer as to the true state of her health. She opened the box, which revealed a Neiman Marcus ivory white knee length monogramed bathrobe with the letters *"BKW"* elegantly embroidered into velvety terry cloth. Kath slipped the new robe over her peach colored pajamas and slowly spun herself in a circle as she modeled the new garment which delighted everyone in the room.

Kath slid the empty gift box to the far side of the bed before she pulled the blankets down and log rolled in under the covers. The guests watched her awkward move in muted surprise as they slid their chairs closer to the side of the bed. Kath cheerfully chatted away, absent any ill will that may have been present in the past. Like most siblings who infrequently visited one another, Kath and her sister delighted in fond recollection of the good old days. But their discussion became increasingly guarded as Kath explicitly defined what her gastrointestinal struggles truly implied.

The enormity of that tale fell upon a preoccupied sister, distracted by the negative impact a delayed dinner might have on her husband's long history of diabetes. For a brief moment Marianne stared off into the distance. Then she politely excused herself and discreetly directed her husband to follow her into the kitchen where they discussed her meal plan. She promptly left the house with the promise of a quick return.

Kath fell asleep while Chuck read the local newspaper at the kitchen table. An hour later, Marianne returned with a large, thick-crusted, double cheese and pepperoni pizza. As the activity in the kitchen increased, the clang of dishes and silverware filled the air, along with the unmistakable aroma of pizza that soon wafted all the way into the back bedroom. Kath slowly awoke to that unique scent, which tortured her taste buds and tickled her sense of smell. She tried not to think of the delectable delight that rested in a greasy box just a few yards away.

Kath reminded herself that the fistula had only been closed for a few days and the collection bag had proved to be more of a habit than a necessity. Kath felt lucky to be in that small group of people with fistulas that actually healed, and she felt a bit guilty that she never fully believed what the doctors promised or her astrologer had predicted.

She visualized the melted, yellow-white cheese as it slowly oozed over the side of the thick brown crust. Her hand felt the warmth of that Italian delight while her greasy fingers guided a triangular piece of an aromatic, steamy pizza toward her eagerly opened mouth. She suddenly found herself standing next to the bed. For a brief moment she stood very still as her nose sniffed the air like a hound-dog in hot pursuit of a scent. The unmistakable aroma filled the room around her, and she tried to resist the sudden urge to have just one, small bite.

The dinner chatter abruptly stopped when Kath sat down at the dining room table she had avoided for over six months. She gazed at the pizza like a junkie hypnotically staring at a bag of pure heroin. Kath broke the silence when she asked the group if a small piece of pizza would hurt her. Her brother-in-law-doctor deferred comment but didn't discourage her as Marianne retrieved an extra plate from the cupboard. "Only you can make that choice," I said.

Kath clearly struggled with the moment but signaled her decision when she reached for the smallest piece of pizza and placed it on her plate. While everyone gaped with pizza-filled mouths, all eyes were on Kath as she slid the narrow tip of the pizza into her mouth, chewed it carefully, and then let out an orgasmic groan before she swallowed. And the crowd cheered!

For the first time in months, Kath smiled as she savored another small bite. Everyone at the table felt elated. But after she chewed a fourth bite, Kath quickly leaned toward the table and spit the partially chewed contents out onto the plate. We all watched in stunned silence as her face filed with horror and she ripped opened her new robe. She lifted up her pajama top and stared in utter disbelief as the collection bag filled with masticated pizza. The room fell into thunderous silence as everyone else swallowed in a collective gulp.

The next day Marianne returned to Ann Arbor, while an emotionally distraught Kath retreated into the privacy of her bedroom and waited for the partially digested pizza to pass through the fistula. She blamed herself for the setback and struggled to find a viable path forward. But with no conventional medical options available to her, she pursued the unorthodox alternative therapies she had always embraced.

The healing scent of lavender emanated from a candle powered oil diffuser that burned on her bedside stand. She retrieved a velvet pouch from the desk that contained various quartz crystals. She emptied the contents onto a tray of sea salt that alchemistically removed any negative energy the stones may have accidentally accumulated, and permeated them with a positive dynamism she believed to be conducive to healing.

Kath laid on her bed with her tortured abdomen exposed and stared at the ceiling for a few moments of silent prayer to Airmed, the Celtic god who healed the soldiers who fell in battle. When she had finished her incantation she reached for the stones and placed them in a circle around her abdomen. She resumed her prayers and visualized the beams of energy emanating from the healing stones, penetrating her battered abdomen. The warmth that grew deep within her belly convinced her of the authentic power of the quartz crystals.

Kath initially supplemented her daily quartz crystal ritual with the long-distance Reiki healing techniques from her old friend Jeanne Jesmore who lived in San Diego, but Kath needed a local practitioner. She enlisted the help of Roy Harding, a fellow Reiki master who lived nearby and worked as a nurse in the intensive care unit at the local hospital.

The former Army Ranger medic with an oversized belly stood tall at five-foot-six. He sported a thick black mustache with a long thin ponytail that flowed from a very baldhead. For years, the southern born Vietnam vet had struggled with PTSD, but somehow in the early 80s had stumbled upon sobriety and completed his nursing degree with honors. A self-taught naturopath, Roy mixed his own essential oils and grew the organic herbs he used in his Native American healing rituals that he incorporated into his Reiki practice.

Dressed in her monogramed pajamas, Kath watched as Roy unfolded his massage table in the center of the living room and prepared the therapeutic aromatic oils before he donned his Native American healer's robe for the Reiki ritual. Roy helped Kath onto the tall massage table where she laid back and buried her head into a down-filled pillow.

Roy removed four large clear quartz crystals from a velvet pouch along with a black Raven's feather and put them on the table next to the essential oils. He rubbed the palms of his hands together for a few moments before he hovered his opened palms over the entire collection and offered up a ritualistic prayer to the healing powers of the universe. The chants continued as he rubbed the individual stones between his hands and gently placed them on the four corners of Kath's abdomen with the umbilicus at the center.

With the fingers of both hands, Roy held onto the quill of the black raven feather and offered it up to the sacred powers, much like a Catholic priest holds up a communion wafer, while he silently prayed to the gods of health. He slowly waved the feather over Kath's entire body and circled her abdomen several times before he placed the plume on top of her pajamas near the collection bag. With his stubby fingers spread far apart, Roy rested his opened hands just above the fistula while he quietly chanted his healing prayers. The scent from the essential oils filled the room. After maintaining that position for several minutes, the beads of sweat that quickly formed on Roy's forehead were readily absorbed by the embroidered, American Indian style headband he wore.

Kath believed the thirty-minute Reiki service helped her tremendously, so twice a week for one month they repeated this ritual. But at the end of the final session, the bile continued to ooze through a persistent fistula that still emptied into a collection bag.

It took a few days before Kath cautiously conceded that the curative effects of Reiki energy had completely failed its metaphysical promise. Forced to reassess her long championed esoteric approach, she persistently searched the online medical journals for non-surgical techniques that might close the gastrointestinal fistula. And she found a couple of endoscopic procedures that just might work.

Kath phoned the company representatives for the two different products and struggled to separate fact from fiction as she listened to their sales pitch. One technique used a procedure that passed a uniquely designed fiberoptic camera through the mouth and into the small intestine to the site of the fistula. Once the entrance to the fistula could be fully visualized, the doctor mechanically inserted a fibrin plug into the hole and permanently sealed the fistula. The other procedure inserted a small catheter through the abdominal opening of the fistula and filled the tunnel with a fibrin-based putty that simply plugged up the channel. Before either method would be considered, a baseline radiographic evaluation of the abdominal fistula had to be completed.

Kath waited two weeks before the fluoroscopic fistulagram could be scheduled and another week before Dr. Wilson personally reviewed the results with her in his office. The radiographic tests clearly outlined a single, thin tunnel that originated in the distal part of the jejunum and exited near the umbilicus. Unfortunately, the total distance from the esophagus to the origin of the jejunal fistula exceeded the entire length of the fiberoptic camera, which rendered that particular procedure useless. The radiographic information also suggested that a mass of adhesions had tightly bound the exterior of the intestine to the surface of the abdominal wall. That significantly increased the likelihood of future bowel obstructions and further complicated any attempt to plug the fistula with the putty-like substanc,e which eliminated the second procedure.

Kath hung on Dr. Wilson's every word as he detailed the test results, but her spirits slowly sank when she eventually realized the nonsurgical techniques would never be implemented. She withdrew into herself as he discussed the deleterious effects the large mass of adhesions would eventually have on the small bowel. His mouth formed words that she no longer heard as unpleasant memories from previous multiple intestinal obstructions flooded her mind. But the harsh reality of the moment abruptly returned when she saw that his lips no longer moved, and she heard the uneasy silence of his unanswered question. The whir of the office ventilation fan filled the room as she blinked herself awake. When their eyes finally met he repeated the question, "What do you want to do now?" Without hesitation she pointed to the collection bag that bulged under her dress and said, "Fix this damn thing!"

A Gun to His Head

31

Months after Dr. Donacheck expressed his reluctance to repair the fistula, the dangers of the surgical intervention that he spoke of echoed ominously in Kath's mind. She needed no reminder from Dr. Wilson about the risk of permanent malabsorption syndrome from the surgical removal of damaged intestines, or the possibility of more fistulas if the resected bowel leaked, or the likelihood of peritonitis and the unfortunate consequences of subsequent blood infections. But she also knew she had no choice.

The limited options for surgical repair of the fistula led Kath to return to the University of Arizona Cancer Center in Tucson, where a year earlier she had received care from Dr. Carol Chen, an expert in Borderline Serous Tumor with Low Malignant Potential. Although the recommended chemotherapy had no effect on the tumor, Kath felt so confident in the Medical Center's culture of care that she made an appointment with Dr. Oscar Gomez, an experienced gastroenterologist with a long surgical history of complex fistula repair. Two weeks later we drove the four-hour trip to the University of Arizona Cancer Center in a rented RV.

After Kath registered at the reception desk, we sat in the atrium located at the intersection of three long corridors that led to distant departments. Kath shifted about in a soft chair, nervously protecting the integrity of the collection bag, and watched the multitudes as they navigated their way through the corridors. A young thin nurse with a long blonde ponytail, dressed in crisp blue scrubs, walked toward us while calling out Kath's name. Kath pushed herself up from the chair and politely shook hands with the woman, as the two exchanged personal information.

After leading us into a windowless exam room in the gyne-cological oncological department, the young nurse assured us the doctor would arrive shortly and closed the door as she left. Kath fidgeted with the collection bag when the doorknob jiggled. The heavy door creaked open, and Dr. Gomez entered with his assistant.

The middle age specialist's huge smile revealed straight white teeth beneath a thick black mustache that matched a full head of dark hair with a touch of gray. He walked towards Kath with an out-stretched hand as he introduced himself with a slight Hispanic accent.

Perched on a three-wheeled stool, Dr. Gomez listened care-fully as Kath told her well-rehearsed, complicated story. When she had finished, he helped her up the step stool in front of the exam table, before he lifted her loosely fitted cotton print sundress and exposed the bag as she lay back on the paper lined table.

After washing his hands, he donned a pair of exam gloves, then gently moved his hands around Kath's entire belly as his fin-gers probed deep into her abdomen. He paused for a moment, then asked for permission to remove the collection bag, and carefully peeled off the apparatus. He cleaned the colostomy paste from around the fistula site with a saline-soaked gauze until he could see the tunnel's exit. He stared at the one-millimeter hole for a few mo-ments before he unabashedly announced that the fistula could be successfully repaired with minimal risk.

Kath stared at Dr. Gomez in disbelief as she held a gauze bandage over the fistula, which oozed small amounts of bile. He re-assured her that his conclusions had not been arrived at lightly. The radiographic test results she had mailed to him, combined with the information he gleaned from his physical examination, convinced him the fistula could be successfully repaired.

Surprised at the unexpected news, Kath's mind shut off the outside world as she tried to remember what it felt like to drink an ice-cold glass of water. She visualized herself seated at our dinner table in front of a steaming, full course meal. The doctor's voice sounded far away as he listed the significant surgical risks associated with a laparotomy of this magnitude. But Kath abruptly snapped back to the discussion when she heard him say the surgery could be scheduled in a couple of days. After awkwardly pushing herself up to a sitting position on the exam table, she said, "I need to think about it. Can I call you in a day or two?"

"Sure. There's no hurry." Dr. Gomez replied. "It's important that you're comfortable with your decision. Please call my office if I can help in any way."

Kath smiled an impish grin when they shook hands, but she felt exposed with the sundress hiked above her waist as she waited for him to leave. She watched as he closed the door behind him while I prepared to apply a new collection system with supplies from the emergency medical bag.

She slid off the exam table and checked the integrity of the new bag before she tugged her sundress down and fluffed it back to its natural position. She wiggled the wig with both hands until it felt right on her head, then pulled a small cosmetic kit from the side pocket of her black leather handbag and, with a small flip up mirror, touched up her makeup.

Back in the RV, we sat at the small kitchen table and talked about what Dr. Gomez had said. But we didn't talk for long. The hot desert air made Kath's mouth exceptionally dry, which interfered with her ability to properly enunciate her words.

Physically exhausted, but buoyed by the sudden change in her prognosis, she laid down in the double bed, as thoughts of a normal life danced in her head. Would she really be able to drink ice water again? But the tranquility of the moment remained short lived when thoughts of going through another surgery stiffened her entire body. She stared at the overstuffed medical bag for a few moments before she pulled it toward her and removed the supplies for an intravenous injection of Ativan and injected it through her PICC line. Her anxiety dissipated as the emotional storm abated, and she slipped under the covers for the long trek home.

We awoke the next morning in our own bed, to the chirping sound of the CADD pump alarm that signaled the completion of the overnight TPN infusion. The sun peaked through the bedroom curtains as I gathered the numerous supplies for the daily morning ritual.

The twenty-minute procedure had become so routine that Kath frequently slept right through it. Her eyes slowly opened when I peeled the collection bag from her abdomen, and she looked around the room in a sleepy fog before she put her glasses on the bed and rubbed her eyes awake. After a brief "good morning" smile, she stared solemnly at the ceiling, and in a serene voice said, "I have history with Dr. Donacheck. I trust him and I want him to repair the fistula."

Two weeks later, Kath felt nervously upbeat as we walked through the June heat of a Scottsdale parking lot toward Dr. Donacheck's office and entered the crowded waiting room. Kath leaned against the counter and tried not to stare at the well-dressed occupants seated there, doing their best to not look ill and wondered if she looked as sick they did. She took a seat in the crowded room that slowly emptied before the medical assistant finally escorted us through a familiar hall to Dr. Donacheck's open office door. The doctor shuffled medical papers back into a folder Kath had sent him and smiled as he reached across the desk to shake our hands before he sat back in his large comfortable chair. He listened politely with his hands folded on his lap while Kath briefly detailed the purpose of her visit. When she had finished, he explained his reluctance to do the surgery and ended with the caveat, "If you put a gun to my head, I'll do it."

The room grew uncomfortably quiet as we exchanged unsettled glances. Kath rose from the chair and stood stoically in front of his desk. She rested her hands on the shiny mahogany top and leaned forward. The two silently stared at each other for what seemed like an eternity before she sauntered around to the other side of the desk and towered over the still seated Dr. Donacheck. He looked up as she deliberately placed the pointed barrel of her index finger against his left temple and wiggled her thumb. The doctor reacted with a barely discernible grin before he threw his hands up in surrender and said, "Ok, I'll do it."

The secretary scheduled the surgery for the last week in June, which left Kath little time to prepare. One week later, on June 27, 2011, we arrived at a large medical center in Scottsdale, Arizona, at 5:00 A.M. for an anticipated one-week stay.

Kath leaned back in the passenger seat of the car as we sat in the empty parking lot well ahead of the scheduled appointment. We watched as the morning sky changed from a black, star-lit cosmos to an orange-red canopy that gradually outlined the giant, dark green saguaros that stood like sentinels against the horizon, before she rehtorically asked if she had just witnessed her last sunrise. The tick of the dashboard clock answered the solemnity of the moment as we stared out the windshield and waited for the appointed hour. She tugged at her sundress to allow extra room for the collection bag and fiddled with the PICC line under her right sleeve. Then with hidden trepidation, she looked at me and said, "Okay. Let's go."

The beautiful sunrise painted itself on the building's glass facade as the shadowed silhouette of a couple walking arm-in-arm grew larger on the oversized entry door that opened automatically when we approached. Alone in the center of a deserted lobby, we found our way to the patient registration area, where a hospital employee cheerfully directed us to an open cubicle in a not so busy office.

A heavy-set, middle-aged woman smiled warmly from behind her desk and offered us the seats in front of her as she shuffled a stack of official papers that awaited Kath's signature. Kath maneuvered herself to the front of the chair, but her eyes stared at the clerk's hot cup of coffee and the steam that danced above it before it dissipated into nothingness. With partially closed eyes she leaned forward ever so slightly. Her nostrils flared open as she breathed in the distinct aroma of a dark roast blend.

A loud thump from a stack of papers that landed in the middle of the clerk's desk snapped Kath back to reality. She slid back into an uncomfortable chair and breathed a silent sigh of relief when her hand confirmed the collection bag remained intact under her sundress. She remained distracted by the steamy cup of coffee that rested on the corner of the desk and never heard the clerk's monotonous explanation of each page as she blindly signed the papers that were handed to her.

When the presentation had finally finished, the clerk placed a plastic name band around Kath's wrist, and an elderly volunteer in a pink candy-striped outfit walked us to the pre-op area. We stopped in front of locked, windowless double doors that she opened with the swipe of her hospital badge, and she escorted us into a brightly lit room that housed a dozen gurneys covered with neatly trimmed white sheets. A single green hospital gown had been placed in the center of fluffy pillow that rested at the head of each gurney. We waited by the desk until a young nurse dressed in blue surgical scrubs stepped out from behind a curtain and introduced herself as Kath's pre-op nurse. She checked Kath's wristband for accuracy and retrieved the medical chart from the nurses' station before they both disappeared behind a curtain.

Dressed in a green hospital gown with a blue bouffant surgical cap that covered her stubbled scalp, Kath lay under the sheets while an intravenous antibiotic infused into her PICC line. Dr. Donacheck peeked around the curtain, then offered supportive words and a warm smile. When he left, Kath closed her eyes and visualized herself without a fistula, as a group of nurses moved her to the surgical suite.

Four hours later, Kath arrived in the recovery room and grinned a sleepy smile as she reached over the gurney's rail for my hand. When Dr. Donacheck arrived a short time later, he said the surgery had proved far more complex than he had anticipated. Large portions of Kath's intestine had become attached to the inner abdominal wall, which he had painstakingly separated without tearing the bowel. This had avoided a colostomy, but he could not salvage three feet of jejunal intestine. It took hours to meticulously remove a tangled web of adhesions that ensnared large areas of the intestine that caused Kath's frequent small bowel obstructions. A large bandage covered a stapled vertical incision that traveled from her pubic bone to the sternum right through her belly button.

Kath drifted off as he detailed his post-operative concerns but her eyes snapped open when he declared her abdomen free from tumors. A painful grimace flashed across her face as she leaned up on one elbow and stared directly at Dr. Donacheck before she asked, "What did you say?"

"I scraped out all of the cancer, and I think you'll live," he replied. Dr. Donacheck smiled as he squeezed her hand in a moment of solidarity while the nurses prepared to transfer her to the oncological floor.

As she rode the gurney to the new room, Kath pondered the implications of what Dr. Janicek had said. She tried to understand how a cancer that been resistant to more than a dozen different chemotherapies and remained untreated for over eight months had miraculously disappeared. Her hands moved inquisitively under the sheets as she felt the outline of the oversized abdominal bandage and tried to imagine what it would be like to go to bed without the hum of a CADD pump or experience the sudden leak of bile on the bed sheets.

As the gurney traveled along the hospital corridors, Kath drifted off in the twilight of anesthetic haze and tasted the subtle sweetness of her mother's chocolate cream cake with a dark roast cup of coffee that always complemented it. When she arrived at the room she awoke with a smile as wide as a child's grin in front of a big bowl of ice cream. As the nurses transferred her from the gurney into the bed, Kath felt the serenity of someone who knew they had just cheated death.

Kath's first foray out of bed brought back unpleasant memories of intense pain from previous abdominal surgeries. But after the nurse gave her IV Dilaudid, she literally pushed herself out of bed and grimaced as she clung to the walker and made her way around the oncology unit. By the second day, the pain improved, but the intestinal peristaltic movement failed to materialize. She couldn't eat Jello until the gurgle of bowel sounds returned.

Dr. Donacheck reminded Kath that she hadn't had a bowel movement since the fistula had first formed eight months ago, and the desiccated stool that still occupied the colon needed to be evacuated. The chronic use of opioids for pain control interfered with the normal resumption of peristalsis and exacerbated the constipation. He discussed various alternatives that might resolve that problem, but he listened carefully when Kath suggested Methylnaltrexone, a new drug that instantly blocked the anti-peristaltic effects of opioids and quickly restored the normal movement of stool through the intestine.

Dr. Donacheck agreed with her suggestion. A short time later the nurse injected the drug subcutaneously in Kath's abdomen, but as the clock ticked on with no immediate resolution, an aura of disappointment descended upon the room. The nurse shuffled in place as she discussed alternative therapies for severe constipation.

After several minutes the conversation suddenly stopped when Kath's eyes grew unexpectedly wide and her face expressed a panicked surprise. Bewildered by the strange sensations that came from deep inside her abdomen, she jumped off the bed and grabbed the IV pole. She pushed past the nurse on her way to the bathroom and slammed the door behind her.

Wow!

The sudden revival of the peristaltic movement signaled unclogged intestines and heralded a return to a life Kath thought had been lost forever. She no longer took for granted the everyday joys of eating or drinking. She savored the robust flavor of a morning cup of coffee while the taste of French toast smothered in butter nearly brought her to tears. Her improved nutritional status rendered the TPN or any IV's unnecessary. As her strength returned, she no longer needed the walker for the laps around the nursing unit. Nearly a week after surgery, the signs of better health appeared everywhere. In the morning, as warm water dripped down her freshly washed face, she stared into the bathroom room mirror with a careful grin and dared to believe the nightmare might finally be over.

She exited the washroom in her pajamas with a colorful headscarf neatly cinched behind her head, which complemented the monogramed blue terrycloth bathrobe that she tied around her waist. She reached for my hand, and we casually strolled the crowded corridors. We stopped in front of the large windows at the hospital's entrance and gazed at the desert landscape lit by the colorful morning sun before Kath silently thanked an invisible power for a second chance at life.

Later, we ambled through the gift shop and looked at things Kath didn't really want before returning to the room in time to watch her favorite midday soap opera, *The Bold and the Beautiful*. As the night slowly replaced the day, we stared out the fourth-floor window and held each other in a long-forgotten embrace, as the local Fourth of July fireworks lit up the sky.

Kath slept well that night and felt rested when Dr. Donacheck's morning rounds interrupted her breakfast routine. He seemed pleased with her progress but expressed concern over a slight increase in her white blood cell count that he noticed in her morning blood work. This suggested a possible infection.

He apologized for an interrupted meal as he moved the tray table off to the side and lowered the head of the bed. He gently lifted her pajama top, which exposed an oversized bandage. He placed a stethoscope on her abdomen and smiled at the symphony of bowel sounds that gurgled in her belly before he gently pressed around the dressing. He carefully removed the heavily taped bandage, which exposed her stapled abdomen and gently pressed along the incision line when a barely discernible look of concern flashed across his unflappable face. He reached for the staple remover that he had placed next to her food tray and opened a pack of sterile gauze that he balanced on her abdomen.

Kath's jaw tightened. A sense of dread flooded over her as he briefly explained the obvious plan to remove the staples. Flat on her back, she stared at the ceiling and couldn't see the small stream of yellow fluid that oozed out from the open wound after he removed the first staple. But when he removed the rest of them, a tsunami of yellow pus flowed out from the bottom third of the newly opened incision. Her nose sniffed the air and quickly recognized the distinctive scent of putrid pus that filled the room. Dr. Donacheck sopped up the purulent fluid with a sterile gauze as Kath pushed up on her elbows to see what had happened. But her head quickly fell back on the pillow in shocked disbelief as her eyes stared blankly into space in a moment of deja vu. She closed her eyes tightly, and after a deep sigh muttered, "Not again!"

Dr. Donacheck packed the newly dehisced hole with sterile gauge and taped a large bandage over it while Kath lay there dumbfounded. He returned the equipment to the bedside tray before he sat on the side of the bed and offered his theory on why the wound had opened up.

Dr. Donacheck explained the extensive nature of the abdominal surgery set into motion an exaggerated series of events that culminated in another infected superficial dehiscence. He predicted the wound vac would totally close the abdominal wound in less than two months but recommended a visit from an infectious disease specialist. Kath's eyes watched Dr. Donacheck's mouth form the words, but she never really heard them as her mind drifted away and struggled to comprehend this latest setback. She had survived a high-risk surgery with all of her bodily functions intact. That, by itself, seemed unbelievable, but to have an abdomen free of cancerous tumors bordered on miraculous. So, in light of all that, this temporary setback seemed very minor.

She awoke from her trance when Dr. Donacheck said that she would probably be home in a couple of days. She smiled, raised herself up on an elbow, and thanked him for everything. He reciprocated with a warm smile and patted her hand, but when he left the room her head flopped back on the pillow in a semi-dazed state.

Later that afternoon, a nurse arrived with all the necessary supplies for the wound vac's airtight seal, and once again the familiar but subtle sound of the machine's rhythmic click played in the background as she settled in for the night.

Kath slept soundly under the thin hospital sheets, but she stirred early the next morning when the door creaked opened and muffled footsteps of soft-soled shoes stopped at her bed. She sensed a presence standing next to her. She looked up through sleepy eyes at a tall, attractive young woman with long, dark blonde hair tied in a ponytail. "Hi. I'm Dr. Schroeder, the infectious disease doctor," she said, with a broad, confident smile.

Kath squinted to read the blurred embroidered name on the white lab coat before she reached for her glasses. She sat up in the bed just in time to see the doctor toss the paper towel she had used to dry her newly washed hands into a garbage can several feet away. "Two points," the doctor exclaimed. Then she reached over the bedrail to shake Kath's hand.

Kath smiled a wide grin at the doctor's unorthodox introduction, and the two instantly bonded as they talked more about the joys of life than the dangers of an infected dehiscence. Dr. Schroeder's contagiously cheery persona helped Kath relax, as the doctor carefully inspected the area around the tightly sealed wound and the fluid that drained though the vacuum tubing. She leaned against the bedrail and declared the contaminated wound could be successfully treated with Zyvox, an expensive oral antibiotic, while the dehiscence would be a small detour on Kath's road to recovery. "I can't speculate as to how your abdomen became infected," she said on the way to the sink. "But you should be able to go home tomorrow," as she dried her hands with paper from the dispenser. Kath flashed a happy smile at the news when Dr. Schroeder spun around in basketball-type fashion and tossed the balled-up paper into a distant trashcan. "Two points," Kath yelled as the doctor waved good-bye.

Anxious to go home, Kath stared into the small, flipped-up mirror tucked into the bedside stand and carefully applied her makeup to a face that no longer seemed worried. Her combed-out wig looked as natural as could be, and her colorful sundress that replaced the drab, itchy hospital gown made her look more like a visitor than a patient, except for the drain tube that curled out from under her dress to the nearby vacuum pump that pulsated at her feet.

The discharge nurse arrived with a wheelchair to take Kath to the hospital exit while I retrieved the car. As we traveled back to

Sedona along the I-17 high desert corridor, the dark cloud of desperation that frequently followed Kath after nearly every oncological visit had been replaced by a strong sense of unbridled optimism. She believed the cancer that had stalked her for over a decade had finally been vanquished, and the sense of dread that permeated her soul had been replaced by a near manic state of euphoria.

When she walked in the front door of our home, the metastatic memories of the last dozen years flashed before her eyes. The sudden avalanche of emotions left her momentarily stunned as she stood in the living room and held the wound vac tightly in her hand. She shook her head in dubious disbelief that the nightmare had finally ended.

Ziggy ended Kath's brief inner sojourn when he meowed his way around her legs and flopped down on the floor for more attention. When she stroked his silky-smooth fur, Kath felt the same emotional tranquility that other cancer patients experienced from their therapy pets. For almost a year, Ziggy had been by her side in the confines of the bedroom infirmary helping her cope with the insanity of the fistula. Now he followed her to the kitchen and sat next to her while she rummaged through the refrigerator.

"I think I'll make a grilled cheese sandwich," she announced, promptly collecting the appropriate ingredients. The wound vac hummed along on the floor as she carefully buttered the outside of the bread and filled the inner layer with a mild cheddar cheese. Kath carried both the wound vac and the dinner plate to the table and settled in to the same chair she had occupied on that disastrous night months ago when the pizza oozed out of the fistula. Smiling broadly as the flavor of her favorite food thundered over her taste buds and the melted cheese dribbled down her cheeks, she closed her eyes and savored every bite.

For months, the constant horror of the fistula had sometimes given way to a sudden surge of panic that sent her heart racing. But since the surgery, an uneasy calm had replaced that deep intangible fear. Suddenly, the subtle joys of life exploded all around her. The aromatic scent of fresh coffee filled the house every morning, and a French toast breakfast soon became the norm. Her expertise at securing a watertight seal over the abdominal wound allowed daily showers that lasted until the hot water ran out. She ignored the suction tubing that remained connected to the wound vac parked on the floor, next to the bathtub. The collar on her blue terrycloth bathrobe still bore the hair dye stains from years ago when she last colored her hair, but the towel that wrapped around her wet head no longer collected the displaced clumps of lost hair. The blow dryer gave what little hair she had some body, as she brushed out the tangles. But she smiled when those twisted strands remained securely anchored to her scalp. She shunned the pajamas during the day and usually selected a loose skirt or sundress that easily accommodated the suction tube and a long sleeve blouse that hid the PICC line in her upper right arm.

A fully visible suction tube connected to an even more obvious machine detracted from any outfit she tried to wear and tested her self-esteem whenever she ventured out from her cloistered world. But she always enjoyed a visit to the local Merle Norman store in Sedona whenever she replenished her cosmetic supplies.

When Kath entered the familiar boutique, she waved to the elderly store manager. Darlene greeted her like an old friend and smiled warmly as they exchanged a hearty handshake. Kath placed the wound vac on the floor and checked the integrity of the suction tubing before she sat on a tall, padded swivel chair in front of the glass display case.

A large professional makeup mirror reflected Kath's magnified image, and she gasped at the numerous facial wrinkles that were completely indiscernible to the casual observer. She busily brushed, dabbed, and polished her face with the various products that Darlene set in front of her until she had achieved just the right look.

Darlene's soon spoke about her husband's ill health and the reality of her forced retirement as the cash register rang up the selected supplies. Kath nonchalantly swiveled the oversized chair from side-to-side but abruptly stopped moving when she realized that Darlene wanted to sell the store at a bargain price.

Kath's previous experience with Arbonne skin care products and the entrepreneurial spirit she'd inherited from her father set her mind in a whirl. She imagined herself behind the counter actively engaged in the business of personal care products until she stood up to pay the bill. The unexpected tug from an over stretched suction tube reminded her of the precarious state of her health.

They each forced a smile as they said their goodbyes. Kath slowly walked away but stopped at the end of the counter and instinctively looked over her shoulder. Their eyes met in a deep, intuitive gaze that acknowledged their uncertainties before she exited through the large glass door.

The emotional milestone of our thirtieth wedding anniversary quickly supplanted the melancholic memory of her cosmetological friend as Kath busily prepared for our anticipated celebratory dinner date at Cucina Rustica, an expensive restaurant in our small town. The outfits that she had bought from her favorite online retailers like The Pyramid Collection hung neatly in her closet while the new cosmetics occupied a significant portion of her bathroom vanity countertop.

When September 4th arrived, Kath finished her makeup and selected an ankle length white on pink satin, pleated skirt. Then she chose a dark, tight fitting, long-sleeved cotton pullover sweater that covered the PICC line but accentuated her figure. She scrutinized her attire in front of the full-length mirror and concluded the ensemble looked great if she ignored the suction tube that trailed out from under her skirt.

The restaurant's maître d smiled warmly at our early arrival and congratulated us on our anniversary before he cheerfully escorted us through a well-dressed crowd toward two open bar stools in a softly lit cocktail lounge to await an open table. Kath tucked the wound vac snuggly under the chair before she cautiously scaled the extra tall barstool and breathed a sigh of relief when the suction tube safely bridged the distance.

Confident the abdominal dressing remained intact, she placed her embossed leather clutch purse on the ornately carved mahogany bar and ordered a flute of Moet Chandon. Kath gently swirled the exotic contents of the tall glass with the air of a sommelier and aptly sniffed its rich bouquet. When the maître d called us for our table, Kath finished the last of the champagne in one giant gulp and returned the emptied flute to the bar.

Kath grabbed her purse as she slid off the stool and avoided stepping on the suction tube but felt self-conscious when she reached under the chair for the wound vac. Embarrassed by a machine that pneumatically chimed out a rhythmic beat for all to hear, she sheepishly looked around the busy room and expected condescending stares from the upper crust crowd. Much to her surprise, no one noticed or cared. She held the wound vac at her side while the suction tube dangled under her skirt, then walked with perfect posture through a maze of occupied tables as she followed the maître d. When we arrived at our table, the neighboring diners continued with their hushed conversations but discretely watched as Kath set the suction machine under the table.

The joy of the moment displaced all of her worried thoughts about the future and the past retreated into the distant background of her mind as she sipped another glass of champagne and slowly savored a medium-rare filet mignon. Her fully restored digestive tract reacted with quiet delight as she savored a full course meal, but the first bite of the tiramisu triggered an audible groan that turned heads from the neighboring tables.

Utterly surprised at the pleasant feeling of a full stomach, she slowly slid her chair back from the table and used a white linen napkin to wipe away the smeared desert from the corner of her mouth. Kath leaned back in her chair and slowly sipped the last of the champagne as she visualized a life free from cancer, which evoked a huge grin that the waiter mistook for anniversary bliss.

Kath politely accepted the waiter's congratulatory wish as he placed the dinner receipt on the table. As she prepared to leave the restaurant, she reached under the table for the wound vac but lingered a moment with the machine nestled on her lap before she stood up and maneuvered her way through the crowd toward the exit.

The next morning Kath awoke to the sound of a wound vac in a bedroom that looked like an infirmary and prepared for the routine replacement of the abdominal dressing. The wound vac ritual had occurred every morning since the surgery and continued unabated for the next few weeks while the wound grew steadily smaller. Eventually, a small sterile gauze bandage replaced the need for the machine and marked a historic moment in her oncological journey.

She never forgot how a dirty hospital shower stall contaminated Dr. Freeman's uncovered and open surgical incision with the virulent strain of Methicillin-Resistant Staphylococcus Aureus (MRSA). She avoided any baths after Dr. Donacheck's surgery, but once the wound had fully closed she duct-taped a strip of Saran Wrap around the PICC line in her right upper arm which created a water tight seal. Then she gathered all of the necessary supplies for a well-deserved hot bath.

She hung her blue robe on the small hook behind the bathroom door and lit the scented candles placed on the side of the tub before she carefully stepped into the steaming hot water. She submerged herself as her right arm carefully rested on the tub's rim and sighed with delight as her tense body immediately relaxed. Through closed eyes, she watched the flickering flames of the candles and whiffed their subtle aroma, as she lay motionless in a tub of tranquility. She was mesmerized by the subtle sound of water as it gently splashed about the tub, and her troubles slowly melted away. She remained in that blissful state for some time before she washed herself with the scented soap. But something felt wrong when her fingertips followed the full length of the distinctive abdominal surgical scar, and her eyes snapped open in alarm. She sat up so quickly that the water splashed over the tub wall and nearly extinguished the candles.

She stared at her abdomen through the soapy water until she saw what her fingers had felt. She had no belly-button. She jumped up in disbelief and carefully inspected her button-less abdomen as the bathwater sloshed back and forth beneath her. She leapt out of the tub, and the water poured from her body onto the floor as she ran to the nearest mirror. Her heart pounded as she leaned against the counter and stared in disbelief at the image of an alien abdomen while the water pooled at her feet.

Fixated in front of the mirror, she was totally aghast until she remembered her conversation with Dr. Donacheck. She'd forgotten that months earlier Dr. Donacheck had casually mentioned that he'd surgically removed her umbilicus, as he feared it might inadvertently infect the abdominal incision. The ever-present wound dressing had concealed that part of her abdomen which kept the umbilical area out of sight and out of mind until she sat in the bathtub.

Frozen in front of the mirror, Kath tried not to be overwhelmed by the peculiar nature of what she saw. She began giggling uncontrollably when she visualized herself in a bikini, reclining on a lounge chair at a crowded pool, holding a glass of champagne.

For the price of a belly-button she had her life back. And to Kath, that transaction seemed more than fair.

33
That's It?

Kath stared into the familiar desert landscape that zoomed by her passenger side window and pondered the possibilities of a cancer-free life as we traveled the two-hour drive to Dr. Schroeder's Phoenix office. We strolled across the asphalt parking lot on a warm October day and breathed a sigh of relief when we entered the air-conditioned office. Kath greeted Helen, the receptionist, with a warm smile of recognition. The two exchanged personal pleasantries while Helen updated Kath's insurance information.

Suddenly, the front door of the office burst open, and Dr. Schroeder scampered in. A blast of hot air blew through the room as she muttered to herself about the unusually warm autumn weather. Trying not to drop the stack of papers she was carrying, Dr. Schroeder abruptly stopped her rhetorical monologue when she looked up and found herself next to Kath. She quickly placed the stack of papers on the countertop and embraced Kath in a way that warmly acknowledged their personal history. They talked and laughed their way down the hall like old friends before they detoured into the examination room.

Kath lifted her blouse with one hand and pulled the waist-band of her pants down with the other, displaying a well-healed scar and a conspicuously absent belly button. Dr. Schroeder felt the scar and palpated Kath's abdomen before she declared the wound completely healed. But she couldn't resist the temptation to joke about the obvious. "Well, I hope you're not into navel rings," she said, as Kath looked up at her in feigned shock. "Hey, I know," Dr. Schroeder said, "You can go as a belly dancer for Halloween."

"Don't even joke about it," Kath humorously chastised her. "Last Halloween I had tampons tucked firmly in that fistula hole. I looked like a hermaphrodite with a misplaced cotton penis." They stared at each other for an uncomfortable moment before Dr. Schroeder said, "Wow, that's weird." And they erupted in simultaneous laughter. "But the good news," she continued, "is the PICC line can be removed."

Kath extended her right arm, and Dr. Schroeder immediately peeled away the sterile dressing. The doctor listened carefully while Kath shared her worries about whether the cancer had been truly vanquished. The doctor refused to opine on the subject and quickly removed the two-foot-long catheter from her arm.

Kath immediately stopped talking. Her eyes grew wide as she anxiously watched for the tail of the catheter to finally exit her arm. Dr. Schroeder placed the catheter on a nearby tray and held a sterile gauze over the exit site while she talked about the need to keep the site clean. Then she said there would be no need for a follow-up visit unless some unexpected complications developed. After a few minutes, Dr. Schroeder dressed the IV site with a small sterile bandage and said, "That's it."

Kath stared at the lifeless catheter that lay on the stainless-steel table, surprised that the decades-long cancer struggle had ended with so little fanfare and wondered whether that was truly "it." She swung her arm around in a giant circle, like a baseball player about to deliver a windmill pitch, and smiled at the unencumbered motion. Kath threw her arms around Dr. Schroeder in a warm embrace when suddenly her stomach gurgled so loud that they instinctively lurched away from each other. Their eyes remained locked in a gaze of mutually embarrassed surprised before they surreptitiously giggled at the obvious acknowledgment of an overactive gastrointestinal tract. They exchanged another polite hug and said good bye.

The excessive heat that had built up inside our closed car did little to erase Kath's irrepressible grin. A tempered euphoria followed her back to Sedona. She felt confident that even if the slow growth tumor returned it would take years, if not decades, before it would threaten her life again.

Happy to be back in her kitchen, Kath inventoried the contents of the refrigerator while Ziggy meowed his way around her legs. She closed the refrigerator door and petted her furry friend, marveling at the freedom she felt without the anchor of a PICC line or a wound vac.

She walked toward the bedroom but abruptly stopped in its doorway and stared into a room that bore the scars of an epic life and death struggle. Debris from that battle remained strewn about the room, with medical supplies stacked in every corner. Eventually, she discarded all of the supplies and transformed the infirmary back into a bedroom, as she tried to resume a life that had been nearly forgotten.

The recuperative nature of the next few months helped re-establish the everyday habits that, on the surface, seemed mundane but provided a sense of normalcy and kept the thought of cancer at a forgettable distance.

The days before Thanksgiving heralded the arrival of the Holiday Season with plenty to be thankful for. Kath wanted to prepare a special dinner. She bought a fresh turkey with all the trimmings from the local health food store and stocked up on ingredients for the many family recipes that she planned to make from scratch. She searched the stores until she found an embroidered linen tablecloth with just the right backdrop for her formal dinnerware and complemented the elegant silver she'd inherited from Grandma Wilson.

She celebrated that Thanksgiving morning with a freshly brewed cup of coffee and sat at the kitchen table relaxing in her pajamas while she studied the recipes her mother had written decades before on paper that had long since yellowed. A wistful smile spilled over her face as she fondly remembered the Holiday dinners at the Wilson family farm with relatives who had passed away.

She basted the turkey as it roasted in the oven and expertly juggled the assorted dishes that simmered away on the various burners. The scent of a delicious dinner wafted throughout the house while the music of Chris Spheeris played softly in the background. When the food neared completion, Kath shed her jeans for a more formal look and proceeded to serve up a culinary feast that filled the table.

Like an artist who searched for imperfections in her work, Kath slowly surveyed the entire length of the Thanksgiving table and offered an approving grin before she sat down on a formal Asian-designed rosewood dining chair with a white linen napkin on her lap. She paused for a moment of silent prayer, then held her Wedgewood Kutani Crane bone china dinner plate in one hand and filled it with samples from every dish until it nearly overflowed. Her hands rested on the table in true Emily Post fashion as her taste buds experienced a gustatory explosion. She proceeded to savor every bite as if it would be her last.

Our dinner conversation remained light and centered on the critiques of the food. She didn't talk about the cancer or TPN or fistula surgeries or the dozen different chemotherapies that she had lived through, or any of the previous holidays. To Kath, the past remained just that, while the future shimmered in a distant promised land that had yet to be navigated. On this particular occasion, she simply lived in the moment.

Kath returned to the buffet three more times and ate more food in a single sitting than she'd ever consumed in her life. When she finally finished, her belly felt incredibly distended. She leaned back in her chair and slowly pushed herself away from the table.

The previous holiday season had left her with a detached surrender, which nearly overwhelmed her. She had not expected to see another Christmas. Photographs from that time captured a resilient spirit who defiantly smiled at her perceived fate while this Christmas season offered the unimaginable gift of a victory over cancer. In celebration, she canceled all of her medical appointments for December. For the first time years, she felt a sense of control over her life.

Her physical ailments had finally mended but her soul remained bruised as she struggled to find the spiritual balance in her life. She became increasingly reflective as the Holiday Season progressed. She preferred the classic music of her youth instead of the usual carols when she decorated the Christmas tree with ornaments that dated back more than thirty years and dozens of small red-velvet bows that she made years ago. She carefully unfurled her mother's home-made tree skirt that had adorned the Wilson family Christmas tree for years and completed the scene.

Kath believed in the Christmas story and always said "Jesus was a Capricorn," but the Eastern philosophy espoused by Paramahansa Yogananda of the Self Realization Fellowship shared an equal space in her mind. For as long as Kath could remember, she had harbored a relentless desire to see God, and that single passion always guided her never-ending spiritual quest. She resumed the SRF meditation techniques and enthusiastically dovetailed those scientific methods with her own Catholic practices.

The ecclesiastical rituals of the Catholic Church had long fascinated Kath, and the Christmas Season certainly offered a myriad of opportunities to experience those holiday customs. Each morning she lit the ceremonial candles of the Advent wreath and read the relevant scriptures before she completed a thirty-minute meditation with selected chants from Paramahansa Yogananda while Ziggy competed for her attention.

She regularly practiced some form of spiritual invocation to a higher power but never asked for, or expected, a miraculous intervention. Although Kath did not believe in predestination, she did believe her karma would be played out exactly as the universe intended, but she had to know the final scene.

Kath filled her days with metaphysical techniques that purported to diviniate the future. She carefully studied the computer-generated astrological charts that cluttered her desk for clues that might be hidden amongst the stars and planets. But the cryptic information she gleaned tended to be ambiguous. She turned to the mysteries of the Tarot to gain some insight into her destiny. She removed her deck of Rider-Waite cards from a purple, velvet pouch packed with small quartz crystals that protected them from negative energies. Sitting cross-legged on the bed, she rubbed a large pink quartz crystal stone between her palms. She then closed her eyes and shuffled the deck, concentrating on the one question that dominated her thoughts.

For three straight nights, she peeled the cards from the top of the deck and laid them in front of her until the Celtic Cross pattern had been fully populated. She placed the remainder of the cards in a neat stack in front of her, then leaned back and carefully studied the messages that the array of colorful cards secretly whispered. Each night the cards of the Tower and the World appeared in the same specific positions on the Celtic Spread. This suggested an end to the cycle of life, and that freaked her out. She abruptly stopped the readings and returned all the cards to their purple pouch. And she never read them again.

On the second Sunday of Advent, Kath wrote Christmas cards. But as the evening progressed, she struggled with the message. She had lost regular contact with most of the people on the list and only communicated with them once a year. After all she had gone through, a cheery note inside the card seemed insincere. She thought about the family Christmas celebrations in the snowy Michigan winters, but most of her relatives had been dead for years. She rarely saw her two surviving sisters, and that left her a bit despondent.

Kath never felt truly close to any one individual. She constantly struggled to cross the great divide of intimacy, and her disdain for small talk compounded the problem. Kath willingly shared certain parts of herself with others, but a fear of absolute honesty prevented the emotional closeness true friends share. She preferred to live in her head where it felt safe. And, as mentioned before, she unabashedly embraced the Greta Garbo line, "I vant to be alone."

Kath resumed her embrace of the Wiccan philosophy and joined an online Wiccan group under the pseudonym of Morgaine Silverhawk. She regularly chatted with her fellow Wiccans but thought of herself as a solitary practitioner. She prepared for the Celtic ceremony of Yule and gathered the robes, chalices, sacred knives, and all the paraphernalia required. But, the Yule log remained the key item on the list. However, the Wiccan custom clearly stated that the log must either have been harvested from the householder's land, or given as a gift... it must never be bought, and she had no idea where to find one. Our property had no logs to harvest, and she knew of no one to ask for a "Yule Log." But she traveled to Crystal Magic anyway, convinced the universe would provide.

She drove the deserted Red Rock highway to Sedona but screeched to a halt when she rounded a bend and stared through the windshield in disbelief at a single oversized piece of firewood lying in the middle of the empty road. She leapt out of the car and scooped up her new found Yule log, but lingered on the highway for a brief moment to silently thank the gods for their timely gift.

Kath celebrated the Winter Solstice in the privacy of her bedroom in true Wiccan fashion. A green cloth adorned her altar with a mistletoe wreath next to a small cauldron that stood in the center of a circle of twelve sacred stones and the Yule log, with white, red, and green tapered candles that fit snuggly into the holes that she drilled. She recited the ceremonial incantations dressed in her long, hooded robe, and she felt very energized when she waved her mystical wand as she invoked her spells. When the ceremony had finished, she stood alone in front of the altar unable to share her delight with anyone.

When Christmas finally arrived, it felt anticlimactic, as Kath spent most of her time alone in bed, cuddled under the blankets with the biography of Freddy Mercury. She read countless books on the rock stars of her day, but she felt irrepressibly intrigued with the profound dichotomy of the singer's personality and couldn't put the book down. She closely identified with the introverted aspects of his private life that contrasted sharply with his wild sexual escapades and flamboyant stage persona. She shared his heartbreaking loneliness and understood the tragedy of his unrequited love for Mary Austin, his former live-in girlfriend. But more importantly, she perceived an emptiness in herself that she believed could only be filled by an elusive perfect love she forever sought but felt she had never found.

We celebrated Kath's sixtieth birthday with a simple dinner followed by the opening of a few gifts. But the double CD of *Queen's Greatest Hits* clearly proved to be the gift that she liked the most. The music blared at full volume as Kath swayed to the beat of the many famous tunes. She gleefully flung her arms about in rhythmic fashion until she suddenly stopped and became somber, as she sat crossed-legged in front of the stereo while the music vibrated the house. She tilted her head back and lifted her eyes to the heavens, silently absorbing every word in the song as the music boomed across the room. Her eyes welled up and tears streamed down her face as she lip-synched the words, "Can anybody find me.....Somebody To Love," from Freddy Mercury's hit song.

She rarely displayed such emotion and felt a bit embarrassed when she wiped her cheeks dry with the back of her hand. Once the song had finished, she offered a sad smile before she excused herself and went to bed.

Her emotional doldrums lasted for a few days. But in the early morning of New Year's Day she emerged from a self-imposed exile dressed in her pajamas. We chatted over a cup of coffee at the kitchen table like we had for the last thirty years, as if nothing had happened. Her fork swirled the last piece of French toast in the pure maple syrup that pooled at the bottom of the plate. She chewed the final bite with obvious ecstasy while she relived the oral history of her favorite breakfast cuisine.

She held the oversized coffee cup with both hands and sipped the dark roast blend as she spoke fondly of past New Year's Eves. But she heartily laughed when she recalled the ballroom dance contest that we inadvertently had crashed many years ago at the San Diego Convention Center.

We had spontaneously attended the very prim affair. We sat at a large formal dinner table with sixty-year-old female contestants who unabashedly tried to recapture their youth with predacious young male dance-school gigolos, who clearly loved their dance partners' money. Their candid conversations embarrassed us, as the matrons fawned over their part-time paramours while the magisterial dancers with numbers pinned on their backs promenaded around the dance floor. We watched in dumbfounded disbelief as the desperate dreams of those mature women unfolded before our eyes, while the blatant unapologetic hedonism of the male youth remained poignantly displayed for all to see.

Kath refilled her coffee and shook her head, remembering the triteness of their behavior, and said, "I wonder how the granny dancers would manage life with cancer, and if their young escorts would be their willing caregivers?"

Kath strongly believed that no one should face cancer alone. She had befriended many chemo patients whose daughters, grand-daughters, or sisters had helped with their care. But she had curiously observed that the male species remained mostly absent.

She leaned against the kitchen counter and smiled at me over the rim of her coffee mug. Holding the cup with one hand, she hugged me with the other and whispered, "You've always been there for me, even though you didn't have to be." Her eyes misted up. She twirled around with her head tilted back and her arms outstretched with the coffee cup in her hand but never spilled a drop, then she disappeared into the bedroom.

Kath's buoyant charm, bolstered by the continued absence of various tubes and dressings, encouraged those around her to be optimistic about her future. But they didn't know, nor did she share, that her appetite had gradually decreased and that her abdomen felt mildly bloated.

No Way

Kath reluctantly ended the month-long healthcare sabbatical and found herself in Dr. Wilson's exam room where she awaited his physical evaluation. She giggled when he burst through the door in his usual Cosmo Kramer fashion. He sat on a three-wheel-stool and then pushed himself across the room with his feet up in the air as he rolled up next to her chair.

He held her hand with both of his as he looked into Kath's eyes, studied her face, and listened intently while she updated him on her current state of affairs. Kath explained with a smile her need for the holiday hiatus, but she quickly lost her cheerful grin when she conceded that the time for a medical follow up had arrived. She told him about her diminished appetite and the uncomfortable bloated sensation within her abdomen, which she attributed to mild constipation. Dr. Wilson had concerns but kept them to himself when he handed her a prescription for blood work. The next day she went to the local laboratory for blood samples and then found her way back to the familiar Imaging Center in Scottsdale for yet another PET-CT scan.

She returned to Dr. Wilson's office a week later and sat nervously in the exam room. He entered the room in an uncharacteristically subdued fashion with a number of papers clutched in his hand. He sat ominously silent next to her and leaned forward with a poker face that spoke volumes. Kath took a quick, deep breath and held it for a few seconds. Her eyes welled up at the unspoken results that she already knew.

The CA-125 had jumped four-fold since the last test, and the radiology scan confirmed what the cancer marker suggested. The disease had aggressively returned and had spread beyond her abdomen. It had metastasized to her liver and lungs where it had never been seen before. The hum of the ventilation fans broke the uneasy silence in the exam room as Kath sat back in her chair with her hands on her lap. Her mind whirled as she tried to focus her thoughts. She instinctively placed her right hand over her mouth, and the air hissed through her fingers as she took a reflexive, deep breath while she stared blankly into space. Dr. Wilson was fidgeting in his chair still holding the test result, when she turned toward him and said, "No Way!" He suggested a return to Dr. DeMarco in Sedona for further chemotherapy, but Kath knew she needed to start with Dr. Donacheck, the one oncological doctor she trusted above all others.

In early February, we once again found ourselves parked in the lot at Dr. Donacheck's Scottsdale office. Several months before, his surgical skills had saved her life, but she doubted he could once again be the magician she desperately needed. She knew the cancer had spread beyond the reach of his surgical knife. And based on the numerous chemo failures in the past, she had little confidence conventional drug therapy would be any more successful. She left open the possibility that a clinical trial might deliver her from this metastatic mess that she suddenly found herself in. She took a deep breath followed by a long sigh before we walked toward the office and sat in Dr. Donacheck's waiting room, filled with women of all ages who shared one thing in common.

The colorful headscarves covering the baldheads belonged to those who had undergone chemotherapy, and their upbeat demeanor usually camouflaged how awful they felt. Those with stubbled scalps and a semblance of regrowth happily telegraphed that they had completed chemotherapy, but lived in constant fear the cancer would return. But those with full heads of well-styled hair knew they had an inescapable date with an alopecic drug.

We watched the anxious reactions of the occupants when the nurse stood at the office door and trumpeted out a name. The respondent and their entourage slowly made their way through the gateway of hope that led to the rest of the office. It took a while before those same clients exited through the same door, but at a quicker pace, clearly anxious to return to the safety of their own homes, leaving behind the harsh realities of an oncological office. The waiting area eventually emptied and we soon found ourselves alone in the spacious room, with smooth jazz playing softly overhead. Soon the nurse stood in the open doorway and beckoned Kath to come in.

She escorted Kath to the exam room and asked that all of her clothing be removed, as she handed her a thin yellow paper gown that did little to keep her warm in the air-conditioned room. She lay on the exam table and restlessly stared at the ceiling while she mentally rehearsed what she wanted to tell Dr. Donacheck. When the door clicked open she recognized the footsteps that abruptly stopped next to her. She nervously looked up from the table as Dr. Donacheck gently reached for her hand and greeted her in a voice that calmed her frantic mind.

At a time when cancer remission seemed only a distant hope, she drew strength from his strong presence and calmly described the cascade of symptoms. He lifted the paper gown, exposing her abdomen, and smiled when he saw a belly without a button.

"Your incision healed nicely," he said. "And I doubt it would have if your umbilicus had remained."

"I look like an alien," Kath replied. "I stand in the shower and my belly's flat. There's nothing there. When I look in the mirror, I feel like a freak. I'm embarrassed. It's a body image thing, you know? You'd think I'd be over that with the fistula, the tampons, the collection bags, the bile, and pizza oozing out of holes. Who doesn't have a belly button?"

"Karolina Kurkova," he replied.

"Who's that?" she asked.

"A Victoria Secret model," he said. "She had it removed as an infant, and her belly looks just like yours."

"Well, lucky her," she retorted.

He slid his hands over Kath's midsection in a massage type motion, and she gave a short gasp when he pushed his fingertips firmly into her belly as he searched for abnormalities. She watched his eyes for any expressions that hinted at what he had discovered, but she was disappointed when he revealed no clues. He then rubbed the working end of the stethoscope between his palms and warmed it up before he asked her to sit up so he could listen to her lungs. Next, he examined her pupils and placed his hands around her neck while his fingers searched for something that his eyes couldn't see. He spoke very little as he conducted the remainder of the physical exam, but when he had finished he asked her to get dressed and meet him in his office

The nurse escorted Kath through the hallway maze and stopped in front of his open office door, where he invited Kath in with the silent wave of his hand. She sat down in a comfortable, chrome legged chair in front of his large desk in full view of an oversized computer monitor with an image of her last PET-CT Scan on the screen. She calmly folded her hands on her lap as he leaned back in his chair and started the conversation with what he found on the physical exam.

He described a number of very small nodules within her abdomen that he defined as probable tumor growth, but he was more unnerved by the fluid that had collected inside of her belly and within the base of her right lung. He then clicked the mouse, which highlighted the image on the monitor, and drew a circle around a specific area on the radiographic image with a special laser pointer.

He went on to describe how the results of the physical exam correlated with the PET-CT that showed many small tumors scattered within her entire abdomen. He highlighted those with the laser, but his voice grew concerned when the laser pointed to the fluid that had built up in areas where it shouldn't be.

Kath clenched her teeth and her eyes grew distant as she tried to assimilate what she had heard. When he had finished, she asked, "What can you do to help me?"

"Unfortunately, there is nothing I can do." He explained that surgery was no longer a viable option, and as a chemotherapy provider, he only offered drugs that had been approved by the FDA. Dr. Donacheck concluded that the cancer had mutated into a more aggressive type of cell, and he recommended prompt enrollment in a clinical trial that used experimental drugs he could not provide.

Kath sat silently stunned for a few minutes, as the subtle sounds of a busy office filtered through the walls. Then she looked at him and asked if the clinical trials at the Cancer Center in Scottsdale would be a good place to start. He leaned forward with his arms on the desktop and simply nodded his head.

Their eyes locked in a silent gaze that mutually acknowledged what they both knew. Kath stood up and reached across the desktop with an open hand. Dr. Donacheck momentarily stared at her hand before he rolled back his chair and walked around the oversized desk toward her. They embraced in a warm, extended hug, and he wished her well in her next chemo adventure. When they had finished, Kath abruptly turned around and walked through the empty waiting room, waving goodbye to the office staff on her way to the car.

What's the Worst That Can Happen?

35

Kath stared out the passenger window and then quietly said, "Before we go home, I'd like to stop at the Virginia Piper Center and check it out." Years earlier, Kath had visited that cancer clinic for potential treatment options. It happened to be next door to the PET-CT radiology center she regularly visited.

We exited the elevator at the Center and entered the waiting room, where a large, stuffed orange tiger attracted Kath's attention. She walked up to the office window and asked to be interviewed for eligibility in a clinical trial.

Kath returned to the room filled with stuffed animals and sat next to the large tiger while she waited for a response from a clinic representative. A young nurse dressed in blue hospital scrubs promptly approached her. Deborah introduced herself as one of the trial coordinators, then sat down next to Kath and asked to hear her story.

Kath recited her well-rehearsed cancer tale and rattled off the dozen different chemotherapies she had received over the course of her long journey, including her unsuccessful enrollment in a previous clinical trial. Deborah listened in sympathetic silence and nodded in agreement when Kath made it clear that she did not want to be part of the placebo group within the trial.

Deborah identified an investigational drug that might prove beneficial and outlined the specific clinical procedures the experimental regimen required. Kath struggled to concentrate on the intricate details that the nurse painstakingly delineated. But once the hope of a new therapy broke through her foggy despair, she became emotionally lost in the possibility of a cure and no longer heard what the nurse said. Her eyes stared blankly into in the distance, and Deborah's words sounded like a muffled conversation that emanated from another room. Kath slowly stirred from her self-induced hypnotic trance in time to hear the nurse say, "We hope you decide to join the Virginia Piper Cancer Center family." Meanwhile, her outstretched hand held a number of papers for Kath to take with her. She instinctively reached for the forms and calmly looked around the room as she reoriented herself to the moment and promised to deliver the necessary information in time for a follow-up appointment in one week.

Kath returned to Sedona with high hopes, but an unsettled ambivalence soon crept in as she collected and reviewed the tremendous amount of personal healthcare information that the clinic required for entry into the trial.

The latest PET-CT scan detailed the explosive tumor growth that correlated with the meteoric rise of the most recent CA-125. The results explained all of her latest physical symptoms and, unfortunately, supported Dr. Donacheck's conclusions. Emotionally, she struggled to accept the irrefutable facts that the disease had rapidly progressed, while intellectually she grappled with the conclusion that her life depended on the success of a clinical trial. She reluctantly returned to Scottsdale for another chemo adventure that she did not want to have.

Kath's heart raced as the elevator zoomed up to the third floor of the Cancer Center. When the doors opened to the clinic hallway, Kath remained frozen in a moment of apprehension before she took a deep breath and proceeded toward her uncertain fate. She walked with confident trepidation down the long hall toward the secretary seated behind a glass partition and announced her arrival.

They exchanged pleasantries while the clerk proceeded with the admission process. When they had finished, Kath handed her an oversize envelope containing all of the requisite forms the Center had requested. When she returned to the waiting room, Kath felt unusually anxious, so she sat alone in the corner next to the large orange tiger. But outwardly she looked as calm as a yogi in a meditative state.

She watched as people passed through the waiting room, waved to the secretary, opened the door, and entered the clinic area. Some of the travelers looked weary shuffling in with their walkers, while others had a determined step in their stride and pulled the door open with purpose. But all of them had a companion by their side.

Deborah entered the waiting room with a salutary greeting and sat down next to Kath as she opened the envelope Kath had previously given to the secretary. The nurse removed the stack of completed forms and quickly flipped through them for accuracy. But she stopped when she reached the "Consent for Treatment" form. The previously signed paper detailed the unpredictability of the experimental drug selected for the trial and listed its many possible side effects. It expressly offered no guarantees for the efficacy of the treatment and released the clinic from all liability associated with any unintended consequences of the intravenous medication, including the possibility of death. Even with all the dangers associated with the trial, the experimental drug offered a ray hope at a time when Kath desperately needed it. Kath knew she would either live or die by this trial, so the legalities of the paperwork meant nothing to her. When Deborah asked if Kath understood the inherent risks of the medication, she tilted her head and with a shrug of her shoulders asked, "What's the worst that could happen?" Deborah replied with an uneasy smile, as she returned the papers to the envelope and escorted Kath into the clinic.

The large patient care area had over a dozen recliner chairs occupied by mostly middle aged to elderly female patients. Most had hair, but a few wore the telltale headscarves of chemo-induced alopecia. All had intravenous medications running. A few appeared ready to vomit, as their wide-eyed companions nervously held a well-placed barf pan just in case. The nurses, dressed in blue scrubs with stethoscopes draped around their necks, moved around the room like clockwork checking on their patients and the corresponding medications. Kath made herself comfortable in the empty chair Deborah had picked out before the nurse briefly departed to find the doctor in charge of her care.

Kath laid back in the recliner with her feet up and tried to get a sense of the clinic's atmosphere. As she looked around the room, many of the patients quietly conversed with their companions, often punctuating their conversations with forced laughter and unnaturally loud giggles. Grocery lists, children's lives, and television programs seemed to dominate the conversations, while the severity of the individual's conditions remained tucked away in the unspoken backwaters of all of the discussions.

Acceptance into the clinical trials was predicated on the fact that every person in the room had previously failed at least two standard chemotherapy regimens and traditional therapies no longer remained an option. The survival rates for most non-localized cancers remained dismal. Everyone in the patient care area fully recognized the distant odds of success, but very few ever talked about that. It seemed everyone adhered to the axiom *You Can't Afford The Luxury Of A Negative Thought,* as their conversations usually centered around an upbeat and positive message.

Kath watched as a small woman dressed in a white lab coat entered the far end of the treatment area and walked briskly past a number of seated patients that she politely acknowledged with a cursory smile on her way toward Kath. Deborah hurried to keep pace behind her. She abruptly stopped in front of Kath's chair and introduced herself as Dr. Rena, a young East Indian physician who spoke with a mild accent. The young doctor smiled warmly as she sat on a small, three-wheel stool and rolled up next to Kath, blindly reaching for the medical chart Deborah had handed her.

Dr. Rena peered through her glasses as she quietly skimmed through the contents of the open chart that rested on her lap and occasionally stopped to read certain pages. Then she flipped the medical record closed with an audible "hmmmm" that others were not meant to hear but caught Kath's attention.

Dr. Rena crossed her arms and leaned back on the stool as she spoke about the significant degree of metastasis highlighted by the PET-CT scan, but she offered some hope that the intravenous medication used in the trial might at least stop the spread of the growth and potentially reverse it. The doctor explained, with great delight, the intricate micro-pharmaceutical details of the experimental drug's toxic molecular effect on the cancer cells that had been grown on laboratory mice, and she hoped the in-vitro success would be translated into a cure for this particular form of cancer. She finished her summation with the caveat of no guarantees.

"Besides," Doctor Rena said, "if that drug doesn't work, there are many others on the shelf ready to go."

"Great!" Kath said. "That's what all the other onco docs said." She abruptly pushed the recliner into an upright position. Her feet landed on the floor with a thud, and she quietly stared at Dr. Rena before she leaned further into the doctor's personal space. "I've searched all over this country for a magical drug that will finally end this nightmare, and this experimental medication will make the thirteenth different chemo drug I've tried. They all promised great things, but they only made me sicker and always ended in failure. I need your alchemy to work because this cancer has gotten worse. I can't do it without you, nor do I have the time to search for another doctor."

After a brief moment of silence, Dr. Rena removed her glasses and slid even closer toward Kath before she said, "I can never presume to know the burden you feel from this dreaded disease. But as long as you're willing to try another experimental chemo drug, I will never abandon you, and I'll do my best to rid you of the cancer." They stared at each other like two gunfighters sizing each other up before Kath flopped back into the recliner, put her feet up on the foot rest, and said, "Let's do it."

A young nurse rolled a portable, stainless steel tray filled with laboratory blood tubes and medical supplies next to Kath. Robin introduced herself as a nurse with three years of experience at the center as she searched through the material on the tray. She found two surgical masks and handed one to Kath.

She discussed the details of the upcoming procedure as Kath tried to listen while she slipped the elastic bands of the paper filter around her ears and pinched the mask snuggly around her nose. Robin then opened a packet of sterile gloves with perfect technique and soundly snapped them over her hands, wiggling her fingers through the snug latex until they stubbornly slid into place.

Kath watched the nurse cleanse the port site with a special solution of chlorhexidine before she inserted a straight non-coring Huber needle into the double lumen chemo port that had been under the skin of her shoulder for years. The port had been accessed hundreds of times since its original placement, but Kath constantly feared a potentially fatal infection from an improperly placed needle. That kept her in a hyper-vigilant state each time someone used the port. Robin completed the procedure to Kath's satisfaction and filled the numerous lab tubes required for the clinical trial without any problems.

Kath removed the mask after the nurse connected a bag of intravenous normal saline to the needle and slowly infused the IV solution. Kath promptly smacked her lips together and said "I can taste the salt." Kath felt the relaxing effect of the intravenous diphenhydramine that Robin injected as part of the medication regime regularly given just prior to the chemotherapy. She closed her eyes as she settled back into the recliner and listened to the muffled conversations in the patient care area while she slowly drifted off from the effects of the Benadryl.

The nurse rechecked the identification label on the chemo drug with a second nurse and obtained Kath's vital signs before she started the IV the medication. Kath never felt any side effects from this particular chemotherapy, and after a brief infusion she left the facility feeling much the same as when she first arrived.

Kath returned to the clinic twice a week with a strong sense of purpose and a bounce in her step. She sat at her usual spot in the waiting room next to the giant orange tiger and fidgeted through outdated magazines, as she warmly acknowledged the other trial participants who joined her in the adjacent seats with broad smiles that disguised everyone's worried faces. The cheery conversation in the crowded waiting room screeched to a hush whenever the clinic door opened but quickly resumed after the nurse called out a name, much like a contestant being picked for *The Price is Right*.

When the mystery voice called out Kath's name, she followed the nurse back into the patient care area where Robin waited for her next to an empty chair. The two exchanged personal pleasantries before Kath plopped into the recliner with her purse on her lap and popped up the footrest in one easy motion while Robin checked her vital signs.

Dr. Rena sat next to Kath and reviewed the most recent medical information from her chart as Kath fidgeted with her purse. The doctor described the latest PET-CT result that showed a rapid progression of the disease, which seemed unfazed by the four doses of the experimental drug. But when Kath heard the CA-125 had climbed to historic levels she let out a gasp. Kath sunk further into the recliner and stared blankly at Dr. Rena as she continued to speak, but she never heard the stark words. For weeks Kath had readily discounted her bloated abdomen as nothing more than severe constipation, but the inability to take a deep breath made all those physical changes harder to ignore. The sturdy protective shell of denial started to crack.

Kath looked around the room at the other patients sitting in their chairs as bags of IV fluids dangled over their heads. They blithely passed the time of day while their caregivers tried to deny what the occupants of the chairs had recognized long ago. Kath stared right through Dr. Rena when she asked for four more weeks of the experimental infusion to give the medication a chance to work. Kath tightened her lips, then nodded her head before she said yes.

The bloom had fallen off the rose, and optimism remained in short supply as Kath struggled through the next three weeks. Emotionally, she found it difficult to accept what the latest PET-CT scan and CA-125 results implied, but she intellectually conceded the experimental chemotherapy simply didn't work.

She looked to the astrological stars for direction but found none. She tried to meditate, but her bloated abdomen made the lotus position impossible, and the distractions of cancer left her unable to focus her mind. She found comfort in reading Paramahansa Yogananda's monthly newsletters, which lay scattered about the bed, and she stared blankly at the ceiling as her hand slowly petted Ziggy who purred louder with each stroke. Her breath quickened and her eyes nervously darted about, while beads of sweat formed on her brow. She felt nearly paralyzed with dread when she heard herself say, "Is this how you want to go out?"

She was pondering that rhetorical question when her thoughts suddenly cleared and she abruptly sat up, sending Ziggy flying off the bed. She dangled her feet off the side of the mattress and a sad smile slowly stretched across her face as she thought about the many family members who had walked that lonely path toward death.

She thought of her thirty-three-year-old niece who died of lung cancer but had never smoked. Kath remembered the many times she sat with Patty at the cancer clinic. The peculiar metallic scent of chemotherapy still lingered in her olfactory memory, and the sounds of that emaciated young woman's intractable retching still rang in her ears. Her eyes grew misty when she recalled how that childless couple had emotionally struggled with Patty's terminal illness while their charade of a normal married life crumbled around them. A sudden epiphany morphed Kath's sadness into anger when she realized that her niece's failed chemotherapy regime appeared eerily similar to her own.

The anger Kath felt from her many years of unsuccessful cancer treatments suddenly collapsed the indestructible wall of denial and revealed the inevitable conclusion of her life. She was going to die from cancer. That surreal admission brought with it a serenity like she had never felt before.

Her sudden acquiescence stood in sharp contrast to Patty's staunch determination to live, and that disparity quickly disrupted the tranquility of the moment. Embarrassed by her perceived cowardice in a fight for survival, Kath's body trembled with adrenalin before she jumped off the bed with clenched fists and a tightened jaw. Her mind recited the mantra that cancer is fought one day at a time as she bowed her head and prayed with folded hands for the strength to fight one more day.

She returned to the Cancer Clinic for the fourth week of therapy and waited in the assigned chair for the lab results. Dr. Rena approached her with a face that foretold failure. She sat on a stool next to Kath and flipped through the papers in her chart as she solemnly recited the unrelenting rise of the CA-125. When Dr. Rena suggested a different clinical trial that might offer some hope, Kath leaned in close to the doctor and stopped her in mid-sentence. "Everyone here at the cancer center has been very kind," she said. "But it is also readily apparent that this cancer will never respond to any chemotherapy, and I need to reevaluate my plan." Kath leaned back and the two stared at each other before Dr. Rena's misty eyes acknowledged the truth of that statement.

Kath stood up, slung her purse over her shoulder and with a long, warm embrace thanked Dr. Rena for her efforts. She forced a smile to Robin and waved goodbye as she went through the clinic door and never looked back.

The End Is Always Near

Kath had anticipated the failure of the clinical trial prior to her last visit at the Cancer Center and had arranged for an evaluation at the University of Arizona Cancer Center in Tucson by a specialist in Borderline Serous Tumors with Low Malignant Potential. One week after she quit the clinical trial, Kath arrived at the Southern Arizona clinic.

She made the uncomfortable, four-hour drive to Tucson reclined in a passenger seat with a bloated abdomen that made it hard to breath and impossible to relax. Once parked, she quickly rolled out of the car much like a nine-month pregnant woman. But as she walked toward the cancer center, the casual observer would be hard pressed to note any abdominal distention that may have protruded through her loose-fitting sundress.

She carried the most recent PET-CT scans along with the latest lab data in an oversized manila envelope as she walked through the parking lot with the poise of a professional model. Once inside, she walked with imperceptible trepidation toward the registration area and sat uncomfortably in a chair as she finalized the tedious but well-known enrollment process. When she finished the forms, Kath stood up with a sigh of relief from abdominal decompression, that the clerk mistook for the welcomed completion of a laborious but necessary bureaucratic task and said, "A lot of papers, huh?" Kath smiled warmly at the secretary and proceeded to the nearby waiting room where she slouched in an oversized but comfortable upholstered armchair to await her summons.

A young woman dressed in blue hospital scrubs walked into the waiting room and loudly announced, "Barbara Wilson." Kath waved in acknowledgement and, after a cursory introduction, followed Miranda through the narrow corridors of the clinic. They stopped at a scale where the nurse recorded Kath's height and weight before she led her to a small exam room that resembled countless others she had visited along her journey.

Miranda checked Kath's vital signs, which appeared to be within a normal range. A petite young woman in her mid-thirties, dressed in green hospital scrubs with the name Dr. Ashley Hunter embroidered just above her left shirt pocket, entered the small room.

Dr. Hunter extended a well-manicured hand to Kath for a friendly shake, but quickly beckoned her to remain seated when Kath courteously attempted to stand and return the gesture. Dr. Hunter rolled the round stool towards Kath and sat down next to her as she touched Kath's arm in recognition of their acquaintance.

Their eyes locked for what felt like hours but lasted no more than a second or two as they peered deep into each other's souls and smiled at the humanity they saw. The strangers felt a deep sense of personal camaraderie as they discovered a profound mutual respect that no longer made them strangers. Dr. Hunter broke the spell, and said, "Tell me your story."

Kath exhaled an extended sigh and looked directly at Dr. Hunter with a face that telegraphed advance knowledge of the last chapter of a story whose final page had yet to been written.

She told her tale in the third person, as if all the described symptoms belonged to someone else. And as the health of the story's central character gradually deteriorated, her tone took on a subtle sense of urgency. The doctor listened respectfully as the drama unfolded and leaned in closer when Kath talked about her bloated abdomen.

When she finished her tale, the doctor helped Kath onto the examination table, unwrapped the black stethoscope from around her neck, and told Kath to take a series of slow deep breaths. She slowly moved the device around Kath's lungs but lingered a bit longer on her lower right side. Then the doctor returned the stethoscope to her neck and helped Kath lay back on the table while her fingertips probed her abdomen.

When she'd completed her assessment, the doctor asked Kath about the latest PET-CT Scan, and Kath pointed to the manila envelope on the chair. After Dr. Hunter had read the contents, she slid the papers back into the packet when a moment of uneasy repose filled the room. The doctor asked a few more questions about Kath's appetite before she excused herself to review all of the relevant medical information with a promise to return shortly.

To Kath the minutes seemed like hours, but Dr. Hunter eventually returned with a face that spoke volumes and eyes that seemed to be misted over as she looked at Kath. Sitting on the stool next to her patient, Dr. Hunter wrapped her hands around Kath's and took a deep breath before she spoke. "The cancer has aggressively metastasized beyond your lower abdomen and spread to your liver, lungs, and pelvic bone. That uncomfortable bloated feeling is the ascitic fluid that has built up inside your belly, and it will only get worse." She went on to describe how the walls of the many tiny blood vessels that fed thousands of marble-sized tumors scattered throughout her abdomen, leaked large amounts of plasma and collected within the peritoneal cavity. The tumors had inadvertently plugged the abdomen's natural drain pipes and resulted in an astonishingly large collection of ascitic fluid.

Kath momentarily closed her eyes and shook her head from side-to-side while she processed what she had just heard. A mere two months ago she'd enjoyed the biggest Thanksgiving dinner of her life, but now she felt sick and bloated, with no taste for food.

When Kath opened her eyes, the doctor's sad eyes were staring back at her. She said, "Your physical exam and lab results confirmed what the recent PET-CT scans suggested, but I wanted to be sure of my findings before I arrived at any conclusions." Her voice cracked with emotion as she struggled to say, "I'm sorry to tell you this, but you have about three months to live, and I suggest that you get your affairs in order."

An awkward moment of stunned silence echoed about the room before Kath said, "How can a slow growth borderline serous tumor kill me?"

"Because it has changed into an aggressively metastatic invasive carcinoma," the doctor said.

"There's nothing that can be done?" Kath asked.

"No," the doctor said. "Chemotherapy hasn't worked. Radiation might work on a single large tumor mass, but these small tumors are too numerous and are scattered everywhere. Even surgery can't fix this. I'm sorry but there is nothing that can be done."

For over fifteen years, Kath had believed the slow growth, low-grade serous tumor would be more of a nuisance than a life-threatening illness. She never believed it would kill her. An uneasy silence filled the room. Kath hands tightly grasped the arms of the chair and she took a deep breath as her eyes stared downward in an empty gaze. The occupants remained frozen in time before Kath suddenly jumped up and stood in front of the seated doctor who quickly rose from the stool and looked her in the eyes. Kath loosely draped both arms on the doctor's shoulders and whispered, "The future's uncertain and the end is always near," (a quote from *The Roadhouse Blues*, one of her favorite Jim Morrison songs.) They lingered for a moment in an embrace, but finished with a tighter hug before Kath thanked the doctor for her advice and left the room.

The long ride back to Sedona was silently somber as Kath sat partially reclined in the passenger seat and stared at the desert scenery that passed by her window. She felt mildly nauseous while the phrase "aggressively metastatic invasive carcinoma" echoed around in her head, and the words "three months to live" dominated her thoughts.

The cataclysmic news from Dr. Hunter didn't square with Dr. Donacheck's conclusions after he had surgically repaired the fistula and declared her abdomen cancer free a mere six months ago. Nor did it square with the scientific literature that strongly suggested that women with borderline serous tumors rarely had problems after the initial tumor had been removed. She suddenly sat up, her hands waving frantically in the air and rhetorically said, "How could I be so unlucky?" Her face remained frozen in a puzzled look for several uncomfortably long moments before she returned to a reclined position and stared out the window. Silence filled the car for many more miles before she quietly said, "I guess this is it." And after a long pause, she suggested that hospice should be contacted once we returned to Sedona.

When Kath entered the house, Ziggy greeted her with a constant meow. Everything seemed surreal as she stared down at her cat while he happily weaved his way around her legs. Her distended abdomen prevented her from petting her furry friend. Her eyes grew misty as she carefully stepped over Ziggy and made her way to the bedroom. She crawled under the covers, still fully dressed and pulled the blankets up to her chin. The enormity of the day weighed upon her as she tried to figure out what to do next. But her mind remained unfocused. She opted for a large dose of Lorazepam, which produced an uninterrupted sleep that lasted until the next morning.

Kath's eyelids struggled to open as she slowly stirred from a medicated haze. In the twilight of a half sleep she believed the devastating news had just been a bad dream, but when she opened her eyes, the reality of the moment jolted her awake. She lay motionless while she stared at the ceiling in disbelief and felt a tear trickle down her cheek when she contemplated how others she had known with terminal illnesses managed their fates.

She remembered how Patty, her niece, had vomited her way through chemotherapy and had defiantly fought for her life when all hope for recovery had been lost. She thought of Lori Michaels, who stopped all treatment after their phone conversation and chose to meet death on her own terms, even though chemotherapy may have added a year or two to her life.

Kath inadvertently chuckled out loud when she recalled how her eighty-four-year-old father, who struggled with severe bouts of paranoia, insisted on making love to his spouse of fifty-seven years one last time before the ambulance unceremoniously carted him out of the house he had built and abruptly deposited him into a nursing home bed.

Kath sat next to him for several days in the dark, cramped, musty quarters of the shared room as she watched the most formidable man of her childhood lay in a confused heap. The nurses blamed his refusal to eat or drink on his dementia, but Kath knew her father understood that his time had come and was doing everything he could to hasten its arrival.

She felt nothing but respect for the man she had both loved and feared, as she wiped away tears of pride. She hoped she had inherited her father's courage to answer death when it called her name.

She found her way into the shower and stood under the hot water as she despondently pondered how her long journey would end. She watched transfixed as the water circled freely down the drain and noticed the lack of hair that usually clogged it up. "At least I'll die with a full head of hair," she said to herself, as she turned the water off and stepped out wrapped in a towel.

She hurried through her makeup and arrived early in Dr. Wilson's office to request a hospice referral, while a part of her hoped he would talk her out of it. She sat in the familiar waiting room holding Dr. Hunter's printed report. She felt a whiff of jealousy tainted with a hint of anger as she looked at the elderly patients, who had lived a full life, seated all around her. Kath responded to her name and completed the routine procedures before she entered the same exam room she had visited countless times before. She slouched uncomfortably withdrawn in a chair as she awaited the doctor's arrival and tried to not think morose thoughts that painted a dismal future.

The door flew open as Dr. Wilson entered the room in his "Cosmo Kramer" fashion, but he immediately sensed her deep despair. He gently touched her arm and softly asked, "How can I help you?"

"You can get rid of this cancer for starters," Kath replied as she handed him Dr. Hunter's report.

He flipped through the papers while Kath filled him in on the findings and the sober recommendation. The room fell quiet except for the rustle of the papers. He put them on the counter top, gestured for her to sit on the exam table, and helped her to its edge.

He unwrapped the stethoscope from around his neck and carefully listened to Kath's lungs but spent a little extra time on the right lower lobes. Then he listened to her abdomen and used his fingers to palpate the fluid that had accumulated deep within her belly. His eyes grew solemn as he helped her off the exam table and pulled his stool close to her.

He told her about the significant ascitic buildup throughout her abdomen as well as a large right pleural effusion, which partially collapsed her lung and made it difficult to breathe. He recommended a CT Scan to confirm his findings and suggested the fluid be drained. Kath understood what the procedures entailed and agreed to them, but she also knew the fluid would return. A lengthy discussion about her future ensued, and Kath conceded to the appropriateness of hospice care.

Dr. Wilson agreed with Dr. Hunter's conclusions that the cancer had accelerated and quickly metastasized to so many areas of the body that it proved untreatable, but he refused to say how long she had to live. They looked at each other in stunned silence before Kath broke the spell, and without breaking eye contact, calmly asked to be enrolled in hospice. He struggled to speak through misty eyes as he matter-of-factly explained what the program entailed. When he had finished, the two silently stared at each before they hugged in a long embrace and the doctor whispered, "I'm sorry."

The CT-scan confirmed that a massive metastatic dissemination of individual marble sized tumors had taken root from Kath's neck to her pelvic floor, and the sheer number of neoplasms rendered any surgical or radiation treatment totally futile. The scan also revealed a partially collapsed right lung from a large pleural effusion and identified an exorbitant amount of ascitic fluid that constricted her diaphragm and left her chronically short of breath.

The unexpected tumors discovered in her liver and lungs heralded a bleak outlook, but the newly diagnosed obstructed bowel from abdominal adhesions explained why her appetite had recently dwindled. This created an urgent nutritional problem that required immediate attention.

The cavalcade of medical issues that needed to be addressed nearly overwhelmed Kath as she waited in the reception room of the radiology department for her lungs to be drained and the ascites to be evacuated. She never heard the myriad of sounds from the busy waiting room or even noticed the many ill patients who sat around her.

The nurse leaned into the doorway and called out Kath's name, which initially went unheeded as she remained lost in thought. This prompted a second summons that slowly rousted Kath back to reality before she belatedly acknowledged her presence with the wave of her arm.

She pushed herself out of the chair with an audible grunt and politely chatted with Candace as they walked side-by-side down a busy corridor toward the treatment area. Kath grew silent when they entered the cramped quarters of the radiology room and stared wide eyed at the large stainless-steel tray filled with medical instruments.

Candace dangled a heavily starched hospital gown from one hand and closed the door with the other as she instructed Kath to remove all her clothing from the waist up. Kath felt a little chilled as she sat on the edge of the gurney dressed in a poorly insulated gown while Candace explained how the thoracentesis procedure drained fluid from around the lungs and the paracentesis emptied ascitic fluid from the abdomen.

Kath heard the heavy radiology door creak open and turned around in time to see a tall lanky man with thick glasses enter the room. The door closed with a clunk as the new arrival dressed in a white lab coat walked hastily toward her with an outstretched hand and introduced himself as Dr. Davies.

He recited his professional credentials while he stood next to her and explained the procedure in detail before he positioned Kath on the gurney for the thoracentesis. Her legs dangled over the side of the stretcher as she leaned her torso forward and placed her head on her folded arms that rested on a pillow on top of a portable tray table. Her skin sensed the sonic wand from the ultra sound machine as the doctor searched her back for the best entry point to drain the pleuritic fluid from her lung. She felt the chill from the chlorhexidine swab that sterilized the selected area and heard the

334

rustle of a large sheet of thick paper that covered her back and served as a protective sterile field while the radiologist carefully centered the precut hole over the planned puncture site.

Kath never saw the three-inch-long needle that the doctor inserted between her eighth and ninth rib nor did she see the 1,500 cc's of fluid that he evacuated from her lungs. But she knew the fifteen-minute procedure had succeeded as her breathing immediately improved. Dr. Davies placed a simple Band-Aid over the puncture site and helped her lie down on the gurney as he prepared her abdomen for the paracentesis.

She watched as he manipulated the ultra sound wand around her abdomen as he searched for the optimal location to insert the needle and meticulously cleaned the carefully selected spot with another chlorhexidine swab before he covered the targeted area. She felt the prick of a large bore needle but could not see the four liters of yellow fluid that quickly drained from her abdomen. Twenty minutes later Dr. Davies replaced the needle with a Band-Aide. Kath felt surprised at the loss of tension within her previously distended abdomen and delighted in the ease of a deep breath as she sat on the side of the gurney in wide-eyed amazement. Everyone in the room celebrated the procedure's success as Dr. Davies helped her off the gurney, but their eyes silently betrayed the unspoken word of the temporary nature of the therapeutic triumph.

Kath's abdomen had felt grossly distended for so long that she'd forgotten what normal felt like until she sat comfortably in the bucket seat of our small car and smiled all the way home. The euphoria of unencumbered breathing continued for a few more days, but the reality of her predicament unceremoniously returned when the hospice nurse scheduled the initial home visit.

Kath faced the appointment with full make up and styled hair as she lay on top of the bed covers dressed in her pajamas, wrapped in a dark blue terrycloth robe, while she awaited the nurse's arrival.

Karen stood in the bedroom doorway with one hand on the extended handle of her small-wheeled suitcase while the other clutched a computer. She cheerfully introduced herself before she entered the room. She unloaded her luggage before she pranced her way along the side of the bed and greeted Kath with an outstretched hand. Karen proceeded with small talk as she dragged a chair toward the head of the bed and sat with a dignified posture while she entered Kath's demographic data into the computer. Kath readily answered all of the mundane questions, but when Karen asked for a detailed cancer history, their eyes locked in a silent stare that seemed like an eternity.

Kath's eyes grew notably distant as she visualized all of the faces she'd met along her oncological journey. She abruptly awoke to a drop that dribbled down her cheek only to find Karen's eyes still fixed on hers. She instinctively wiped away the single tear and proceeded to tell her lengthy tale.

When Kath had finished, she felt a moment of kinship with the hospice nurse who had professionally controlled her moistened eyes. In a slightly cracked, business-like voice Karen said, "The intractable abdominal adhesions have permanently blocked your intestines and severely compromised your nutritional status. Are you interested in TPN?"

When she heard the question, it occurred to Kath that she had not eaten real food in several days. She leaned on one hand and rubbed her abdomen with the other as she stared off into the distance, lost in a moment of deep contemplation.

In the dark days of the fistula, when all hope of recovery seemed lost, she had actively explored the requirements for physician-assisted suicide in Oregon. She'd repeatedly said if the cancer ever became terminal, euthanasia would be a viable option.

After the fistula surgery removed the threat of cancer, she had returned to the life she'd once lived and forgotten about physician-assisted suicide until Dr. Hunter's dire prediction. She stared quietly at the word "Hospice" embroidered on Karen's white lab coat and remembered how Lori Michaels had talked defiantly about her death before she stopped all oncological intervention. She never met her brave friend in person, but her memory reminded Kath that life becomes more precious when there's less of it to waste. Kath's once cavalier attitude toward death and physician-assisted suicide now seemed unacceptably stupid as she sat upright in bed and said an emphatic "Yes" to the TPN.

Karen busily tapped away on the computer keyboard before she looked up and asked, "Are you having any pain?" Kath tilted her head slightly while her eyes glanced upward and reflected on the nature of the question as she searched for words that quantified the subjective nature of pain.

She remembered the pain from her knee surgery when she'd cursed like a sailor and unceremoniously demanded pain meds. She never forgot the sharp pain she'd felt when she walked the hospital hallways after four different abdominal surgeries and winced with each step, as the pain medication dispensed by the nurses remained largely ineffective. She'd lived with the physical demands of a colostomy bag that collected excrement from a fistula for eight months and never complained of pain, but the complete absence of food or drink for the entire duration nearly destroyed her. In the dismal days of the fistula, she never used a fentanyl patch or the "break-through" intravenous morphine for pain control. Rather, she used them to cope with the relentless emotional stress and the unrequited desire to simply savor a cold glass of water. She refocused her icy stare at Karen and answered with an abrupt, "Yes, I have pain."

"A fentanyl patch is usually ordered for pain control," Karen answered, "with Morphine or Dilaudid to be used for break-through pain."

"The pharmacy filled Dr. Wilson's prescriptions and supplied me with fentanyl patches and intravenous Dilaudid," Kath said. "While the patches have been helpful, I haven't needed the Dilaudid…yet."

The nurse tapped away on the keyboard as Kath silently withdrew inward and searched for the words that precisely described what she wanted from the hospice program. She abruptly sat straight up and blurted out, "I don't want to die in this bed!" Startled, Karen calmly peered over the top of the computer and suddenly found herself locked in an emotional stare with her client. "Where would you like to die?" Karen asked softly.

Kath flopped back into the bed and thought of the only place that fit her dreams. A little country town in the English Cotswold's on the banks of the River Eye in the tiny hamlet of the Lower Slaughter just outside of Bourton on the Water. She had visited that English hamlet on her final trip to England when she stood on the grassy banks of that stream and realized for the first time that cancer would eventually take her life. She felt herself transported back to the banks of that tiny river, under the shade of a huge English Oak tree, and heard the water as it cascaded over a small dam. "That's where I would like to die," she quietly whispered. Her grimaced lips matched a furrowed brow when she realized the implausibility of that request. For a brief moment she felt the cool breeze of the English countryside on her cheeks and her facial tensions eased. When she opened her eyes, Karen was staring back at her. "What did you say?" she asked.

"Nothing," Kath answered. "I just don't want to die in this bed. Surely, there must be a hospice house somewhere nearby where people can go to die."

"There are in Phoenix," Karen replied, "but none around here."

"I can't die in this bed," an exasperated Kath said.

"But that's what hospice does," Karen replied. "We keep people comfortable so they can pass peacefully at home."

"No," Kath insisted. "You don't understand."

"Then help me," Karen answered.

Kath pushed herself up and leaned toward Karen before she said, "When I'm dead and buried in the family plot at Oak View Cemetery in Royal Oak, Michigan, and Jim gets remarried, I don't want him to look over at his new wife asleep in this bed and think, "That's where Kath died."

Their noses remained inches from each other in an uncomfortable moment before Karen replied, "Well, I don't know how to fix that."

"Then what good is hospice?" Kath asked and flopped back into bed.

"All hospice homes are actually assisted living centers that offer a percentage of their rooms to hospice patients and charge an average monthly out of pocket expense of $3,500, which is not reimbursed by insurance," Karen said. "Every one of them has a waiting list to get in, but there's no waiting for me to come to your home once a week, or more often if you need it, and the price is right."

"What does that solve?" Kath asked.

Karen replied with raised eyebrows and shrugged shoulders as she placed the stethoscope in her ears and listened to Kath's abdomen.

Kath stared silently at the ceiling and felt the gentle pressure of the stethoscope as it moved around her belly. "I won't die at home," she muttered to herself.

Kath surprised herself with the adamancy of her statement. She had always believed she would simply out live the slow growing cancer and die peacefully of old age. But since Dr. Hunter's dismal prognostication, her emotions had vacillated between the accepted family tradition that a stoic Wilson somberly faced their eventual demise, and a frightened cancer-ridden person who feared that even the slightest acknowledgement of the inevitability of her looming death would only serve to accelerate it. As she struggled to focus her eyes on the word "hospice" embroidered on Karen's lab coat, Kath realized how that single word said it all, and an unexpected sense of peaceful surrender suddenly filled her soul.

Kath pushed herself up in the bed and dangled her legs over the side as she watched Karen pack her things into the small suitcase. Then in a sincere voice, Kath said, "I look forward to your next visit."

Karen smiled in response and said "I'll be back next week. But please call if you need me sooner." They exchanged soft hugs and warm smiles before Karen left the room with her small suitcase in tow.

Kath mindlessly swung her legs as she listened to the squeaky wheels that slowly faded into the distance. She stared absentmindedly down the hall for a few minutes before she breathed a long sigh and flopped back into bed. Ziggy cuddled up next to her.

In the days that followed, Kath preferred the silent sanctuary of her own bed. She lay under the covers and read numerous biographies of her personal heroes or took refuge in the distractive cinematic marvels of Netflix but seldom ventured out of the house.

37
Damn!

Kath always believed that if the ascites remained dormant then she had a chance to beat the cancer, but as she lay under the blankets and gently rubbed her abdomen, she knew the ascitic fluid had returned in the two short weeks since the paracentesis. Her mind raced to rationalize what her hands had found, but her thoughts suddenly screeched to a halt when she remembered Dr. Hunter's prediction that proved impossible to dismiss.

Every sentient being possesses a primal life force whose sole job is to do whatever is necessary to ensure its survival, but that self-protective instinct leaked out of her soul much like the air that hissed out of a punctured tire. That frenetic self-preserving energy had been replaced with a surreal, almost celestial calm that permeated every cell of her being. The uncomfortable acceptance of her inescapable death quickly crescendoed into a full awareness that her inevitable demise had nearly arrived. Through clenched teeth, she muttered a single word, Damn."

That Buddhistic Bodhi experience temporarily opened her spiritual third eye in a way that none of her previous meditations had ever done, and for a brief ironic moment she felt rapturously happy. She had no bucket list written on the refrigerator door and felt no need to cram anything extra into what remained of her life other than to place a picture of Paramahansa Yogananda's "Last Smile" on her nightstand.

Medical science had no permanent solution for the incessant build-up of ascitic fluid that continually flooded her cancer-ridden abdomen, and the misplaced fluid lowered her blood pressure enough to make her dizzy every time she stood up.

She once again remained totally dependent on nightly TPN infusions through a newly placed PICC line that never fully replenished all of her nutritional needs..

Her doctors discouraged any surgical intervention to correct that intestinal blockage, as it would likely prove fatal. Even though Kath readily recognized these events as a precursor of Dr. Hunter's dire prediction, she tried not to notice the dark clouds that gathered on her life's horizon and struggled to live like she always had.

Janet Jenson, a nurse who had cared for Kath during one of her many hospitalizations, regularly extended an open invitation for Kath to visit a newborn foal from Janet's prized show horse at a ranch in the nearby town of Camp Verde, but Kath respectfully declined every offer. Abraxas, her father's thoroughbred racehorse that Kath had known in her youth, always held a special place in her heart. She didn't know how she would handle the emotional response she knew she would feel at this stage in life if she stood next to a such an animal again.

Kath declined many opportunities to get out of the house even when she felt good. Her interest in the outside world had long since faded. She preferred to live uninterrupted in her secluded sanctuary tucked safely under the covers with Ziggy snuggled by her side and a book on her lap.

The periodic paracentesis successfully drained the protein rich, ascitic fluid that built up within her abdomen and allowed her to breathe easier for a few days. But the significant loss of protein contributed to her overall malnutrition that could not be completely replenished by the nightly TPN infusions

Kath felt unusually exhilarated after one of her many paracentesis treatments and abruptly decided to take a day trip to escape her self-imposed lockdown exile in an attempt to reestablish a sense of normalcy in her life. She chose to visit the newly created

Bearizona Wildlife Park that boasted of self-guided automobile tours through various animal enclosures.

Kath sat upright in the passenger seat for the ninety-minute ride and talked about her life's plan as if she had a long cancer-free future. She grew visibly energized when we approached the park entrance and eagerly chatted with the gatekeeper about the exhibits. She used the tour map to guide us through the enclosures and grew visibly excited when we drove past the different animals lounging on the side of the road. After the auto tour we parked in the main lot and walked to the remaining smaller expositions, but her enthusiasm quickly faded as the trek to the first exhibit proved further than her endurance allowed.

Totally winded, she sat down in front of the baby bear enclosure and anxiously waited for her breath to slowly return. Her eyes grew sadly distant as she stared at the cubs frolicking in their enclosure. Wiping a tear from her eye, she quietly said, "Let's go home."

Kath said nothing as she leaned the passenger seat back for the long ride back to Sedona. She withdrew into herself and tried to control a sense of panic that bubbled up within her as she silently grappled with the indisputable fact that she was dying. A near hysterical frenzy was abruptly replaced with an absolute calm that filled every cell in her body as she suddenly knew, deep in her soul, that in a very short time her life would be over. Her logical mind no longer searched for some way out of this untimely demise. She serenely acquiesced to the inevitable and calmly watched the high desert scenery zoom by the car window for the last time.

The familiarity of her bedroom sanctuary helped ease the impending sense of doom that lurked just beyond her emotional horizon, while the intravenous use of self-administered hydromorphone helped her cope with everyday life.

Each morning Kath awoke to the chirping sound of the TPN pump that signaled the completion of the overnight infusion. She carefully disconnected the IV tubing and secured the PICC line with a SaranWrap-like cover that protected it from water before she stepped into the hot shower. She ritualistically applied her makeup and properly primped the wig that covered her straggly thin hair only to spend the rest of the day under the blankets, dressed in her pajamas.

The bed offered a cloistered reprieve from the unseen mayhem that swirled around her every waking moment. She continued to read the numerous biographies of her personal heroes and took refuge in the movies offered by Netflix, but when the persistent realities started to overwhelm her, she escaped into a self-administered opioid induced nap.

Her ill-fated future created an uncomfortable angst that gave most friends or neighbors a convenient excuse not to visit. But when the occasional guest did call, the visitors uncomfortably brought with them a gift of genuine congeniality that helped Kath momentarily escaped the tediousness of a terminal disease.

The infrequent guests cautiously navigated around the subtle awkwardness of the elephant in the room while the fatal nature of Kath's deteriorating condition remained the unspoken utterance in any conversation. As the disease progressed, Kath had fewer days when she felt up for visitors. But when guests did arrive, she actively engaged them regardless of how awful she felt and tried to focus the discussion on their personal interests to help them feel less awkward.

Sandra Moker instantly connected with Kath during one of her many stays at the hospital and, as a nurse, Sandra excelled in the art of conversation. She knew when to speak and when to listen. They shared a common interest in stylish attire and the proper application of expensive makeup. When Sandra visited, her husband, Russell, often sat quietly in the chair as the two women discussed the fine art of cosmetics, wig care, and hairstyling. They fitted four different types of wigs over Styrofoam mannequins' heads strategically arranged on the bathroom vanity and studied the texture of the hair like two beauticians in a salon. They discussed technical approaches to accentuate the wigs' stylistic themes as Sandra used a hairbrush and a blow dryer, like an artist with a paintbrush, to complete her masterpiece and concluded the job with a special finishing spray.

Kath inspected each of the wigs before she carefully slid them over her wispy thin hair while Sandra brushed in the final touches. Kath stared in the mirror and surveyed the finished look with an approving grin. They repeated the ritual with the other wigs, but when she tried on the long black "Cher" wig they momentarily stared at each other with their mouths wide open before erupting into uncontrollable laughter as Kath pranced around the room and comically impersonated the famous singer.

They inspected a collection of new clothes that Kath had bought on-line, consisting of loosely fitted dresses that accommodated her ever-changing girth. Kath modeled the apparel as they critiqued the color, style, and compatibility with the various wigs before the garments ended up back in the closet with the price tags still attached. Kath never wore most of the clothes she bought, but Sandra understood that the ritual of shopping eased Kath's troubled mind.

Jim Scheid was another nurse-friend who visited. They first met during one of Kath's many hospitalizations, and he impressed her with his ability to pursue an intelligent conversation on topics other than medical or oncological issues. A recent diagnosis of ALS had forced Jim into an early retirement from his nursing career. Their deadly diseases granted both of them distinguished admission to a very exclusive club that no one wanted to join, but this created a unique camaraderie that only fellow members understood.

They chatted about Jim's love for live theater and critiqued the latest Hollywood movies but avoided any discussion of the obvious. The only veiled reference to an untimely end occurred when Kath quietly said under her breath, to no one in particular, that he would probably outlive her.

The cancer's debilitating effects advanced so quickly that Kath became less interested in visitors and more interested in narcotics. The numerous bottles of prescribed drugs that currently filled her medicine cabinet, closely resembled her father's. He relied on many different prescriptions to control his hypochondriacal or paranoid states. But Kath was not a hypochondriac or paranoid, and the IV Dilaudid temporarily blurred the approaching shadow of death.

Kath never feared life's final moment, but she dreaded the slow-motion odyssey that relentlessly carried her ever closer toward the end. Solitary meditative practices and literary escapes no longer dispelled the ever-growing cloud of doom that gradually gathered around her. She tried to read but frequently awoke from an unexpected nap only to find the book had tumbled face down into her lap. And the once sacred act of meditation no longer provided any spiritual solace, as her mind saw only darkness. Time slowed to a crawl as the days dragged on. The nights proved to be nothing more than a series of short medicated naps as she stared blankly at the bedside clock while the red digits flipped to the next number that solemnly marked the passing of another sixty seconds of her life and a minute closer to death.

Clinical depression had haunted Kath for most of her adult life, but as the cancer progressed she never bemoaned her final fate or felt sorry for herself or treated others badly when she felt miserable. Instead, she retreated into a self-reflective state and quietly withdrew from the outside world, much like she had done in normal times.

Kath had shared a perpetual disdain for the mundaneness of light conversations and preferred in-depth discussions on any of the countless books she'd read or the nuances of the many mythological rituals she had studied over the years. Kath never shared her personal thoughts or fears about her approaching journey to the other side of the River Styx. As her physical condition deteriorated, her limited social world became smaller and smaller, and she interacted with very few people on a regular basis.

Karen, the hospice nurse, visited once a week but never stayed long, as Kath purposely remained emotionally distant and never discussed any end-of-life issues with her.

Carol Higgins, an experienced home care assistant, dutifully attended to all of Kath's needs for six hours a day, twice a week for three consecutive months, but Carol's persistent presence reminded Kath of her dependent state and created a sense of resentment and despair.

Close to Kath in age, Carol tried to establish a positive rapport with her client, but Kath felt they shared little in common and gently ignored all attempts at small talk. She purposely retreated into her books or took self-medicated naps, but Kath never discussed her unfortunate prognosis with her nurse's aide.

Crystal Johnson replaced Mika and proved to be the only person that Kath energetically interacted with. She developed a close relationship with the twenty-two-year-old slender, blonde housekeeper whose young life swirled in the innocent dramas of a twenty-something. Once a week Kath traveled with her from room to room as she eagerly listened to Crystal's latest romantic escapades over the clamor of the house cleaning equipment and offered sagely advice for the girlish problems of the week. As her health slowly deteriorated, Kath could no longer follow Crystal around the house and spent most of her time asleep in bed.

On one such house cleaning visit, Crystal carefully crept into the bedroom with an arm full of supplies, but the clank of her equipment inadvertently stirred Kath from a Dilaudid-induced slumber. Kath slowly sat up on the side of the bed with her head scarf slightly askew but with her makeup intact and gently rubbed her reluctant eyelids open while Crystal apologized profusely for the unintended intrusion. Kath responded with a warm smile and repeatedly tapped the mattress with her hand, as she gestured for Crystal to sit next to her on the side of the bed.

Crystal dumped the cleaning supplies on the floor and sheepishly sat next to Kath. Her feet swung nervously over the side of the bed while Kath carefully repositioned the babushka that covered her straggly hair. They shared a brief but intense visual embrace when Kath's nose suddenly sniffed the air for the source of a familiar scent.

"Are you still smoking cigarettes?" Kath asked.

"Not as much," Crystal replied.

"Well stop that!" Kath sternly replied. "You wanna get cancer or something?"

They looked at each other with a surprised, wide-eyed look followed by a howling laugh as Kath leaned back on her outstretched arms to relieve the pressure within her distended abdomen. "Life rarely turns out the way you think it will," Kath said, as the two friends sat quietly next to each other.

Kath spoke with Crystal about the turbulent times of the late sixties long before her protege had been born. She explained how the newly developed contraceptive methods triggered the sexual revolution along with the unintended consequences associated with it, but that information seemed like old news to the latter-day millennial.

In 1960, the FDA approved the first the oral contraception pill, but only married couples could legally acquire it. That left millions of women in twenty-six states without access to the new pill until a 1972 United States Supreme Court decision legalized birth control for all citizens. The initial hormonal dosage of the new contraceptive pill eventually proved to be unnecessarily high, which led to unintended consequences and the rise of the intrauterine device.

"All of those things made me infertile and gave me cancer," Kath declared. "I told Jim numerous times he was free to leave me, but he never did. I'm in this spot because of stupid decisions I made long ago. Be careful what you do to your body because one day it will come back on you. So, stop smoking," Kath vehemently declared. "And don't get an I.U.D!"

As her health worsened and the intravenous Dilaudid became part of her therapy, Kath considered an intentional overdose as a possible option. One night while we were lying in bed, she said, "I don't know how things will end for me, but if the pain becomes so bad that I decide to give myself enough Dilaudid to hasten the end and I'm physically unable to inject it, would you help me finish the job, if I asked?" We stared at each other in an extended awkward moment. I gave a silent but affirmative nod before she offered a tortured smile and patted me briefly on the shoulder. Then she rolled over and fell asleep.

Fortunately for me, she never asked.

Kath spent her days in a Dilaudid-induced state but remained extremely cognizant of her surroundings. She retrieved her old books on Padre Pio and re-read them all. She knew every aspect of that humble Friar's life, who had been canonized on June 16, 2002. She firmly believed this man knew God. She dog-eared certain the pages of the books that contained her favorite passages, but one stood out above the rest: *Through the study of books, one seeks God; by meditation, one finds him.* She saw her life's goal in that quote and that phrase rang true to her soul.

The Friar also rekindled her desire to pray the Rosary. She found the Rosary Beads given to her long ago by Father Merisman when she was baptized as a Catholic in Salt Lake City. She obsessed over the proper procedure for reciting that extended prayer and kept a laminated "cheat sheet" on the bedside stand. It listed the specific day of the week when one of the three traditional mysteries, the Joyful, the Sorrowful, and the Glorious should be prayed. The card delineated each of their associated five mysteries for a total of fifteen, which are meditated on prior to the start of each decade of the Rosary. Kath always had a penchant for rituals, and the proper recitation of the rosary brought her joy.

Kath longed for the melancholic days when she had actively studied the doctrines of the Catholic Church with Father Merisman in the halls of the Cathedral of the Madeleine. She chuckled when she recalled the time she nervously attended Mass in the back pew of St. John Vianney, the local Catholic Church in Sedona, and prayed the fistula bag under her dress wouldn't burst its biliary contents all over the floor.

As Kath lay in bed and paged through biblical passages in between naps, she decided to receive the Sacrament of the "Last Rites" and asked her long-time friend, Mary Londry, to arrange it. The two women first met years ago at the Sedona Library where Kath had volunteered. They shared an immediate, deep-seated, ecumenical connection that had persevered over the years. Mary had been a long-time parishioner in good standing at St. John Vianney and intervened with the pastor, who agreed to bring the Sacrament to Kath.

Kath prepared herself in extraordinary fashion with her favorite wig combed to perfection, her make up precisely applied, and a colorful comfortable sundress that complimented a pair of dress shoes. She approached this sacred occasion with a clear mind, absent the effects of IV Dilaudid, as she sat in the living room and read her favorite sections of the Bible.

She greeted the pastor at the door. They had never been formally introduced, so they sat together on the couch and became acquainted. The priest said a prayer and read some biblical passages before he heard her confession. After a moment of silent-prayer, they recited the Apostles Creed together before he asked her to lay on the couch while he prepared the sacred oils and draped a purple stole around his neck.

He prayed aloud the canonical verses long described in the ancient tradition of Catholicism while he anointed the seven parts of her body with his holy oils. When he had finished, he helped her up into a sitting position, then flipped open the lid from a small round, gold container and offered her Holy Communion.

Kath initially hesitated to receive this sacred gift, for she had abstained from all food or drink for many weeks and didn't know what would happen if she ingested anything. But she quickly closed her eyes, opened her mouth, stuck out her tongue, and received the Lamb of God.

She easily swallowed the bland wafer that slowly dissolved in her dry mouth, and after a few closing prayers, the priest concluded the ceremony. He packed up his ministerial supplies and shared a warm embrace before he exited as quickly as he had come.

Kath stood in the doorway and watched him drive away, but she continued to stare at the empty street while she tried to process all that had happened. She half hoped some celestial event would shake the heavens, or that she would feel a surge of cosmic energy charging down her spinal chakra. But nothing extraordinary happened.

She took a slow deep breath followed by a long sigh, and then quietly closed the door and walked toward the bedroom. She carefully placed her wig on the mannequin's head, and snugged the headscarf tautly around her scalp. She returned the shoes to their proper place and hung the sundress neatly in the closest filled with multiple sets of clothes.

Dressed in her monogramed pajamas, she sat on the side of the bed with her head tilted back and stared at the ceiling for a few moments before she reached into the bedside drawer to retrieve a small bronze statue of Ganesh. She held the Hindu deity in the opened palm of her hand and said a silent prayer to the remover of all obstacles before she placed the figurine on top of the stand next to her bed. She then prepared a dose of IV Dilaudid that she self-injected through the PICC line before she crawled under the blankets and promptly fell asleep.

The subtle background beat from the TPN pump did not interfere with her sleep that night. But when the sun rose the next morning, she suddenly sat up, wide-awake, and stared at me with a look that suggested she had something on her mind.

Her solemn face gazed softly at mine with eyes that whispered a litany of unspoken words. She leaned forward with a wistful smile and gently rested her hand on my shoulder before she said in a voice filled with hopeful conviction, "Don't go to work anymore." Our eyes remained locked in a whimsical stare while her words lingered in the air as the silence echoed about the room before she softly added, "Stay with me."

Her voice hid the fear she felt, and her face masked the terror, as her misty blue eyes spoke of her need to no longer be alone. The deafening silence remained unbroken while that emotional moment eclipsed all words. But my single silent nod confirmed that her call had been heard and resolutely answered.

A previously negotiated leave of absence from the hospital where I worked had been unconditionally granted and allowed me to be with Kath full time, and rendered any further outside assistance unnecessary. I remained at my new post, fixed in a chair, perched at the foot of the bed with a computer in my lap and dutifully watched over her as she occasionally glanced at me over the mound of blankets before she returned her head to the pillow with an imperceptible smile.

Kath withdrew into herself and never said much, as terminal cancer had a way of limiting most conversations. She never complained of pain but frequently commented on the uncomfortable nature of the distended abdomen, for which she received regular paracentesis, only to have the fluid return a few days later. She never shared her thoughts on the fragility of her situation nor suggested any direction in terms of emergency care or the specific parameters for CPR. I never asked, but it remained conspicuously implied that when the time came the answer would be self-evident.

Kath increasingly withdrew from all social interactions and progressively retreated from life. She never talked on the phone or emailed her friends and spent most of her time in bed. The daytime hours seemed particularly difficult, as she no longer read books or made predictions from her astrological charts. She gradually increased the use of I.V. Dilaudid and simply napped the daytime hours away.

The evening's ritualistic preparation for the intravenous nutritional potion became routine and separated the nighttime activities from the day. The genre of movies we rented from Netflix rarely mattered as she seldom stayed awake long enough to watch the entire film.

Kath had never been a restless sleeper and often greeted the morning in the same position she had fallen asleep in. The relaxed nature of her sleep defied the anxiety she must have felt as she laid motionless in bed but remained wide awake with her eyes closed. In the still of night, she thought about the things a person with a terminal diagnosis thinks about while the TPN pumped rhythmically in the background.

Once, as we lay in bed well past midnight, long after the movie had finished and the Dilaudid had worn off, I sensed the powerful presence of a loving energy that penetrated my unconscious state and stirred me out of a deep sleep. I struggled to open my sleepy eyes and found Kath wide awake, lying on her side with her chin cupped in the palm of her hand, and her eyes locked on mine.

We shared an intensely reverent stare that mutually acknowledged the undeniable beauty of the moment when her blue eyes welled up with a look that evolved into an emotionally powerful but amorous gaze that caught me by surprise. "I love you," she said, with a confident and tranquil voice. She continued her silent stare for a few more precious moments before she turned away and rested her head on her pillow without any further comment.

A mechanical beep unceremoniously signaled the end of the overnight intravenous TPN infusion and the start of a new day. She disconnected the IV tubing and stood in front of the vanity mirror as she absentmindedly slid her thumbs between the pajama's waistband which reaffirmed her distended abdomen had grown. She shook her head in passive surrender and carefully brushed her straggly thin hair before she tied the colorful scarf around her head.

She leaned her face closer toward the mirror and grinned a huge smile as she surveyed the condition of her teeth that no longer needed the Invisalign braces before she reached for the toothbrush that stood upright in the chrome holder. She retrieved the toothpaste from the vanity drawer and methodically squeezed the paste onto the brush in such a purposeful way that the empty part of the tube looked like it had been flattened with a rolling pin. She vigorously worked the brush, which temporarily alleviated her perpetually parched mouth, and rinsed with water that could never be swallowed. She once again leaned in closer toward the mirror and checked her lips for any residue before she returned the brush and tube to their original place.

She turned the hot water spigot on and slowly unbuttoned her pajamas as she prepared for a sponge bath while the steam swirled in the air. Her head shook in disgust as the mirror reflected breasts that no longer looked round and firm, but flat and droopy much like a ninety-year old woman, while the PICC line dangled precariously from an arm that no longer held a youthful shape. Her outstretched hands rested on the counter top while she bowed her head in resignation and pondered her fate. Kath always believed that she would grow old, as her mother had, but the fate of Lori Michaels never drifted far from her thoughts.

Only one percent of all borderline serous tumors ever turned aggressively malignant. Why this benign cell had suddenly exploded into a ferocious monster remained a mystery to every medical person she met. When the familiar small, domed-shaped bumps erupted around her abdomen, just under the skin, and she could actually touch the alien invader, she knew the end was near.

Kath buttoned her pajama top and snugged the headscarf tightly around her head before she returned to bed just like she did every morning. But with each day that passed, she felt noticeably worse.

Most days she stared at the ceiling lost in her thoughts, before she pulled the covers up to her chin, but the soft cotton blankets offered little protection from the harsh realities of her fate. She searched in vain for the ethereal calm she'd heard in Lori Michael's voice on her last phone call, but Kath never achieved that final state of grief that Dr. Elisabeth Kubler Ross described as "acceptance."

Her drug-induced somnolence dampened all personal interactions and exacerbated her natural propensity to withdraw from the daytime world, which only deepened her despair. And that toxic mix inadvertently conspired to create the fourth stage of grief described by Dr. Kubler-Ross as depression. The nighttime shadows spawned their own demons as she pretended to sleep under the cover of darkness but remained wide awake, alone with thoughts that she never shared.

In health, Kath preferred a solitary existence alone with her books or a home cooked meal with friends who dined at her formal table. Occasionally, she participated in a rare, fun-filled drunken night on the town where she humorously lost her inhibitions and reveled in the attention she received. But in sickness she simply wanted to be alone.

Family members had been concerned about her well-being since the initial diagnosis, but their geographical distance prevented a full appreciation of her precipitous decline. Throughout most of her illness Kath resisted their visits, but given Dr. Hunter's terminal prognosis she relented.

Kath dreaded the inevitable social awkwardness she knew would accompany the family visits, as they feigned a jovial discussion of the old times while they vigorously avoided the word "death." She knew that congenial pretense would continue until the very last moment when everyone's eyes would tear up as they said their final good byes before they uncomfortably exited the room.

Dr. Kubler-Ross's stages of grief affected both patient and family, but the amount of time the individuals spent at each level were always different. Denial seemed to be the hardest to get through, as both patient and family begrudgingly accepted the diagnosis but steadfastly believed a cure quickly would return their life to normal.

Everyone is a cheerleader after the first chemo treatment, and no one whispers a negative thought. As the disease proliferates and new medications follow failed chemo drugs, the oncological team inevitably launches the silver bullet theory in their endless quest to promote hope, as they proudly proclaim, "There is always another drug to try." This medical mantra insidiously escalates an innocent scenario where all parties involved unwittingly commit themselves to a plan where success is just around the corner, while the cheerleaders chant, "You can't quit now, after all you've been through."

As the side effects escalate and the disease progresses unabated, the anger stage often overlaps with denial. But Kath never expressed anger. Not once! Neither at God or at those around her.

When the chemo treatments are finally halted, a profound sense of helplessness descends upon the patient who is suddenly propelled past the stages of denial, anger, and bargaining, and is thrust into depression. The patient inevitably reflects on their life's accomplishments and failures. This either helps them move on to acceptance or pushes them further into a depressive state.

Once the family objectively recognizes the debilitating effects of the multiple surgeries, the countless chemotherapies, and the consumptive nature the disease has heaped upon the patient, they too transcend into depression. This stage for the family is often mixed with bargaining and is usually marked by incessant prayer and deal making with God.

If the patient is fortunate enough to reach the final stage of acceptance, that monumental achievement often helps the family find their own peace. The spiritual aura around the person who has accepted death can be very powerful, as Kath discovered with Lori Michaels.

Unsure of what they would find, my brother, David, and his wife, Linda, arrived from San Jose for an overnight stay. Kath had meticulously prepared herself for their visit and greeted them with a broad smile when they arrived. She sat up in bed with pillows that cushioned her back against the headboard and her legs stretched out under the covers. She placed a pillow across her lap that discreetly covered her distended abdomen, and flashed her bright eyes in a greeting that defied any hint of the Dilaudid she had injected just prior to their arrival.

They sat in chairs at the foot of the bed and promptly engaged in the pleasantries of small talk. David jovially spoke about their role in our wedding that had taken place in their home over thirty years ago, and reflected on other shared moments, while Kath mainly listened.

After a few hours it became obvious to all that Kath had grown weary. They also felt the emotional strain as they struggled to find a graceful way out, when Kath said, "I know why you came." She thanked them for accepting her into the Sesnak family and for the loving friendship they had shown her over the years. They struggled with their goodbyes before they shared a final embrace with Kath. They awkwardly stood at the side of the bed not wanting to leave but knowing they had to. They silently stared at each other through misty eyes that understood the magnitude of the moment, which they acknowledged with one last unspoken farewell before they walked out, unable to look back.

Kath watched them leave with great sadness as they disappeared down the hall and the sound of their footsteps faded into the distance. She wanted to run after her friends and ask them to stay for a glass of wine, like she had in days gone by. A cloud of melancholia descended over her when she heard the front door close, and a flood of memories made her smile in the midst of tragedy.

The harsh reality of her destiny severely tested her emotional stability, and the continued deterioration of her physical status compounded the conflict. The intravenous Dilaudid steadied her inner calm as she wobbled on the edge of the abyss, and the drug offered some relief from the deep peristaltic pain in her abdomen.

She spent all of her time in bed except during her morning makeup routine, which continued unabated regardless of how poorly she felt. But personal interactions had become very distant and disjointed. A calamitous convergence of abdominal complications and significant opioid consumption noticeably diminished her clarity of mind.

Periodically, she stirred from a deep slumber and stared blankly at a piece of paper taped on the wall next to the bed that documented in large letters when the next Dilaudid dose came due. But that reminder never consciously registered with her. She seemed to look right past it when she asked in a weakened voice for another dose before she nodded off again.

Marianne always kept current on her sister's condition and became increasingly concerned, as Kath's health rapidly declined. She arrived from Ann Arbor prepared to say her final goodbyes, but even Marianne's best poker face failed to conceal her surprise when Kath greeted her sister in a euphoric upbeat fashion.

She sat in bed with her makeup and wig perfectly placed and projected an emotional energy that defied Marianne's expectations. After the pleasantries subsided Kath quickly grew tired and quietly laid on her side, as Marianne sat in a chair near the head of the bed and held her hand. Kath closed her eyes but did not fall asleep as Marianne stared in disbelief at her younger sister. Tears streamed down her face as her mind slowly scrolled through their shared history. Marianne wiped the tears away with her free hand as she quietly uttered the Wilson family motto "When things get tough, you soldier on." Kath responded with a noticeable half smile.

Blessed with the gift of gab, Marianne entertained Kath for hours and recounted the stories of their lives from her bridesmaid days for both of Kath's weddings to the drunken encounters at an Ann Arbor bar when they both continuously flashed their breasts at the patrons before they were asked to leave. Kath lay uncomfortably on her side and tried to listen through the haze of the Dilaudid injections.

As she held Kath's hand, Marianne noticed her sister's nails needed a manicure and decided to open up the "Wilson Salon" with supplies gathered from the vanity drawer. Marianne told old family tales while she filed her sister's nails with a large emery board and trimmed her cuticles before she finished with a nice shade of glossy, clear polish.

As the day wore on Kath became increasingly tired, and the time for Marianne's departure became self-evident. When the time came for their final farewell, the emotions in the room grew incredibly palpable. Marianne hugged her dying sister with a warm embrace that transcended words, while Kath recognized the solemnity of the moment. She returned a weak hug as both sisters fought back the tears. Kath knew she would never see her sister again, but her emotional restraint concealed her true sentiments as she watched her sister walk away.

Marianne stood in the doorway and looked at Kath for a final farewell through watery eyes. Kath offered a weak smile with a single nod of her head that silently messaged her sister to "soldier on." Marianne left for Ann Arbor fully aware that a she would soon return to the land of the Red Rocks while Kath self-administered another dose of Dilaudid and went to sleep.

The rapid proliferation of adhesions slowly strangled Kath's intestines and increased her abdominal pain, while the meteoric rise in the number of tumors flooded her peritoneal cavity with more ascitic fluid that dramatically distended her abdomen. This misplaced fluid caused her blood pressure to drop to dangerous levels, and the frequent use of Dilaudid exacerbated her hypotensive state.

Kath felt no ill effects from the low blood pressure recorded by the nurse as they prepared for another paracentesis at the outpatient radiology clinic, Kath had become well acquainted with Candace, the tech who helped her over the course of many such procedures. They chatted like two women having lunch while she drained four liters of fluid from Kath's abdomen.

Kath returned home a bit wobbly, much like a punch-drunk boxer at the end of a twelve-round match. She promptly crawled into bed grateful to breathe easier but was physically debilitated by a relentless abdominal pain with intractable nausea that neither I.V. Zofran nor Dilaudid mitigated. Every ninety minutes she haplessly tried to pick herself up off the pillow as her head bobbed about in a stuporous state with unfocused eyes and weakly asked for more Dilaudid before she plopped back down and fell asleep.

Her drug-induced slumber did little to prevent a very troubled night. She uncharacteristically tossed about the bed while the I.V. pump rhythmically infused the TPN. At three in the morning her eyes abruptly popped open followed by a panicked look that flooded her face before she loudly proclaimed, "Oh, my God!"

In one single motion she rolled out from under the blankets and stood beside the bed. Her hands thrashed anxiously in the air and her legs nervously danced about as the IV line precariously tugged at the connections. Her hands came to rest on the side of her face as an expression of overt shock slowly morphed into humiliation. She stared at her urine-soaked pajama bottoms and looked at the large, round, wet spot that stained the bed sheet. Then she cried out, "I pee'd the bed! Oh my God! I pee'd the bed!" Kath felt so embarrassed that she grabbed the I.V. pump and ran into the bathroom, where she sat on the commode for nearly an hour.

Eventually, she crept back out dressed in new pajamas with the I.V. pump in one hand and the supplies for another dose of Dilaudid in the other. She sat on the side the bed and nervously prepared the medication for self-injection, and then laid down on clean sheets and an absorbent pad. She pulled the covers up over her head and slept until the alarm on the I.V. pump signaled the start of the morning routine.

She's a 38 DNR, Right?

O ver the next few days Kath's anxiety swelled into a volatile emotional state. The intravenous Dilaudid temporarily relieved the agitation, but one day it suddenly boiled over.

It started in the morning as Kath nervously fidgeted under the blankets and continually checked the progress of the TPN while she impatiently waited for the infusion to finish. Once the I.V. pump signaled the bag had emptied she quickly disconnected the tubing and scurried off into the bathroom where she sat on the commode for nearly thirty minutes. When she finally exited, she nervously paced around the bedroom dressed in her pajamas. Her eyes seemed distant and unfocused as she quietly mumbled about her inability to poop.

In reality, the deep abdominal discomfort that she misinterpreted as an urgent need for a bowel movement originated from an intestinal obstruction caused by abdominal adhesions. She had been without food or drink for nearly two months, and her colon had long since been emptied. But her bowel obsession transcended all rational thought. She insisted on repeated soap-suds enemas to get cleaned out.

She anxiously paced about the room embarrassed by the impending procedure but desperately hoped that it would relieve her symptoms. Absorbent pads covered the bed as she lay on her side and grimaced as the awkwardness of the rigid plastic enema tube made its way into position, but cramped in pain when the fluid flowed in. She did her best to retain the soapy liquid until the very last moment when she rushed into the bathroom and forcefully expelled the contents into the commode. Unfortunately, only clear soapy water emerged. She repeated this procedure a few times but the result remained the same. No poop.

She left the bathroom with increased abdominal pain but mistakenly attributed the sharp rise in discomfort to the repeated enemas that the Dilaudid failed to resolve. She lay in bed and appeared shaken as the lack of results bothered her more than the procedure had.

As the day progressed she increasingly withdrew into herself and spoke very little. She stared blankly at the paper on the wall that listed when the next dose of Dilaudid came due. But the information did not compute as her cognitive function had greatly diminished.

Kath went to bed at the usual time but experienced a fitful and disturbed sleep. Just after midnight she suddenly awoke, and was very confused. She rolled out of bed and tried to walk around the room but she nearly pulled the PICC line out of her arm as she forgot to take the TPN pump with her. Her eyes had a distant, frightened look, and appeared dazed. She found her way to the vanity mirror and stared blankly at her reflection. Her hands primped the wig on her head while the IV line bounced with the movement.

She reached into to the drawer for a brush to finish the job before she retrieved her cosmetic accessories and carefully applied her Merle Norman makeup. When she was satisfied that all looked well, she resumed her walk around the bedroom, but she failed to comprehend the words that I spoke and her verbal responses made no sense. Something had dramatically changed.

Her panicked sense of urgency concerned me, as her unfocused eyes chaotically darted about. Her reluctance to return to bed raised many alarm bells, but her deteriorated behavior suggested a more insidious medical reason for her unusual agitation.

I watched in dismay as her erratic behavior escalated before I called Sandra Moker for help in the very early hours of the morning. Kath's agitated antics quickly dissipated when Sandra arrived twenty minutes after the call.

She stopped pacing when Sandra entered the room. Kath initially stared at her friend with a bewildered far-away look but quickly followed with a huge smile and a warm extended embrace. They sat together on the side of the bed and chatted like two old friends over lunch, but Kath never questioned why Sandra was sitting next to her in the middle of the night.

Sandra rubbed Kath's neck in a moment of friendship and camaraderie, but she gave an audible gasp when her hand felt a large bump at the nape of Kath's neck. Kath's demeanor suddenly changed when Sandra asked about the lump, and the room fell silent when Kath pulled up her pajama top and pointed to numerous golf-ball-sized tumors that had recently appeared on her abdomen, back, and neck. Kath nervously jumped up and walked around the room as she struggled to emotionally manage the enormity of the moment, and then she slipped further into a confused state.

Kath repeatedly went in and out of the bathroom in a near maniacal need to poop, but nothing passed, not even gas. Her temperature and blood glucose checked out to be normal, but a low blood pressure with an elevated pulse raised our concerns. We finally coaxed Kath back to bed, but her unrestrained panic quickly returned.

The underlying cause of the current crisis remained unknown. It may have been a simple matter of dehydration, or an infection that could be easily treated and return Kath to her normal state of ill health. It had been nearly three months to the day since Dr. Hunter had announced her haunting proclamation, and that fact loomed large in all future life saving decisions.

What we didn't know was that Kath had become septic from either an ischemic bowel or from a bacterial peritonitis, possibly acquired from the previous paracentesis. Both involved further studies to appropriately direct advanced hospital care. But if left untreated, either of those conditions often had a fatal outcome. Her near delirious state created a sense of urgency, and her emotional request that she "not die at home in her bed" filled my thoughts when I called 911.

Minutes after I notified emergency services, I saw the flashing lights of the EMS fire department and intercepted them outside, while Sandra remained with Kath. I relayed Kath's history to the crew chief as the fire crew followed us back to the bedroom. The room quickly filled with young firemen as the crew chief talked with Kath and assessed the situation. Kath sat next to Sandra on the bed and answered his questions as best she could. But she clearly fumbled on many of the answers, as her nervousness came across in a maniacal self-conscious chuckle.

The crew chief turned to me and said, "She's a DNR right?" But the answer remained problematic because Kath had never officially consented to a full DNR (Do Not Resuscitate). Thirty years of intimate history filled my mind, and everything around me moved in slow motion, as I stared at my emotionally and physiologically depleted wife. I desperately searched for another way out of this labyrinth, but I knew that if she went to the hospital she would never return. The time for a life or death decision had finally arrived, but I questioned my ability to make it.

The crew chief gruffly repeated the question "Is she a DNR?"

"Well, not technically," I said.

He grimaced his lips and dropped his head as he looked at Kath before he said, "What I see here is a transport issue, and we are not a transport company."

Sandra and I exchanged a look of professional surprise with a touch of indignation while Kath remained totally aloof from the drama that unfolded in front of her. The room grew silent as I walked toward the crew chief. Standing directly in front of him, close enough to feel his breath, I said, "There are no documents that state she is a DNR, and she is clearly unable to make that decision. As her spouse of thirty years, I'm telling you that she is a full code, and everything must be done to save her."

We exchanged a silent but tense look for what seemed like an eternity until he relinquished his stand and directed his crew to prepare her for transport. Kath remained aloof, but she seemed to understand the implications of the discussion as she nervously looked around the room.

Her anxiety quickly escalated to near extreme while the men tried to prepare her for transport. I intervened and offered her an intravenous Dilaudid, which would help calm her down for the thirty-minute trip to the hospital.

The crew chief gruffly shouted, "No IV drugs. I can't transport her with recently dispensed I.V. narcotics."

Sandra and I looked at each other with a surprised but incredulous look. I put the drug in my shirt pocket and said, "Kath, let me take you to the bathroom so you can pee before you go." I quietly reached for the IV pump that infused her TPN, and Kath replied with a confused smile as we walked through the crowd of men into the bathroom. Sandra helped her onto the commode as I said to the crew chief, "We'll be right with you," and closed the door.

I injected the Dilaudid just as I had done countless times before and returned the syringe to my pocket before I flushed the toilet. We waited for a few moments before I opened the door and said, "She's ready now." The crew chief stared at me with utmost contempt but ordered his crew to load her onto the gurney.

The Dilaudid had its intended effect. Kath relaxed as the men loaded her onto the stretcher. Strapped in the gurney, she searched the room in moment of clarity to say a final good bye to Ziggy, but he had long since scampered away. She smiled sadly as she surveyed the bedroom for what she knew would be the last time she would ever see it. Her smile suddenly turned into a devilish grin. She laughed a cute giggle and said, "Wow, look at all these good-looking fire guys around here!" The men responded with a group chuckle, as they wheeled her out the door and into the ambulance.

I met Kath at the local hospital as they were unloading her from the ambulance. I grew concerned about her level of consciousness as her head bobbed weakly with each movement of the gurney, and she was completely oblivious to her surroundings. She responded to my questions with stuporous one-word answers as I held her hand and walked with the EMS crew as they rolled her through the busy hallway of the ER.

The nurse greeted her when we arrived at the room, but Kath kept her eyes closed and vaguely acknowledge the salutation. The EMS crew gently transferred Kath to the bed and wished her well before they left, while the nurse checked her vital signs.

Kath lay on her back, dressed in her famous monogramed pajamas, with the wig still neatly in place. The TPN infusion pump continued its mechanical cadence as she feebly responded with half opened eyes to the nurse's questions. Her temperature was normal, but her blood pressure remained low with an elevated pulse.

The nurse studied the bag of TPN before she obtained blood samples from the PICC line for a standard battery of tests, as I explained Kath's extended history and requested a dose of intravenous Dilaudid. The nurse looked at Kath lying motionless on the bed, and then at me, before she reiterated that a low blood pressure precluded the dispensation of Dilaudid. I reluctantly agreed.

Kath appeared comfortable, but I couldn't tell if she pretended to be asleep, had actually fallen asleep, or had lapsed into a semi-comatose state.

If Kath was pretending to sleep and had emotionally withdrawn from the outside world because end of life issues simply overwhelmed her, then she met the criteria for depression, the fourth stage of grief in Kubler-Ross's model for death and dying.

If I believed she had actually fallen asleep from extreme exhaustion and would return home after the blood tests showed everything to be normal, then I met the criteria for denial, the first stage of grief.

If I believed her altered consciousness stemmed from an overwhelming cataclysmic event that would quickly lead to her death, and she would finally see God, *and* I felt an inner peace, then I had reached acceptance, the final stage of grief.

Shortly after Kath returned from a CT Scan, Dr. Walkner entered the room and introduced himself as the ER physician in charge of her care. The young doctor had a gracious bedside manner as he stood next to Kath and asked her questions that she half responded to. She lay motionless while he listened to her lungs, but she gave a slight grimace when he pushed on her abdomen. He palpated the lumps on the back of her neck, reached under her pajama top and felt the bumps on her abdomen. He shined a light in her eyes and humorously joked, "Is anybody in there?" She responded with a wryly smile. When he had finished the examination he politely excused himself and asked me to join him in the hall just outside the room.

He stood with his back against the wall, and I stood in front of him, still able to see Kath as she slept. Dr. Walkner said the blood work showed an elevated white count, which suggested an infection somewhere in her body, and in r nd hepatic enzymes, which pointed toward significant liver involvement. The CT scan revealed multiple tumors scattered throughout her abdomen, lungs, diaphragm, liver, and various areas around her back and neck with bilateral pleural effusion and a belly full of ascites.

He had read the voluminous medical notes dictated by Dr. Wilson over the years. He paused for a short moment that seemed like an eternity before he said with a most somber face, "Her condition is poor, and the cancer has spread everywhere. I know from the CT that she has an intestinal obstruction and most likely an ischemic bowel that would require surgery to repair, assuming she would survive the procedure. I need to know what you would like to me to do. Do I extend her life with every possible medical treatment, which quite honestly wouldn't help her live much longer, or do I just make her comfortable?"

While I listened to his words, I scrutinized Kath's face for any subtle sign that might have answered the doctor's question, which I assumed she heard. But her eyes remained closed as she lay on the bed with her head elevated and offered no response to the query.

Even when her body started to fail she could never bring herself to say aloud, "Stop everything," and give up. Instead, Kath reached an unspoken compromise with herself and never consented to a "DNR," but left it to me to utter the fateful words that she could not.

Dr. Walkner patiently waited for me to answer his question as he leaned stoically against the wall while I stood in front of him and watched Kath through the door. Everything suddenly appeared in slow motion. The quiet of the busy ER nearly deafened me as I bore witness to the final scene of a tragic play that had already been written when I heard myself say, "Stop everything."

The doctor grimaced an empathetic acknowledgment of my tortured answer that Kath must have heard. I carefully watched her for any kind of reaction but saw none.

The doctor ordered in-patient comfort care for Kath that included intravenous Dilaudid, and the hospital supervisor arranged for her to be transferred to a room in the Intensive Care Unit where I worked. The ICU personnel knew of Kath's long health history and greeted her with sympathetic smiles when she rolled into the unit. She appeared dazed and somnolent with eyes half focused on those who gathered around her. But she managed a smile when they called her name as they transferred her to the new bed.

The night remained uneventful, as she slept undisturbed with the help of Dilaudid. Her stuporous state persisted well into the morning when the nurse disconnected the PICC line from the TPN pump for what proved to be the last time.

Kath remained largely unresponsive when the dawn's early light turned into day. She sleepily rebuffed the nurse's gentle efforts to provide some kind of morning care, but she slowly rejoined the conscious world when Dr. Wilson abruptly rousted her awake.

He sat on the bed and waited until she focused her eyes on his before he said in his uniquely delightful way, "Good morning. How are you feeling?"

It took a few seconds before Kath oriented herself to the moment, but she quickly sat up in bed and self-consciously adjusted her wig as she struggled to answer his question. She still felt the need to poop but couldn't. Her abdomen felt like she'd swallowed a giant watermelon, and certain parts of her belly hurt more than other areas. The ascites pushed up against her diaphragm and left her unable to take a deep breath while the bumps that suddenly appeared all over her body provided an eerie visible reminder of the uninvited alien that lived within her.

The callousness of the cancer's relentless progression validated Dr. Hunter's grim forecast that she had accurately predicted nearly three months ago to the day. Kath remained deceptively calm as a myriad of terrifying thoughts raced through her mind. But she calmly looked at Dr. Wilson and simply said, "I'm okay."

Dr. Wilson knew his patient well and responded with a heartfelt, "I'm glad. For a minute I thought you might be in trouble!" They exchanged a knowing smile. The doctor completed his physical exam while he asked her questions that helped him piece together an accurate picture of her current condition.

He wrapped the stethoscope around his neck and sat next to her as he explained in easy medical terms the findings that she already knew. He paused for a moment and carefully studied his long-time patient, reflecting on the unique physician-patient bond they had carefully nurtured over their many years together.

He paused to gather his wits before he suggested that further medical intervention would not be in her best interest. He simply wanted to keep her comfortable. She bobbed her head in agreement before she nodded off.

I'm not sure she ever saw the sadness that filled his face when he spoke those words. He couldn't shake the horrible feeling that every good physician experiences as he stood next to her bed, his eyes on the verge of tears. He silently conceded his inability to defend his semi-conscious patient from the darkness of death that knocked at the door and silently apologized for being powerless to stop it.

He stared at her for a brief moment before he softly whispered that he'd see her tomorrow, but he instinctively knew that he'd just said his final goodbye and simply walked out of the room.

Morning had moved into the afternoon when our neighbors Janet and Glen stopped by to offer their well wishes. But they seemed a bit befuddled when they realized their friend seemed completely unaware of their presence. They nervously shuffled their feet and spoke in subdued tones, so as not to disturb her sleep, as they slowly realized that Kath's condition was far worse than they ever expected.

A group discussion of her prognosis proved to be an uncomfortable topic. The visitors gave an audible gasp when they learned that nothing more would be done and nervously asked the unanswerable question of, "How long?"

An air of somber silence filled the room as nervous eyes searched for a comfortable place to stare. The discussion eventually moved on to the fond memories of the many dinner parties we had shared over years, and the inevitable spirited discourse fueled by alcoholic beverages. The boisterous conversation eventually dwindled away and quickly led to an uncomfortable silence that filled the room.

The guests nervously fidgeted in their chairs before they gave each other an imperceptible nonverbal look that signaled a mutual desire to leave. They stood together next to the bed in stunned silence before they solemnly wished their unresponsive friend a heart felt goodbye. They never looked back as they closed the door behind them.

I sat alone with Kath and listened to the sounds of her shallow breathing, which broke the uneasy silence that echoed about the room. The subtle movement of her chest offered a reassuring clue that Kath's soulful spirit still inhabited her earthly body.

A loud knock preceded a slow squeak of the room's large hospital door that creaked open and announced the arrival of an unexpected visitor, who walked past the privacy curtains and stood like a sentinel at the foot of the bed.

Carla silently stared at her long-time friend and neighbor lying motionless under the blankets before she declared her presence with a heartfelt, "Hello, Kath!" It took a few moments before Kath opened her sleep-encrusted eyes and slowly pushed herself upright in bed as she focused her eyes on the newly arrived visitor. Her blank expression slowly morphed into the grin of someone who recognized an old friend.

It had been several weeks since Carla had seen her friend and neighbor in the sanctuary of Kath's bedroom where Carla had performed her sacred rituals of shamanic healing that had been ancestrally handed down to her through the many generations of her Native American heritage.

Carla had enthusiastically performed that solemn ceremony many times, and Kath believed the mysterious esoteric energy improved her well-being. Kath instinctively adjusted her wig as she sat up in bed and shared a warm embrace with her longtime friend. Carla stood at the side of the bed while they reminisced like two old friends sharing a cup of coffee at Starbuck's. Carla humorously recalled a particularly funny episode when Kath had smoked pot at Carla's dinner table the night before our trip to England. Kath had discovered an uncharacteristic gift of gab and verbalized her THC induced flight of ideas in an extended monologue, to the amazed chuckles of the dinner attendees.

Carla said goodbye when she saw the weariness in her friend's aura. Their eyes reflected a deep warmth only close friends share, while Carla spoke of a return visit. Kath suddenly experienced a deep sadness as she sensed this would be a final farewell. Her eyes misted up when Carla left the room. She pulled the blanket up to her neck and closed her eyes.

Kath never again had a lucid talkative moment, as the afternoon sun turned into the evening twilight. She remained flat on her back, comfortable under the covers, with closed eyes that stared up to the heavens. She never moved except for an occasional grimace of pain followed by a barely perceptible groan, as one or both of her hands made a half-hearted attempt to rub her distended abdomen.

The darkness of the night filled the room with only the soft glow of an indirect light that silhouetted her face. She had no intravenous fluids for hydration, and for the first time in months the rhythmic hum of the TPN pump remained glaringly absent. Her blood pressure remained low with or without the Dilaudid, and her urine output ominously dropped off to zero. She had no EKG leads to monitor her heart rhythm or a nasal cannula for supplemental oxygen. As a nurse whose job had always been to provide the basics of life support, I had a hard time sitting back and watching my wife, friend, and lover of over thirty years simply fade away.

Her gentle shallow rhythmic breath abruptly changed to a rapid tortured rate. Her face changed from a comfortably relaxed and radiant state to one of angst. She never opened her eyes, but I could see the exaggerated REM movement under her closed eyelids. As this drama unfolded I prepared for what I thought would be her final exit from this Maya-filled life.

The night nurse complied with my request for more Dilaudid, but it made no difference in what I witnessed. Her anxious state continued for another hour, until two in the morning, when her breathing suddenly slowed and her face relaxed into an almost angelic state, which remained unchanged until the dayshift nurse arrived.

Janet, the nurse who had long ago invited Kath to visit her newborn colt, opened the door and asked in an odd sort of way if Kath still remained in the land of the living. I felt somewhat taken aback by her question, as I quickly rechecked Kath's chest movement and assured her that the final moment had not yet arrived. Janet waved a silent signal for me to step out of the room.

I reluctantly left Kath's side and stood in the hall with the door closed behind me as Janet explained her request. She was assigned to be Kath's nurse for the day and told me about the dream she'd had last night.

Janet stood alone in a grassy meadow with slight rolling hills holding the reins of her horse, Vegan, who stood next to her. In the distance she watched a figure appear over the crest of a hill, sauntering toward her through the tall grass. Dressed in jeans and a beautifully colored buttoned blouse, with shoulder length hair that flowed in the breeze, the figure walked toward them. Her fingers cheerfully brushed through the many daisies that sprouted up through the grass. As the figure drew closer, theirs eyes met across the distance and Janet recognized the figure as Kath. Kath smiled when they silently acknowledged each other's presence. Kath reached out her hand to brush Vegas's mane and patted his broad neck, but said nothing as she admired the beautiful colt. The silence seemed to last a long time before Kath looked at Vegas and said, "I have to go now." She patted Vega's forehead before she turned and walked away into the tall grass and disappeared over the hill.

I asked Janet what time she dreamt this, and she said, "I suddenly woke up all sweaty and looked at the clock, which said 2 A.M." A cold shiver ran down my spine as I reiterated my tale about Kath's unusual activity that had occurred at that exact same moment. Our eyes grew wide. We stared at each other with a profound sense of awe when we both recognized the significance of an obviously transcendental event that we had independently witnessed and would never forget.

Janet left me alone in the room, as I held Kath's hand and watched her breathing slow down to almost nothing. It had been 364 days since her fistula surgery, when she had smiled at the promise of life. But now it became abundantly clear to me that the end drew very near. The silence of the room overwhelmed me, as I felt the life energy of my wife and best friend be slowly released into the universe. Kath seemed calm and comfortable, lying perfectly still on her back, with her face pointed to the heavens. I tightened my grip on her hand and watched in sad horror, as the time between her breaths grew ever greater, until finally she breathed no more. I looked at the clock which read 9:20. I continued to hold her hand and cried my eyes out, as she soldiered on into her next life.

Epilogue

Kath had the funeral service she never wanted, attended by a crowd she never thought would show up. She made the final journey back to Michigan and rests in the family plot next her mother and father. Her sister, Roberta, eventually succumbed to alcohol related illness which left Marianne the sole survivor of the Wilson clan. To this day, Marianne dutifully attends to Kath's grave.

As for me, I never wallowed in despair, but I certainly experienced grief and sadness. After the burial, I took a road trip up Highway 1 from San Diego to Victoria, British Columbia, and pretty much cried the whole way. When I returned home to Sedona, I set about the task of cleaning out Kath's things, her clothes, make-up, and medical supplies. It all proved difficult but cathartic. I briefly attended a local grief support group which was therapeutic. But after I spilled my guts out, it was time to move on. All the heartbreak and turmoil I had witnessed over the years convinced me not to squander the time I had left. I made a conscious decision to move on.

The dating scene proved scary, but I met Alice and found the happiness I thought was lost forever. We soon married and I was blessed with a step-daughter, Shawni, and her fraternal twins, Brenna and Aydin, who light up my life.

The dream of a family that Kath and I had tried to create decades ago finally came to fruition. And I have no doubt that she is smiling down from Mantra heaven on the happiness I have found. My new life has been forged from the crucible of tragedy, and I consider myself to be the luckiest guy on the planet.

Acknowledgments

Special thanks to Charles Grosel, Write for Success, who helped me with the intital edit, and to Marion Johnson of The Memory Works, who helped me with additional edits and kept me on the grammatical path.

Made in the USA
San Bernardino, CA
22 April 2019